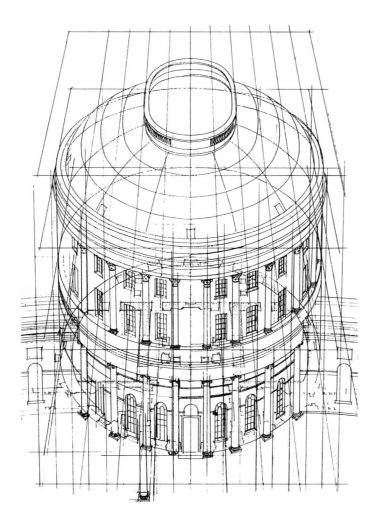

THE ENGLISH COUNTRY HOUSE IN PERSPECTIVE

The English Country House in Perspective

GERVASE JACKSON-STOPS

Illustrations by
BRIAN DELF, PETER MORTER, MEL WRIGHT

Published in association with The National Trust

GROVE WEIDENFELD
New York

For my mother, and in memory of my father, who both taught me to love buildings

Published by Grove Weidenfeld
A division of Wheatland Corporation
841 Broadway
New York, NY 10003-4793

Published in Canada by General Publishing Company, Ltd.

Library of Congress Cataloging-in-Publication Data

Jackson-Stops, Gervase
    The English country house in perspective / Gervase Jackson-Stops.
        1st American ed.
            p.   cm.
        "Published in association with the National Trust."
        ISBN 0-8021-1228-5
        1. Country homes—England.   2, Gardens—England.   I. Title
NA7562.J3   1990
728.8′0942–dc20   89-77420
                                                              CIP

Typeset by Florencetype Ltd, Kewstoke, Avon

Color separation by Fotographics Limited, London and Hong Kong

Manufactured in West Germany

First American Edition 1990

10 9 8 7 6 5 4 3 2 1

Conceived, designed and produced by Toucan Books Limited, London

Contents

Endpapers: The coffered ceilings of the Saloon and an alcove at Kedleston
Title pages: Ickworth; the Rotunda in section

Introduction

THE COUNTRY HOUSE is – like Shakespeare, parliamentary democracy, afternoon tea and a few other national institutions – among Britain's greatest contributions to western civilization. So it is hardly surprising that it has been the subject of a vast and ever-increasing literature. Some have naturally seen this as a sign of retrogression, attacking what they call the 'heritage industry' as part of an unhealthy obsession with the past. But unlike the theme-parks spreading like a rash along our motorways and offering the public a spoon-fed, sanitized, strip-cartoon version of history, the country house can offer us a direct and unadulterated link with our ancestors. In its architecture, planning and decoration, we can see how many of our basic attitudes were formed, and how different aspects of our own way of life were evolved. Its stones and timbers, bricks and mortar, can bring to life the dry records of the history books, showing us the events and personalities of the time in vivid detail.

This backward look is not something we should be ashamed of. The death of the Modern Movement, long overdue, has released us from the stultifying Marxist ideology of determinism; the idea that progress can only be achieved by making a clean break with the past. Indeed it has questioned the very idea of progress, encouraging a humbler, more empirical attitude, which sees history rather in terms of 'swings and roundabouts' – a process of evolution in which there are simultaneous gains and losses.

All this gives the country house a new relevance today, especially at a time when architecture has become a matter for public debate, no longer restricted to the professionals. Without wanting to go backwards, to make replicas or pastiches of our historic buildings, we need to know how these houses evolved, how they answered the needs of their time, and what practical or aesthetic solutions their builders arrived at, faced with new materials, new requirements, new stylistic influences in every generation.

The greater involvement of the general public with architecture, and the increasing popularity of competitions, has at the same time led to a welcome revival of the perspective drawing as an art form. Like the models, 'prospects' and 'birds-eye' views, which first became popular in the seventeenth century, they can be immediately understood where plans and elevations (even for the expert) take time to work out. Applied to existing country houses, views of this sort can also capture the character of a place, and, as the film *The Draughtsman's Contract* suggested, show far more than the human eye or the camera can ever hope to see.

The exquisite drawings by Brian Delf, Peter Morter and Mel Wright, which are in many ways the *raison d'être* of this book, have the fascination of those two great doll's houses which have survived from the eighteenth century, at Uppark in Sussex and Nostell Priory in Yorkshire. With their façades removed or their roofs lifted, we can see how these buildings actually worked and, like Gulliver watching the Lilliputians, find parallels with our own civilization that may amuse as well as instruct.

By choosing a series of twelve archetypal houses, changed as little as possible since they were first built, the aim of this book is also to give an overall 'birds-eye' view of the development of British architecture over six centuries: from Bodiam, built during the Hundred Years' War, to Castle Drogo, still being constructed during the First World War. All twelve of these houses are now in the care of the National Trust, and so regularly open to the public, but it is good to know that six are still inhabited by the families who built them.

The Trust has never consciously tried to build up a 'portfolio' of houses, which would represent different styles and dates, like pictures collected for a great national museum. On the contrary it has acted, and continues to act, as a safety net for outstanding houses and collections which might not otherwise be able to survive intact. It is therefore largely by chance that it owns so many country houses which characterize the taste of a single moment in our history – while others that are more complex, representing the work of many generations (like Chatsworth, Woburn and Longleat), still remain in private hands.

A few of the houses dealt with here may fall into the last category, notably Knole and Petworth (and to a lesser extent Stourhead), but even here the different layers are quite easily separated, and they have been chosen because one period still dominates: Knole as a Tudor courtyard house; Petworth as a Baroque palace; Stourhead as a Palladian villa. Tempting as it is to put these houses into tidy compartments by date and style, however, it is the individuals who built them – idiosyncratic, if not downright eccentric – that these buildings recall, just as much as the architects in their employ. If their presence can still be felt in the houses they created, it is only right that they should loom large in the following pages.

Many people have helped with this book, notably my colleagues in the Historic Buildings Department of the National Trust. I am particularly grateful to Martin Drury, the Trust's Historic Building's Secretary, for allowing me the time to write it, and for his constant encouragement, and to Margaret Willes, the Trust's Publisher, who helped to conceive the book, and read it in manuscript. In any book of this kind, one is of course indebted to others who have researched the history of these houses: in particular Leslie Harris at Kedleston; Catherine Morton at Bodiam; Christopher Rowell and Jeremy Lake at Little Moreton; Mark Girouard and David Durant at Hardwick; Kenneth Woodbridge at Stourhead; Edward McParland at Castle Coole; Sheila Pettit and Andrew Saint at Cragside; and Michael Trinick and Hugh Meller at Castle Drogo. In addition, I should like to thank Rosalind Westwood for allowing me to make use of her detailed (and unpublished) research on the Belton archives. David Thackray, the Trust's Archaeological Adviser, and Peter Marlow, Historic Buildings Representative in Northern Ireland, also helped with the chapters on Bodiam and Castle Coole respectively. Christine Vincent undertook the picture research, assisted by the staff of the National Trust Photographic Library.

Maggie Grieve not only typed the book, but acted as research assistant, production supervisor, and general tower of strength. I am also very grateful to my agent, Caroline Dawnay, and to Robert Sackville West, John Meek and Jane MacAndrew of Toucan Books for their patience, kindness and immense efficiency.

Bodiam Castle

E A S T   S U S S E X

ANYONE who has ever built sandcastles will feel an immediate affinity with Bodiam. Symmetrical, four-square, surrounded by a wide moat, it seems at first sight to have an appealing child-like simplicity. With a round tower at each corner, and a square one in the centre of each side, battlemented and turreted it looks like the work of bucket and spade on a gigantic scale. Unlike most sandcastles, however, washed away by the first incoming waves, Bodiam has been left high and dry in the green meadowland of East Sussex. And if it has begun to crumble gently, that is the effect of time rather than tide.

The smell of salt water and the cry of the gulls may have gone, but the sea is still vital to an understanding of this extraordinary island fortress and its origins, half military and half domestic. The River Rother, which flows only a few hundred yards to the south, was in the Middle Ages and long before a tidal estuary, navigable as far as here and offering one of the few safe passages for large vessels from the coast through the treacherous marshes round Rye and Winchelsea. Only in the late seventeenth and eighteenth centuries did it lose its importance as a thoroughfare with the silting-up of the river bed, combined with the effects of land reclamation and drainage. Excavations have revealed that a thriving port was already established here during the Roman occupation of Britain, continuing in operation from the first to the third centuries AD. This was probably used for the export of iron ore, since Bodiam lay at the point where the Roman road from the Sussex ironfields crossed the Rother, on its way north to join the Watling Street at Rochester.

The strategic importance of Bodiam must also have been realized at an early stage, for the village (though it probably derives its name from an Anglo-Saxon word meaning low-lying or marshy) is at the south-west corner of a triangle of high ground, bounded by the Rother on the south, the Roman road on the west and the Kent Ditch, still the boundary between Kent and Sussex – on the north. As usual the parish church was built on the highest point, but between it and the Kent Ditch is the remains of a circular moat, probably marking the site of a fortified saxon hall which 'Aelfer' (or Aelfhere) held from Edward the Confessor, according to Domesday Book.

After the Norman Conquest the manor was granted to a son of Hugh d'Eu, who took the name of 'de Bodeham', and afterwards passed by marriage to a member of the Wardeux family. Once again the strategic importance of the manor house, commanding the Rother Valley, probably led to its rebuilding on a new and higher site south-east of the church. In the mid-fourteenth century Elizabeth Wardeux, herself an heiress, brought Bodiam as part of her dowry to her husband, Sir Edward Dalyngrigge, a soldier of fortune and the creator of the present castle, which lies on yet a third site near the river bank half a mile to the south.

Sir Edward's character and his career help to explain how he came to build this masterpiece – at the very end of a great tradition of English castle-building, yet at the beginning of a new fashion for courtyard houses that was to flourish in aristocratic circles well into the sixteenth century, and even beyond. A member of an old Sussex family from Dalling Ridge near East Grinstead, he had gone to France in 1367, soon after his coming of age, and entered the service of one of the most celebrated English 'freebooters' of his age, Sir Robert Knollys.

The rewards to be made from plunder and the ransom of prisoners at this stage in the Hundred Years' War were prodigious. Ten years earlier, Knollys' campaign on the Loire is thought to have earned him one hundred thousand crowns in one season alone. Nor was this equivalent of twentieth-century oil money the only attraction, for active service was the one way which men not of the highest social rank could reach positions of the greatest power. From his château of Derval in Picardy Knollys ruled almost as an independent prince, siding sometimes with the king of England and sometimes with Charles of Navarre. Appalling rapine and pillage accompanied his progresses or *chevauchées* through

Bodiam from the south-east. The castle may have been partly modelled on the Château de Villandraut, near Bordeaux.

Normandy, Brittany and Aquitane, like those of John of Gaunt and the Black Prince, but there was also a keen sense of the honour and glory of knighthood on the Arthurian model as celebrated in the chronicles of Froissart, and this too must have impressed itself on the young squires in his retinue.

Edward Dalyngrigge evidently prospered as one of Sir Robert's right-hand men, particularly after the accession of the weak Richard II in 1377. In 1380 he was made an 'Overseer of the State of the Kingdom' and Chamberlain of the Royal Household, and in the following year played a key part, with Knollys, in the suppression of Wat Tyler's rebellion. In 1390 he was one of the royal commissioners empowered to make peace with France, and in 1393 became Constable of the Tower of London.

Meanwhile the severity of English reverses in France was what lay behind Knollys' and Dalyngrigge's return to London. In 1372 the Earl of Pembroke's fleet was destroyed by Castilian galleys off La Rochelle, effectively giving control of the Channel to the French for the next fifteen years; this was perhaps the lowest point of England's fortunes in the whole course of the war. Rye and Hastings were sacked and burnt in 1377, Winchelsea in 1380. So the navigable part of the River Rother, regarded as part of the port of Winchelsea, was left particularly vulnerable to invaders. It was for this reason that a royal licence, dated 20 October 1385, was issued to Sir Edward by Richard II 'to strengthen and crenellate his manor house of Bodyham near the sea in the County of Sussex with a wall of stone and lime, and to construct and make thereof a castle in defence of the adjacent countryside and for resistance against our enemies'.

From the wording of this document one might have expected Sir Edward simply to fortify his existing moated manor house, like his contemporaries Sir John de Cobham, who had remodelled Hever in Kent in 1384, and Bishop Rede of Chichester, who had made Amberley (at the highest navigable point of the River Arun) into a castle a year or two earlier. However, licences from the king were not like today's planning permissions; rather they were an expression of trust in a subject, allowing him almost total freedom of action. So in the end Dalyngrigge decided to construct a wholly new castle a quarter of a mile to the south of his old manor house, close to the river from which any French attack would come.

The age of royal castle-building had ended with the death of Edward III, and the sudden need for a national scheme of coastal defence depended on individuals like these, who were prepared to build for patriotic motives and not just for personal aggrandizement. John de Cobham of Hever, for instance, also built a fortress at Cooling in the north Kent marshes in 1381, helping to control the approaches to the Thames, and the inscription which he had inscribed on copper and fixed to the gatehouse could just as well apply to Bodiam:

> *Knouwyth that beth and schul [are and shall] be*
> *That I am made in help of the cuntre,*
> *In knowying of whyche thyng*
> *Thys is chartre and wytnessyng.*

Cobham and Dalyngrigge were both protégés of Sir Robert Knollys and both had close connections with the court. So it is tempting to think that the royal master-mason, Henry Yevele, who is known to have worked at

Cooling, might also have designed Bodiam – a building of equal sophistication.

The major difference between the two castles is that the former was built for purely military purposes, while the latter was always intended as one of its owner's chief seats – despite the fact that he inherited another house at Bolebrooke, near Hartfield. It is this that gives Bodiam much of its fascination. Like a crab, whose hard outer shell conceals a complex mass of nerves and living tissue, it demonstrates two contrasting sides of late medieval architecture: on the one hand, the ultimate development of the castle as a machine for defence, the perfection of a form that looks back to the experiences of the earliest crusaders, to Saône and Krak des Chevaliers; on the other

hand an early attempt to rationalize the living quarters of a noble household that looks forward to the great courtyard houses of the fifteenth and sixteenth centuries, to Thornbury Castle, Knole and Audley End.

Military and strategic considerations were certainly uppermost in Sir Edward Dalyngrigge's mind when he chose the site and started construction in 1385, and they remain uppermost in the visitor's mind today when approaching Bodiam from the west, as the foreign invader might have done and seeing the solidity of its massive towers reflected in the still surface of the moat. To begin with, Dalyngrigge was fortunate in having some of the best and most durable building materials in England ready to hand: oak spars from Ashdown forest to the west,

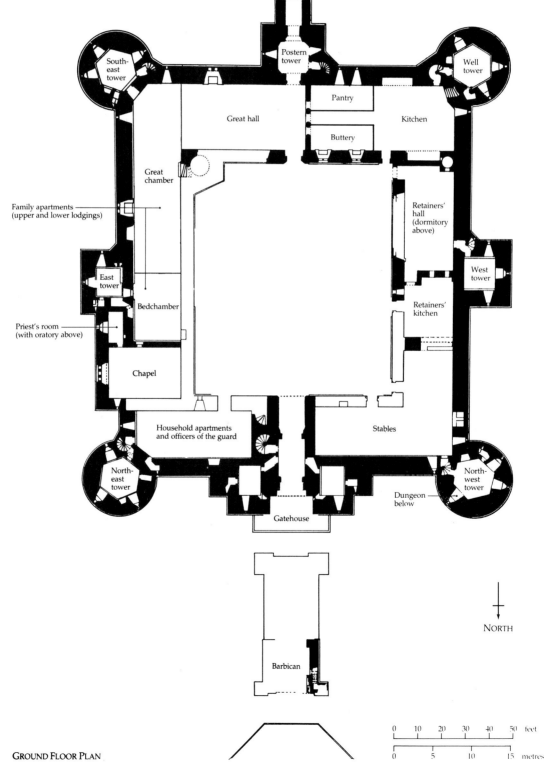

GROUND FLOOR PLAN

and Wealden stone, the oldest of all the Sussex Cretaceous sandstones, brought by barge from Stonegate only ten miles up-river. Cut into massive squares of fine-grain ashlar, their greys and fawns now subtly varied with green and yellow lichen, these giant's building blocks are still among the wonders of Bodiam – used to construct walls which average 6 feet 6 inches thick, and which stand 41 feet above the water. Water was of course the key to Bodiam's defences, and to its planning. Sir Edward's aim in building low down near the river was not only to guard the all-important wharf below Bodiam bridge, but also to make use of the springs here to fill a really substantial moat, up to 8 feet deep. New skills in mining, developed particularly by the French, had made dry moats a liability by this date, just as they had encouraged the building of round towers, which were structurally sounder than square ones.

Separated from the southern edge of the moat only by a narrow strip of land was a substantial harbour, still clearly seen as a dip in the ground some 30 feet by 250 feet. In 1823 the hulk of a medieval vessel was dug up from the mud only a few miles down the Rother, and its dimensions (64 by 15 feet, with a 9-foot keel) suggest that a number of similar boats or even larger cargomen or ships of war could have found a berth here at the same time. It was standard practice for medieval castles to have two gates – one acting as a means of escape in emergency – and at Bodiam there was an obvious symmetry about having the main land gate on the north, and the postern on the south guarding the river approach.

High above these two gates are carved stone shields, which would originally have been painted in bright heraldic colours and which are the only purely ornamental feature to be found in the whole building. As might be expected, Sir Edward's own coat-of-arms and unicorn's head crest occupy the central place on the great gatehouse, flanked by those of the Wardeux family for his wife and by the six martlets of the Radyndens, another powerful Sussex family to which he was connected. Less predictably, the central arms and crest above the postern gate, set between two blank shields, are those of his old commander, Sir Robert Knollys: perhaps not only an acknowledgement of feudal loyalty, and a talisman to strike terror into Frenchmen's hearts, but also an expression of gratitude for the concept of the whole castle.

Sir Robert's own fortress of Derval has long since perished, but Bodiam bears a striking resemblance – if on a smaller scale, to the Château de Villandraut, just south of Bordeaux, where Knollys and his followers (including the young Dalyngrigge) had joined the court of Edward, the Black Prince, in 1369. The idea of adopting a French model was nothing new. Another veteran of the Norman and Breton campaigns, Sir John Delamare, had returned to build a similar four-square, symmetrical castle at Nunney in Somerset in 1373, while the 5th Lord Lovell used Concressault, between the Loire and the Cher, as the basis for Old Wardour in Wiltshire, licensed in 1393.

In the previous century Edward I and his Savoyard architect, Master James of St George, had first brought such continental forms of castle-building to Britain.

The carved stone unicorn and coat-of-arms of Sir Edward Dalyngrigge, flanked by those of the Wardeux and Radynden families, above the main gate. Originally they would have been painted in bright heraldic colours.

Their Welsh fortresses such as Harlech and Beaumaris dispensed with the old Norman idea of a central keep protected by a motte and bailey (as can still be seen at Windsor and Rochester), and established high curtain walls with projecting towers, like the Byzantine forts which the crusaders had seen in the eastern Mediterranean and which the Hohenstaufen emperors copied in southern Italy and Sicily. In form, then, Bodiam has a well-established European pedigree, and what it lacks in size compared to an elder cousin like Frederick II's grim Castello Ursino in Catania it makes up for in the refinement of its detail and the multiplicity of its defences. A toy castle it may look, but contemporaries must have been in no doubt as to its lethal potential.

Donning imaginary suits of armour, it is high time we tried to penetrate those defences ourselves. To begin with, we have to picture quite a different approach. Instead of the straight causeway which now leads to the Great Gatehouse, there was originally a series of bridges beginning on the west rather than the north side of the moat, at the point where an octagonal stone pier still survives. If we should succeed in getting across the first drawbridge at the water's edge, we should still have to run the gauntlet of a long timber walkway with our right (unshielded) sides open to raking horizontal fire from the garrison in the north-west tower and gatehouse. Reaching the octagonal islet or *tête du pont*, which still exists (but which would then have had castellated walls all round it), we would then have turned at right-angles, crossed a second drawbridge and passed – at our peril – under the arch of the barbican. Only a fragment of this gatehouse tower now exists, but a watercolour of 1784 shows it much more complete, and we can still clearly see the grooves for a portcullis on the north side, and stays for heavy double doors on the south. Finally, we should have to negotiate a third drawbridge before arriving at the forbidding archway of the great gatehouse.

The isolated 'keep' of the early Norman castle may have

been made redundant by the curtain-wall castles of Edward I and his successors, but in many ways its role was taken over by the main gatehouse. Here at Bodiam it is twice the size of the other towers, with two massive rectangular projections standing like sentries either side of the central arch. The gun loops in the walls, with circular openings for cannon below and vertical sighting slits above – rather like inverted key holes – were a comparatively new development when Bodiam was built. Most of them are placed at about head height, since raking fire had a better chance than plunging (which if it missed

would hit the ground). Never a feature of castle-building in the north of England, they were a response to the growing sophistication of French firearms: a development which would shortly sound the death-knell of the feudal castle. One such bombard was excavated from the moat during the nineteenth century and is now in the Rotunda Museum at Woolwich Arsenal. However, a copy can still be seen at Bodiam, together with some of the stone cannonballs it might have fired, weighing up to 150 pounds. Both the gun loops and the castellations along the parapets may have been equipped with wooden

The castle as it might have appeared around 1400. The original bridges connecting the castle to the west of the moat were replaced by a straight stone causeway running from the north of the moat to the Great Gatehouse.

shutters on hinges to protect the gunners and crossbowmen until they were ready to fire.

Machicolations, or holes pierced in the overhanging parapets of the gatehouse tower, and in the top of the wide arch that unites them immediately above the entrance, were an older feature, which would have allowed the defenders to drop missiles or pour boiling and corrosive materials on their adversaries. The same principle applied to the series of *meurtrières* (or 'murder holes') in the vaulted ceiling of the passage beyond the first portcullis. The gatehouse at Bodiam is unique in

having had three portcullises, the first of which still survives – a grid of oak beams encased in iron plating that could be raised and lowered by means of a winch in the guard chamber above. Immediately behind it was a pair of solid oak doors (replaced at a later date), and this same arrangement was repeated at the other end of the vaulted passage which originally led straight into the courtyard.

At some later date, Sir Edward or one of his successors evidently decided to extend this passage southwards and make a battlemented platform above. This was doubtless used for watching games or sports in the court below during peaceable times, but it may also have been intended to strengthen the defences of the gatehouse, since a third portcullis and pair of doors was constructed at the far end. The fact that these doors opened only from the inside meant that the gatehouse could thus be held against treachery from within, or against a foe who had somehow scaled the walls or forced the postern gate.

The postern facing the river and for much of the time protected by men-of-war anchored in the harbour, was less likely to be stormed than the great gatehouse. But it too was protected by machicolated parapets, another portcullis and set of doors, and two drawbridges – one at either end of the timber bridge that originally connected it with the southern shore of the moat. There is no evidence that any of the five drawbridges at Bodiam were made to lift up, and it is more likely they were literally 'drawing' (or sliding) gangplanks, about 10 feet in span.

Lord Curzon, who bought the castle in 1916 in order to restore it, discovered the footings of the original bridges after he had drained the moat. A large stone ball, 42 inches in circumference, was also found in the mud and serves as a reminder of the huge catapults known as mangonels or *trebuchets* that were used by the attackers, along with the elaborate siege engines with their curious animal names – the cat, the ram, the bear and the mouse. Fearsome weapons such as these, which made the Hundred Years' War infinitely bloodier than any previous conflicts, go far to explain the elaboration of Bodiam's defences. Nostalgia for the great days of his campaigning with Sir Robert Knollys may have inspired Dalyngrigge to plan this 'ideal' French castle, but real need must have dictated the construction of such a costly building in this most English of settings.

In the event, Bodiam was never properly put to the test, and that explains the marvellous state of preservation of its external walls. The English regained control of the Channel in 1387, before the building work can have been completed, and the next serious danger came almost a century later, in 1483, when its then owner, the Lancastrian Sir Thomas Lewknor, was attainted by Richard III. On 8 November the King authorized the Earl of Surrey and others 'to besiege the castle of Bodyham which the rebels had seized', but it must have been swiftly surrendered, since the new royal constable took up residence on 12 December.

Objects found during Lord Curzon's excavations prove that the castle continued to be occupied until the mid-seventeenth century, but at the time of the Civil War it had the misfortune to belong to a leading Royalist, John

An aquatint of Bodiam dated 1778, showing the postern gate on the right. Although less likely to be stormed than the Great Gatehouse, the postern was also protected by machicolated parapets.

Two watercolours painted by S.H. Grimm in 1784 showing (above) the barbican, now almost completely destroyed, from the bridgehead, and (right) the vaulted passage with its meurtrières – *or murder holes – in the Great Gatehouse.*

Tufton, 2nd Earl of Thanet, and it was almost certainly at that time, and probably in 1645, that the interior was plundered, razed and fired by parliamentary troops.

Today, only a few of the tower chambers remain in anything like their former state, but it is easy to work out how the rooms would originally have been used, and with what ingenuity they were planned. Sir Edward and his entourage were certainly housed in style. No fewer than thirty-three fireplaces are still visible, cut into the outer walls – and more must once have existed, served by chimneystacks on the courtyard side. Twenty-eight separate garderobes or latrines have been found, each with its own drain shaft to the moat – another possible deterrent to would-be attackers – while there are ten stone spiral staircases and traces of several others made of timber.

Given the crowded conditions of medieval life, when privacy was possible only for the grandest, Bodiam must have teemed with life when Sir Edward was in residence. Counting his wife and immediate family, and the core of well-trained men who comprised his 'fighting household', high-ranking officials like his carver, cupbearer and server, and lesser attendants like armourers, minstrels, trumpeters, huntsmen, falconers, painters and joiners, there could have been as many as 150 inhabitants, swelled to even greater numbers by the retainers called in to man the castle in time of danger – yeomen farmers each with their own band of followers. Women numbered only a tiny proportion of this total. Apart from Lady Dalyngrigge, her daughters and their attendants, kept in a kind of purdah in the family apartments, wives and families were expected to live outside the castle, often working their husband's smallholdings in their absence.

As might be expected, the great hall in the south range was the hub of everyday life, as it had been in domestic buildings since before the Norman Conquest. Two storeys high and with an open timber roof, it would have been entered from the so-called 'screens passage' at its western end: a wide corridor on the central north–south axis of the castle, that must also have been its busiest single thoroughfare, separating the family's apartments to the east from the servants' to the west. The timber screen itself (almost certainly supporting a minstrels gallery above) has long since gone. But the great stone arched doorcases at either end of the passage survive – that on the south leading to the postern gate, and that on the north leading across the centre of the courtyard to the great gatehouse. On the west wall, too, can be seen three further arches: those on the left and right entering the pantry and buttery respectively, and that in the centre leading down a narrow passage between them to the kitchen.

Although the great hall still counted as one of the family apartments – indeed the chief of them – Sir Edward Dalyngrigge would probably only have dined there on major feast days, otherwise preferring to eat less publicly in his own rooms in the adjoining east range. The poet Langland lamented this tendency in a famous passage from the *Vision of Piers Plowman*, written in the 1360s:

> *Elyng [lonely] is the halle each day in the week*
> *Here the lord and lady liketh not to sit*
> *Now hath the rich a rule to eat by themselves*
> *In a pryvie parloure for pore mennes sake*
> *Or in a chamber with a chimney and leave the chief hall*
> *That was made for means, men to eat in.*

The reference to chambers with chimneys suggests that the great hall continued to have the old-fashioned feature of a central hearth, as still exists at Penshurst – with the smoke rising to a louvre high up in the rafters. Certainly there is no sign that the hall at Bodiam ever had a chimneystack.

Even if Sir Edward and his family had retired to eat in their own apartments, the high table, placed crossways on a dais at the east end, remained as a symbol of his authority, and was occupied by his deputies, the senior officers of the household. There are parallels here with Oxford and Cambridge colleges, where the master or

A bombard, excavated from the moat in the nineteenth century, now in the Rotunda Museum at Woolwich Arsenal. It would have been capable of firing stone canonballs weighing up to 150 pounds.

Bodiam Castle

1 North-east tower
2 Great hall
3 Postern tower
4 Kitchen
5 Well tower
6 Retainers' hall
7 Retainers' kitchen
8 Retainers' and garrison quarters
9 West tower
10 North-west tower
11 Principal guard-chamber (dungeon below)

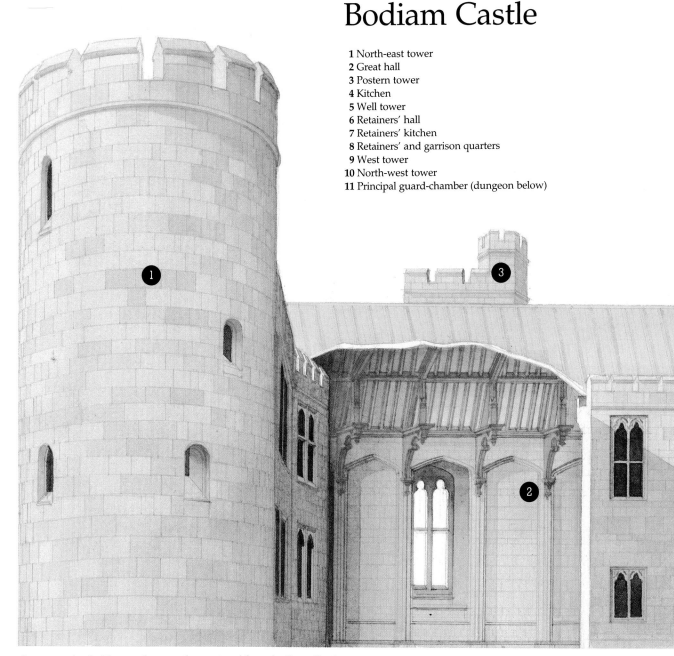

A cross-section looking south across the courtyard from the Great Gatehouse.

warden still generally eats in his own lodgings, while the dons (the equivalent of his upper household) continue to sit at high table. The undergraduates' tables, set against the walls, would at Bodiam have been occupied by the younger squires and yeomen.

The importance of the dais was also stressed by the sunlight which must have fallen on it, from the big four-light window in the south wall – the largest of all those punched in the thick exterior walls of the castle, apart from the east window of the chapel. As in almost all the other rooms, the rough stone walls above the panelling here would have been plastered and lime-washed, giving a far lighter effect than we might suppose. They may also have been hung with arms and armour, although by this date a separate armoury would have housed most of the garrison's weapons, perhaps in a room adjoining the great gatehouse.

The family apartments in the east range were divided into two main suites of rooms or lodgings, one above the other, connected only by a spiral staircase at the south-east

corner of the courtyard which also gave access to the dais end of the hall. Each of these suites consisted of three principal rooms: an anteroom, a great chamber, and a bedchamber beyond, stretching as far as the chapel. Beyond these bedchambers were small closets, equipped with cupboards and garderobes, in the square east tower. The upper suite was undoubtedly the most important of the two. To begin with, there are more (and bigger) windows, and a far more elaborate chimneypiece, in its great chamber. But it also has an oratory (above the ground-floor sacristy) from which its occupants could look down through an internal window to the sanctuary of the chapel, and an extra chamber at the top of the east tower, reached only by a spiral staircase from the closet below. The upper tower rooms both had fireplaces, while the lower one was cunningly heated by the flue from the fireplace in the adjoining bedchamber.

Evidently these upper lodgings were what would later become known as 'rooms of state' – usually occupied by Sir Edward, his wife and family, when they were in

16

residence, but yielded by them to the king or to anybody of superior rank who might be visiting. On such occasions the Dalyngrigges would move to the lower lodgings, otherwise generally inhabited by the constable of the castle, or the steward, who was responsible for running the estates. The family apartments were completed by three substantial hexagonal chambers (again with fireplaces and garderobes) in the round south-east tower, approached by a spiral stair from the lower gallery. They could equally have been given to high-ranking household officials, many of whom were doubtless Sir Edward's near-relations in any case. Huge vaulted cellars running below the whole east range probably provided living quarters for the lower household attendants, as well as storage for the more valuable goods, perhaps including a treasury and armoury.

The furnishing of all these rooms is less easy to imagine today than that of the great hall, but their contents were essentially movable, accompanying the owner of the castle wherever he went. Woven hangings (occasionally

tapestries, but more often strips of plain woollen or mohair fabric joined together) gave colour and warmth to the bare stone or plastered walls, while canopied beds were put up and taken down just like the tents on a military campaign. Whole families often slept together in one room, so beds of this type were also essential for privacy, at a time when pages, or grooms of the chamber, would also sleep on pallets (straw mattresses) at their master's door. Tables and benches were made with draw-leaves so as to extend when in use, and folding stools were also popular. Sir Edward and his wife may have had a pair of X-frame armchairs, similarly made to fold flat; these would have been like thrones for special occasions – presiding over the courts held in the great hall, or receiving guests on a dais in the great chamber, with a canopy erected above – instead of being for everyday use. Many of the window bays have stone seats in them, which would have been lined with cushions. The floors would normally have been covered in rush matting.

Apart from the great hall, the chapel, between the

family apartments and the north-east drum tower, was the one place where the male population of the castle could come together – with the ladies taking part, but concealed from view, in the first-floor oratory. Its siting could hardly be improved, not only for that reason, but because the altar faces east, satisfying liturgical requirements, and because the big three-light lancet window above it, once filled with leaded glass, is on the side of the castle least vulnerable to attack. Two storeys in height, and raised above a crypt, the chapel would have had an open timber roof and its walls may well have been painted with brightly coloured murals. The sanctuary, separated from the nave by a wooden screen, was paved with blue, yellow, green and brown glazed tiles, excavated by Lord Curzon and now in the museum. On the south wall of the sanctuary is a piscina or basin in which the priest rinsed the chalice after Mass, and some steps beside it lead up to the door of the sacristy, which he would have used as a living room, not merely as a vestry.

The apartments in the north-east range, between the chapel and the great gatehouse, are almost as well supplied with fireplaces and garderobes as the family lodgings, and it is probable that these were occupied by the officers of the guard. To examine the living quarters of the lesser orders, however, we should return to the

A view inside the south-east corner tower. Three hexagonal chambers in this tower formed part of the family apartments.

screens passage of the hall and the three arched doorcases in its east wall. The room on the right, with two windows still surviving on the courtyard side, has an underground cellar below, and was therefore the buttery or 'butlery', where ale and wine were stored and dispensed, while the one on the left was the pantry, where bread, tableware and other necessaries were kept. Both would have had solid oak doors with hinged or sliding hatches, and the

The south front of Bodiam, with a Second World War gun emplacement on the left: still part of a national defence system after 450 years.

seneschal or comptroller of the household and his officials (including the butler and 'panter') probably occupied the chamber above, with its surprisingly grand four-light windows.

The central stone corridor between the buttery and pantry led to the kitchen, another huge two-storey interior at the south-west corner of the castle. Two great fireplaces, each 12 feet wide, face each other on the side walls, the one on the north with an oven adjoining it – and both lined with tiles set edgeways so as to resist the heat. Thanks to the architect's ingenuity, however, there is also just room for a door into the courtyard at the north-east corner of the room, with a giant four-light window above it; the only other source of light being a tiny opening high up in the west curtain wall – too dangerous a situation to make any bigger.

The south-west tower behind the kitchen and opening from it contained two vital adjuncts of castle life: the well in the basement (rediscovered by Lord Curzon), 8 feet in diameter and 10 feet deep; and the pigeon loft in the top storey, which contained some three hundred nesting boxes, two-thirds of which survive. As in France, keeping pigeons or doves was a strictly guarded right of the lord of the manor, resented by many smallholders whose crops they ravaged. But as a ready source of eggs

and poultry, even at a time when the estate was besieged, they were an essential rather than a luxury. Two other well-appointed rooms in the tower, with fireplaces and garderobes, would presumably have been occupied by the clerk of the kitchens and his lieutenants, higher-ranking officials than one might suppose. Despite a popular notion that medieval lords lived entirely on roasts (usually of venison), bread and sack, the most elaborate dishes were prepared with the most exotic ingredients. *The Forme of Cury*, a roll of recipes compiled about 1390 by the master cooks of Richard II, reads rather like the Escoffier of its time, and proves that the English did not lag behind the French in the culinary arts, as they were later to do.

There was no way through from the kitchen to the rest of the lodgings in the west range, but these had their own doors onto the courtyard – again reminiscent of the Oxford and Cambridge quadrangle system. The rooms in this part of the castle housed the retainers: the farm labourers or 'hinds' from Sir Edward Dalyngrigge's estate, who would double up as troops in wartime, supplemented by other mercenaries. As serfs rather than freemen, these would not qualify to eat with the rest of the household, and they had their own hall and kitchen on the ground floor of the west range.

There is no sign of a fireplace in the retainers' hall, and it may simply have been warmed by square holes or vents, cut through from one of the two great hearths in the adjoining kitchen. The upper floor was reached by a timber staircase still traceable along the west wall, and probably consisted of one large dormitory, with further rooms for bailiffs or sergeants in the mid-west tower. This side of the castle was most prone to attack, so it was appropriate that it should be manned by troops, and explains why the few windows in the outer walls are no more than slits.

The north-west corner of the castle is the least complete part of the building today, but the stables were almost certainly here, next to the great gatehouse, with more accommodation for grooms, stable boys, farriers, the smith, the falconer, the armourer and other craftsmen such as masons and carpenters in the rooms above. The north-west drum tower also contained the inevitable basement dungeon, entered by a trapdoor from the guard room above.

Re-crossing the moat, and taking a last look at the balanced symmetry of its towers and walls, Bodiam seems not just 'the most fairy of English Castles' as Lord Curzon called it, but a masterpiece of practical planning. A weapon as formidable in its day as the most advanced aircraft-carrier, it is also a 'machine for living', in Le Corbusier's famous phrase, perfectly adapted to its inhabitants' daily needs. We may be tempted to go further, and to see Bodiam standing at the end of a war-like age, looking forward to more peaceable times. But before reaching this conclusion, perhaps we should pause at the concrete gun-emplacement near the path that leads back to the village; a relic of a more recent invasion scare, and a reminder of a Warden of the Cinque Ports more celebrated than any of his predecessors.

As so often in the history of the English country house, *plus ça change, plus c'est la même chose.*

Knole

K E N T

IF EVER a house was made for the 'bird's-eye view', it is Knole. Seen from the ground it can certainly look immense, 'like a medieval village', as V. Sackville-West described the view of it from the deer park to the north, 'heaped with no attempt at symmetry'. Nor could one fail to be impressed by the great length of the south front rising from green lawns and flower beds on the other side, its rows of gables and chimneystacks marching to a more regular drumbeat, no longer sombre and frowning, but of 'an indescribable gaiety and courtliness'. However, it is only by taking wing, and in imagination flying with the swallows which dart in and out of the clock tower and wheel high above the rooftops, that we can make any sense of this vast building, and appreciate its essential unity.

Unity may seem a curious word to choose for a pile of stone and brick and timber covering nearly four acres, begun in the twelfth century or even earlier, and with subsequent additions by different owners – kings, archbishops and courtiers – right up to the early nineteenth. Indeed it may seem strange to find such a pile included at all in a book devoted to 'archetypal' houses, most of them built at one date and in one style. But, as we shall see, Knole is essentially a late medieval creation, whose main lines were complete by 1548, and the important changes made to it in the early seventeenth century were ornamental rather than structural. Halfway between the era of the fortified castle and the era of the compact country house (E- or H-shaped in plan), it remains the best-preserved of the spreading courtyard mansions, which Sir Francis Bacon held – even in James I's reign – to be the only suitable residences for great noblemen and officers of state.

Moreover Bacon's contemporary, Thomas Sackville, 1st Earl of Dorset, who was responsible for those seventeenth-century changes, was backward-looking in more ways than one. Given the tactful nature of his alterations, he would almost certainly have agreed with Bacon that 'it is a reverend thing to see an ancient castle or building not in decay'. The kind of life that he and his successors led at Knole, recklessly extravagant, surrounded by almost as many retainers as their cousin, Queen Elizabeth I, was thus deliberately calculated to continue ancient ideas of feudal power, at a time when new men and new ways were threatening the old social fabric. Beneath the Renaissance trappings – the resident musicians, the travelling players, the latest French and Flemish fashions in costume and in decoration – we are in fact looking at a late medieval lifestyle, not so very different from that of a great magnate like the Duke of Buckingham, builder of Thornbury Castle in Gloucestershire, a century before. The dream was to be ended only by the Civil War, when Knole was sacked like its peers, Audley End and Holdenby: the defeat of the court also spelt the death of the courtyard house.

The courtyard is certainly the key to an understanding of Knole. There are no less than seven of them, and legend (which wraps itself like ivy round the weathered fabric of the place) suggests that they correspond with the days of the week, while the fifty-two staircases represent the weeks, and the 365 rooms the days of the year. It would be cynical to check such romantic sums, but that they are not wholly impossible gives some indication of the size of the house. There is also a mystic aspect to the whole idea which would have appealed to the sixteenth-century mind: time and again in the literature of the period there are references to the household representing a microcosm of the state, which was in turn a microcosm of the universe. Thus God's role at the centre of the universe could be paralleled by the king's at one level (a perfect argument for divine right), and by the nobleman's at another (emphasizing his status as judge and local law-giver). As well as sanctioning a strict hierarchy within the household, these theories encouraged a new symmetry in the architecture of the period, for it was thought that balance reflected the harmony and order of the universe. We have already seen a form of symmetry emerging in the outer walls of

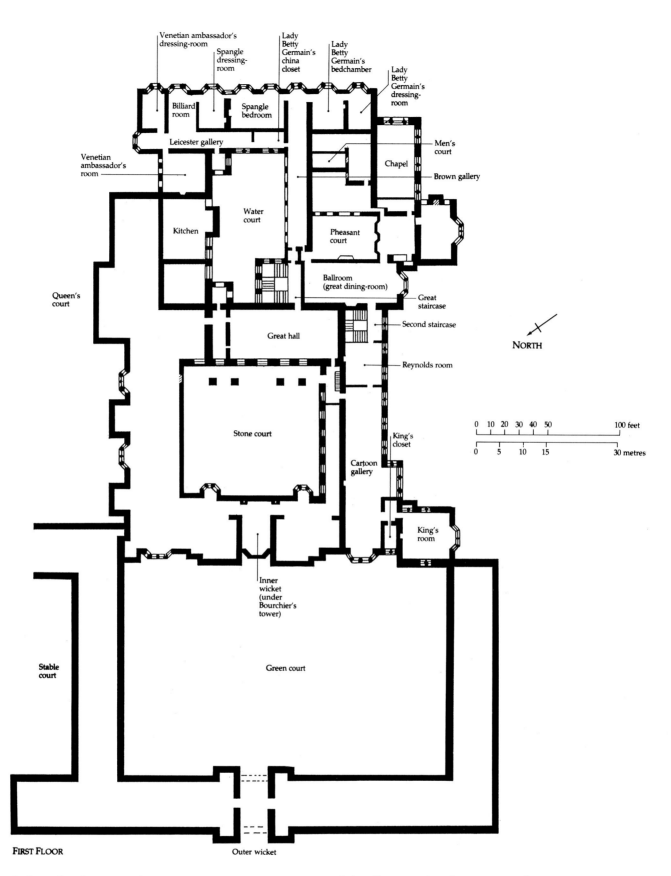

Venetian ambassador's dressing-room

Spangle dressing-room

Lady Betty Germain's china closet

Lady Betty Germain's bedchamber

Lady Betty Germain's dressing-room

Billiard room

Spangle bedroom

Leicester gallery

Men's court

Venetian ambassador's room

Chapel

Brown gallery

Water court

Kitchen

Pheasant court

Queen's court

Ballroom (great dining-room)

Great staircase

Second staircase

Great hall

NORTH

Reynolds room

Stone court

King's closet

Cartoon gallery

King's room

Inner wicket (under Bourchier's tower)

Stable court

Green court

FIRST FLOOR

Outer wicket

0 10 20 30 40 50   100 feet

0   5   10   15   30 metres

Bodiam, but for practical, engineering reasons more than for aesthetic effect. When defence was no longer necessary, as at Little Moreton, symmetry was largely abandoned, although a balance was struck by the ingenious counterpoint of different elements.

At Knole, for the first time, there is a real symmetry about our approach on the main axis, through the central gatehouse on the west front, across the Green Court, the largest of Knole's quadrangles, through a second gatehouse into the Stone Court – and only then a small diversion as we look for the door to the Great Hall on our

left: off-centre, since it must enter the screens passage at one end of the room, in approved medieval style.

The long south front too has a regularity about it, with the arcade of what was once an open loggia in the centre framed by projecting bays and towers – even if the elements beyond, the chapel on the east, and orangery on the west, hardly balance each other. The east front is completely different in character, with its timber-framed upper storey jettied out, and with eight wide pedimented oriel windows, crowned by gables: more like the mansion of a great City merchant within hearing of Bow Bells than

The arcade in the middle of this drawing, with its pillars of different-coloured marbles, is a Renaissance ornament in a late medieval setting.

a courtier's country seat. Yet it too has a surprising uniformity, given that it was never considered a show front and that it masks building work of several different dates. Only from the park on the north, where we caught our first glimpse of the 'medieval village', is there no attempt at symmetry whatever. A jumble of buildings of every shape and size, with the clock tower as the only recognizable feature, rising like the belfry of a parish church at the centre, this was always the service side of Knole: the stables and barns, the mason's yard, the blacksmith's and joiner's shops – like the engine room of a great ship. Yet here too, in the immense thickness of the Kentish ragstone walls, patched and buttressed, are signs of Knole's earliest origins.

Although the county historian Hasted gives the estate a distinguished Norman pedigree of ownership, from the Bethunes and the Mareschals, Earls of Pembroke, to the Bigods, Earls of Norfolk, the first house on the site (on the rounded hill or *knoll*, from which it takes its name) may not have been built until the thirteenth century: perhaps by Robert de Knolle, whose heirs William and Roger are recorded in a document of 1281. Some of the outbuildings on this north side of the house seem to incorporate fragments of an early gatehouse, and it is possible that this was built by Geoffrey, Lord de Say, who acquired Knole about 1370 and who may also have constructed a great hall on the site of the present kitchen. Had his descendants decided to go on living here, Knole might have ended up as a comparatively modest, semi-fortified manor house, like nearby Ightham Mote, or like Broughton Castle in Oxfordshire where they still live today. But a more glittering future lay in store when, on 30 June 1456, William Fiennes, Lord Saye and Sele, sold it for £266 13s 4d to Thomas Bourchier, Archbishop of Canterbury.

The great-grandson both of Edward III and of his Chancellor, Robert Bourchier, ancestor of the Earls of Stafford, Thomas was born to the purple and as a prominent Yorkist rose swiftly in the Church. Of course, the archbishop's power was territorial as much as spiritual. Besides Lambeth Palace, he owned at least four substantial houses – Charing and Otford in Kent, Mayfield in Sussex, and Croydon in Surrey. But Knole was to be his special favourite, constantly visited and added to, and the place where he died in 1486. To understand his contribution, and its importance to the future development of the house, we should stand first of all in the Green Court, with our backs to the outer

gatehouse, and look at the higher range straight ahead: the original west front of Bourchier's house. Forgetting for a moment the Jacobean bay windows which flank the inner gatehouse, and its playful clock tower (half Gothic and half Chinese) added in the late eighteenth century, we can clearly see the character of Bourchier's architecture. Massive, austere, castellated, it would invite comparison with the north front of Bodiam were it not for the smaller square towers at either end (that on the right enlarged at a slightly later date), obviously not built for serious defence, and the beautifully carved stone oriel above the central gate that breaks right through the machicolations, as if purposely demonstrating their uselessness. The charming angels carved in the spandrels of the arch below carry

shields that would doubtless have been painted with the Bourchier arms – and can never have expected to see boiling water or molten lead poured down from above on the heads of assailants. Despite the continuation of the Wars of the Roses, the practical necessities of castle architecture had, in other words, become merely ornamental by this time. Inside the room lit by the oriel, stone corbels carved with the Bourchier or Stafford reef-knot, and with the symbol IHS, even suggest that it was an oratory rather than the more usual guard chamber.

The archbishop's other major contribution to Knole was a new great hall on axis with his gatehouse and of prodigious size. Lord Dorset somewhat lessened its impact by putting a ceiling in below the massive open timber roof, and thus creating the so-called Retainers' Gallery above, in the early seventeenth century. But it still bears comparison with some of the greatest Oxford and Cambridge college halls. An unusual feature of the screens passage is that it has only two doors, serving the

buttery and pantry, on the north wall. The kitchen, instead of lying behind them as one might expect, is placed at right-angles to the hall, on the north side of a third courtyard, and is approached from the far end of the screens passage by way of a large servery, once equipped with a 'master cook's gallery'. There are several good reasons for this arrangement: first, the way the ground gives sharply to the north, making it a difficult site for a construction of any size; second, the proximity of the well in the courtyard to the east, still known as the Water Court; and third, the likelihood that Thomas Bourchier made the old Saye and Sele great hall into his kitchen – a solution favoured by others in their aggrandizement of earlier medieval buildings.

Behind the 'beautiful, decent simplicity' of the west front – as Horace Walpole described it – the courtyard mansion gradually unfolds over an area of nearly four acres.

The disposition of the rest of the house in Bourchier's day cannot have been radically altered by the Sackvilles. His great chamber must, like theirs, have been the present ballroom, but approached only by a small stair off the dais end of the hall. This stair still exists, although its painted *grisailles* by Mark Anthony Hauduroy, dating from 1723–4, lead many visitors to think of it as Georgian. Below the great chamber lay a parlour, which the 1st Earl of Dorset later panelled, and which is now hung with portraits of the poets and dramatists in the 6th Earl's circle – Dryden, Pope, Prior and Wycherley among them. Even here there is continuity, for according to one of the archbishop's contemporaries, he 'opened his house to literary men, whose society he much enjoyed' – a tradition that has been upheld by generations of his successors at Knole.

Bourchier's private apartments may have been between the great chamber and the chapel, which he could survey from a gallery at the west end. The so-called Duke's Tower here is evidently slightly later than the chapel, but records of new towers being built at Knole as early as 1467 could account both for this and for the enlargement of the King's Tower, which then balanced it at the south-west corner of the house. The principal apartment, reserved for the most important guests and in particular the sovereign, probably lay to the west of the great chamber, as it still does: consisting of a withdrawing room (the Reynolds Room), a gallery (now called the Cartoon Gallery) and a bedchamber in the projecting King's Tower. The east range has been much altered since Bourchier's day, but it appears that he may have built a gatehouse on this side too, providing entry to the Water Court, which was then much bigger. The smaller Pheasant Court (used to breed

Lord Amherst's golden pheasants, brought back from his embassy in China in the early nineteenth century) and the tiny Men's Court (overlooked by footmen's rooms) were the result of later sub-divisions in the Elizabethan and Jacobean periods.

Thomas Bourchier bequeathed Knole to the see of Canterbury, and his successor John Morton may have made some small additions before his death in 1500. On the other hand William Warham, who became archbishop four years later, wished 'to leave to posteritie some glorious monument' of his own, and spent a fortune on the improvement of Otford, only three miles away. By now the Reformation was at hand, however, and the next incumbent, Thomas Cranmer, was unlucky enough to lose both these plums to his royal master. Henry VIII seems often to have stayed at Knole, first as a guest of Warham in 1510, and later on his visits to Hever, Anne Boleyn's family home; Cranmer also entertained the King's daughter, Princess Mary, there for six months in 1533. The archbishop's secretary, Ralph Morice, has left us a fascinating account of how Henry VIII actually acquired the two houses in 1538: 'My lord, minded to have retained Knole unto himself, said that it was too small a house for his Majesty. Marry, said the King, I had rather have it than this house, meaning Otford; for it standeth on a better soil. This house standeth low, and is rheumatick, like unto Croydon, where I could never be without sickness. And as for Knole, it standeth on a sound, perfect and wholesome ground; and if I should make abode here, as I do surely mind to do now and then, I will live at Knole and most of my house shall live at Otford. And so by this means both those houses were delivered up into the King's hands.'

In the event, Henry was not content to have his attendants quartered at Otford, and a large new courtyard – the present Green Court – was tacked on to the west side of Archbishop Bourchier's house to lodge them. As with the similar Base Court or outer quadrangle at Hampton Court Palace, the large number of doorways and small windows almost give the appearance of almshouses, and the pots of geraniums outside each entrance, with milk bottles and mail boxes, remind us that many are still separate dwellings, occupied by estate staff. The planning of these units, with a staircase rising behind each door, and rooms leading off on each side, recurs exactly in the Inns of Court and the Oxford and Cambridge colleges of the period. That should hardly surprise us, as these institutions were founded by the owners of great country houses – whether kings, bishops or noblemen – and their organization and architecture was based on the same medieval concept of the extended family.

The new outer gatehouse, broad and four-square, like Holbein's famous image of the King, has a porter's lodge, again on university lines, and is still generally known at Knole as the Wicket – after the little door cut into the great oak gates, which provided the everyday entrance and exit for pedestrians. Only when important guests were received, and allowed to ride through the two gatehouses to the hall door, would the gates themselves

The Stone Court has tanks beneath its paving, used to store water for the house since the seventeenth century.

The Sackvilles were an old Norman family, who had held estates near Withyham just over the Sussex border from the early thirteenth century. Thomas's father, Sir Richard Sackville, earned the punning nickname Fillsack for his shrewd purchases of monastic and other lands during Henry VIII's reign, and, as a first cousin of Queen Anne Boleyn also obtained immensely valuable London properties by royal grant. Thomas himself started life as a poet, and his *Gorboduc*, or *Ferrex and Porrex*, described by his descendant, V. Sackville-West, as 'a five-act blank-verse composition of unbearable dullness', is recognized as the first regular tragedy written in English, and an important influence on Spenser and Shakespeare. Succeeding his father in 1565 at the age of twenty-nine, however, he swiftly abandoned poetry for politics, rising to become ambassador to France and the Low Countries, Lord High Treasurer and Lord High Steward to Elizabeth I and James I respectively.

Although he was granted Knole by the Queen as early as 1566, sub-tenants appointed by Lord Leicester remained in occupation until 1603, when Thomas Sackville finally bought out the balance of the leases. Between then and April 1608, when he collapsed and died during a meeting of the Privy Council, vast amounts of money were expended on bringing the great house up to date – softening its severe, late medieval lines with Renaissance ornament, and leaving it very much as it remains today. Lord Dorset's architect is unknown, but the fact that he employed so many craftsmen from the King's Works, including the Master Carpenter, William Portington, and the Master Plasterer, Richard Dungan, suggest someone like Simon Basil, the Surveyor-General, who collaborated with Robert Lemynge on the designs for Hatfield House in the same decade. The twenty-three great shaped gables crowned with obelisks and surmounted by the Sackville leopards (the supporters of the family coat-of-arms), which were added to give rhythm and unity to the south and west fronts and the Stone Court, can be closely compared with those at Hatfield and at Blickling, Lemynge's later masterpiece. Greater regularity was also achieved by replacing earlier windows all over the house with large two- and three-light mullions, occasionally enlivened by projecting bay windows: two flanking Bourchier's gatehouse on the Green Court, and two more added to the King's Tower and Duke's Tower on the south front.

Perhaps the most startling exterior feature of Lord Dorset's work was the loggia of seven open arches in the centre of the south front, with the pillars and ornaments in different coloured marbles – some of them possibly of Italian origin. Here again there are parallels with Hatfield, though the design of the simpler Doric colonnade in the Stone Court (helping to disguise the lack of a central door to the great hall) is more reminiscent of Robert Smythson's Hardwick. By this date, the old well in the Water Court was not considered adequate to supply the entire house, and the rainwater pipes from all around were made to discharge into great tanks just below the flags of the Stone Court. The lead rainwater heads here and all round the rest of the house bear Lord Dorset's monogram and his

Thomas Sackville, 1st Earl of Dorset, totally remodelled the house which had been given to him by his cousin Queen Elizabeth.

have been flung open – and a beadle's mace still propped up in a corner here reminds us of the solemn processions that would be formed on such occasions, with escorts of liveried attendants, and high officials of the household each holding their wand of office. The north range of the Green Court is still known as the King's Stables, though in Henry VIII's day it would probably have housed the master of the horse, the equerries and armourers, conveniently placed backing on to the huge stable court to the north.

Henry VIII's successors used Knole as a reward for their favourites rather than a residence for themselves: Edward VI granting it to the Duke of Northumberland; Mary I to Cardinal Pole; and Elizabeth I to the Earl of Leicester (one of Northumberland's younger sons). The Leicester Gallery in the east range, overlooking the Water Court, goes under the same name in the earliest known inventory of the house, made in 1645, so, in spite of its later panelling, there may be some truth in the tradition that Lord Leicester added or remodelled this part of the building before 1566, when he returned Knole to the Queen. However, this was as nothing compared with the alterations made by his successor Thomas Sackville, Lord Buckhurst, later 1st Earl of Dorset.

Knole

1 Green court
2 Bourchier's tower
3 Stone court
4 Great hall
5 Great staircase
6 Brown gallery
7 Leicester gallery
8 Water court
9 Kitchen
10 Chapel
11 Ballroom
12 Reynolds room
13 Cartoon gallery
14 King's room

North

The Great Hall, where lattice windows in the upper part of the carved oak screen at one end conceal a musicians' gallery.

Order of the Garter, the date (most often 1605) and various heraldic emblems – usually made in pairs, but no pair the same as another. Superb examples of their type, they must be by the plumber William Halsey, one of the leading craftsmen whose names fill the account books.

Inside the house, as we have seen, Lord Dorset put a plasterwork ceiling and frieze in the great hall, below the rafters of Archbishop Bourchier's open timber roof, so as to create a new 'Retainers' Gallery' above. He also had a vast new oak screen carved by William Portington for the northern end of the room, smothered with heraldry and architectural ornament, much of it taken from Flemish pattern-books like those of Wendel Dietterlin and Martin de Vos. Stripped at a later date, this screen wall may well have been painted to resemble different stones and marbles, far lighter in effect than it now appears. Behind the lattice windows in the upper part is the musicians' gallery, where Lord Dorset's private orchestra of ten or more players would often have performed. It is easy to imagine the screen as a backdrop to the plays and masques regularly performed here. Seen as a piece of stage scenery, its almost barbaric vigour and theatricality are also more easily appreciated. Unfortunately William Portington's equally flamboyant chimneypiece and overmantel, seen in an old painting of the room, were removed in the late eighteenth century, probably to make room for the giant Wootton picture showing the 1st Duke's procession as Warden of the Cinque Ports, brought from the family's London house.

We can only understand the scale and elaboration of the 1st Earl's work at Knole if we realize how old-fashioned were his basic aims. What he wanted was a setting for a medieval way of life, however strong his addiction to Renaissance architecture and ornament. As one of his obituaries put it, 'he kept house for forty and two years in an honourable proportion. For thirty of these his family consisted of little less, in one place or another, than two hundred persons. But for more than twenty years, besides

workmen and other hired, his number at the least hath been two hundred and twenty daily, as appeared upon check-role. A very rare example in this present age of ours, when housekeeping is so decayed'. His grandson, the 3rd Earl, who succeeded in 1609, lived no less magnificently, and another fascinating document that survives at Knole is a 'catalogue' of his family and household between 1613 and 1624, showing precisely where they all ate. As one would expect, members of the immediate family (eight of them only) dined 'at My Lord's Table' in the Great Chamber; a further twenty, including the chaplain, the steward, the Gentleman of the Horse, 'Mr. Matthew Caldicott, my Lord's favourite', and 'Mr. Josiah Cooper, a Frenchman, Page', dined in the Parlour, immediately below. 'The Clerk's Table' at the dais end of the hall was occupied by upper servants, such as the clerks of the kitchen, the yeomen of the buttery and pantry, the baker, brewer, gardener and groom of the wardrobe, while the lower servants sat at the 'Long Table in the Hall' (which still survives), from yeomen and grooms, farriers, falconers and huntsmen, down to 'Solomon, the Bird-Catcher', and the 'Men to carry wood'. Elsewhere there was also a nursery table, a laundry-maids' table, and, lowliest of all, one for the kitchen and scullery, given to such colourful figures as 'Diggory Dyer', 'Marfidy Snipt' and 'John Morockoe, a Blackamoor'.

Because the great hall had now become the servants' domain, except on special occasions such as great feasts or entertainments, it was important to have a grander processional way up to the great chamber, replacing Bourchier's small – probably spiral – staircase behind the dais. Lord Dorset's answer was to build an entirely new staircase in the south-west corner of the Water Court, with three flights leading from a Doric arcade at the bottom to an Ionic one above. This grand architectural display was made still richer by the painted decoration which covers virtually every surface, and which is almost certainly the work of Paul Isaacson, employed by Elizabeth I and James I, and later Master of the Painter-Stainers Company. His allegorical scenes include the Four Ages of Man at ground-floor level, after engravings by

Heraldic Sackville leopards, holding the family coats-of-arms, surmount the newel posts of the Great Staircase. Many more – in stone – crown the gables of the south and west fronts of the house.

Mary Curzon was Governess to the children of Charles I, and married Richard Sackville, 4th Earl of Dorset.

Crispin van de Passe; pairs of mythological figures representing types and anti-types on the stair itself; and on the upper landing, six of the Seven Virtues. In other words the physical ascent was equated with a moral one, typical of the workings of the Renaissance mind: refinement and culture were necessary if one was to leave the world of the hoi-polloi below, and rise to the level of the great and good on the floor above. The turned balusters and the newel posts surmounted by the Sackville leopards are echoed in *trompe-l'oeil* on the outer walls, an early use of feigned architecture looking forward to the later achievements of the Baroque scene-painters.

At the head of the stairs is the door to the Great Chamber. Now called the Ballroom, and filled with furniture, pictures and porcelain in a crowded Edwardian arrangement, it was always known as the 'Great Dining Room' in the eighteenth century, a truer reflection of its original function. In the 1st Earl's day it is unlikely that the room would have contained any pictures, which helps to explain the extraordinary elaboration of William Portington's carved panelling and frieze. These may originally have been painted and gilded to match the rich polychrome effect of the marble and alabaster chimneypiece and overmantel, carved by a mason of Flemish origin named Cornelius Cuer. The quality of his sculpture is in amazing contrast to the crude mermaids and chimaeras of the wood-carvers either side, and this combination of the sophisticated and the naïve is an interesting reflection of the adolescence of English culture, still striving to attain the maturity of France and Italy.

At this time, it would be normal to find the king's arms above the Great Chamber fireplace, not just as a symbol of loyalty, but because this would be the first room of the sovereign's apartment in the event of a royal visit. The large marble plaque in the centre of the overmantel may therefore have born a painted and gilded heraldic achievement. The delicate garlands of musical instruments which flank it are particularly appropriate, for the 1st Earl's musicians must have performed more frequently here than anywhere else in the house. The importance he attached to them can be judged from his will, where he singled out those he had chosen, 'some for the voice and some for the instrument, whom I have found to be honest in their behaviour and skilful in their profession, and who had often given me after the labour and painful travels of the day much recreation and contatation with their delightful harmony'. Richard Dungan's beautiful plasterwork ceiling has a complex geometrical pattern of bands, itself like the rhythmic symmetry of a galliard and the weaving in and out of dancing couples. The delicate branches of flowers and foliage in between must also have reflected the sweet-smelling herbs and rushes strewn on the floor below.

To the west of the Great Chamber, across the landing of the smaller staircase, lay the Withdrawing Room – now called after the splendid series of Reynolds collected by the 3rd Duke of Dorset. By the end of the sixteenth century this room had largely replaced the bedchamber as the private sitting (and eating) room of the family, to which only favoured company would be admitted. The diaries of the 4th Earl's wife, Lady Anne Clifford, often refer to her dining there, particularly in the winter, when the room must have been much easier to heat than the Great Chamber. Thus on 4 April 1617, she records: 'This day we began to leave the little room and dine and sup in the great chamber' – while later in the month, the earl 'dined abroad in the great chamber, and supped privately with me in the drawing chamber'. The walls of the Withdrawing Room are likely to have been hung with tapestry, now replaced by an eighteenth-century stamped woollen velvet known as 'caffoy', giving an equally warm effect. The chimneypiece and overmantel are again by Cuer, and masterpieces of their kind, carved with putti riding on the backs of sphinxes and holding great trophies of arms – a symbol of the power of love over war, and of Venus over Mars, thoroughly appropriate for a room where the ladies of the family would have congregated.

Beyond the Withdrawing Room lay the principal gallery and bedchamber, probably little changed since Archbishop Bourchier's day except for the addition of bay windows in both, along with new plasterwork, panelling and chimneypieces. The first of these rooms has been known as the Cartoon Gallery only since 1701, when the copies of Raphael's tapestry cartoons, attributed to Mytens, were first hung on its walls. But by happy coincidence, William Portington's marvellously carved Corinthian pilasters on the window wall are also Raphaelesque, derived from the artist's famous

The Cartoon Gallery, with its massive oak floorboards, is so called after the copies of Raphael's tapestry cartoons which hang on the walls.

grotesques in the Vatican loggia – with caryatid figures, birds, monkeys, garlands of fruit, and the ram's mask (the Sackville crest) added at the top. In March 1608 the painter Paul Isaacson received the huge sum of £100 'for painting and guilding worke in Y^{or} lo[rdship's] Gallery at Knoll', which must have included the naturalistic colours in which the pilasters are still picked out, and the *trompe-l'oeil* arabesque panels of the dado. Richard Dungan's plasterwork ceiling differs from those elsewhere in having

no square or intersecting panels, merely serpentine ribs which give a marvellous rippling effect of light and shade seen down the whole length of the gallery. Even if we disagree with her dating, we can sympathize with Maria Edgeworth's raptures on seeing the vast oak floorboards in 1831: 'What inlaid floor of modern parquetry could give the sublime feeling one has in walking upon a floor that was laid before planes were invented, with all the identical clumsy nails of King John's time?' Early inventories refer

With its timber-framed upper storey, the east front resembles the mansion of a city merchant rather than the country house of a courtier.

to this as the 'Matted Gallery', however, so it is unlikely that the boards were intended to be visible.

The bedchamber at the far end of the gallery has always been known as the King's Room, traditionally to commemorate a visit by James I but more likely because this was always the principal apartment in the house, prepared to receive the sovereign on one of his royal progresses, though given at other times to any distinguished guest of higher rank than his host. The 1st Earl may have created the little dressing room and closet adjoining it, and he was certainly responsible for the plasterwork ceiling – this time with bound laurel leaves in square panels, a tribute to the fame of the state bed's occupant. The bed itself, like so much of the furniture in the state rooms, is a royal piece which the 6th Earl of Dorset obtained as Lord Chamberlain to William III – more than compensating for the losses of the Civil War.

Lady Anne Clifford's diaries reveal that the various galleries at Knole were the hub of everyday life, where children played, ladies of the household embroidered, read or played cards, and gentlemen took exercise – including games of billiards, shove-halfpenny and shuttlecock. An early billiard table can still be seen in the bay off the Leicester Gallery, together with the rope of a dumb-bell hanging from the ceiling. Connected to a windlass in the attic above, this could be pulled up and down to exercise the arm muscles as in bell-ringing, but without the consequent noise. The open colonnade in the centre of the south front, almost immediately below the Cartoon Gallery, fulfilled much the same role for the family apartments on the ground floor. Indeed this arrangement of a closed gallery above an open one was common at the time, as can be seen in Mytens's famous portraits of the Earl and Countess of Arundel: he sitting in the open sculpture gallery at Arundel House, and she above in the picture gallery. The Brown Gallery at Knole also had an open walkway below it leading from the foot of the great stairs to the Chapel – but like the south colonnade this was filled in at a later date.

Like the Cartoon Gallery, the Brown and Leicester Galleries each led to a bedchamber, dressing room and closet, forming a separate suite or apartment for high-ranking guests. The galleries themselves were ideally suited for the series of portraits then coming into vogue.

A visitor to Lord Burghley's house, Theobalds, in 1598, described the long gallery as 'one side all emperors beginning with Caesar; th' other the pictures of the Chief in Europe'. In the same way, Lord Bindon was to write to Robert Cecil asking for his portrait, 'to be placed in the gallery I lately made for the pictures of sundry of my honourable friends, whose presentation thereby to behold will greatly delight me, to walk often in that place, where I may see so comfortable a sight'. The portraits in the Brown Gallery, forming a survey of European history up to the mid-seventeenth century, seem to have been commissioned by the 4th Earl of Dorset, mostly from the artist Jan van Belkamp. Based on well-known likenesses by Holbein, Cranach, Eworth and others, they are particularly strong on the leading Protestant theologians, explaining why early inventories call this the 'Reformers' Gallery'.

The bedrooms and dressing rooms beyond were probably always intended to be hung with tapestry. However, most of the splendid examples now on view are once again royal perquisites acquired by the 6th Earl, like the unique array of X-frame chairs and stools in the Brown Gallery – once used as thrones at Hampton Court and Whitehall, and given away as 'perks' when they became outmoded. Outside the scope of this survey, they all add to the romantic beauty of the place: a beauty that successive owners have appreciated to the full, never, even when they had the means, wishing to impress their own taste at the expense of previous centuries.

Above all other English houses, Knole stands for the continuity of our landed families. In the 3rd Duke's passion for Italian opera, and for the charms of Madame Baccelli, the Italian dancer lodged in 'Shelley's Tower', we look back to the masques and galliards played by the 1st Earl's musicians; in the books and verses of V. Sackville-West and her cousin Eddy, 5th Lord Sackville, we look back to the author of *Gorboduc* and the jolly Restoration dramatists gathered in the Poets' Parlour. The tide of life still ebbs and flows through the old house with visitors, as it once did with servants and retainers, and watching them from our bird's-eye vantage point above the rooftops we can agree once again with the ingenuous Miss Edgeworth – 'there is so much good taste in keeping up this fine old mansion in its dear old style'.

Little Moreton Hall

C H E S H I R E

WHY IS IT that the English – and the Americans – have developed a passion for Little Moreton? So much so that a bank in a suburban town, a semi-detached on a cheerless by-pass or a stockbroker's mansion overlooking a golf course will suddenly shock its prim sash-windowed neighbours by sprouting gables and bargeboards, leaded lights and a riot of black-and-white beams, in the weirdest of liquorice allsort patterns – all inspired by some half-forgotten lithograph of this ancient Cheshire manor house.

Respect for the obvious age of timber-framed buildings has something to do with it. Soaked by rain and parched by sun, the old beams have warped and twisted over the centuries so that there is hardly a straight line in the whole structure. Swelling here and sagging there, some of its great windows apparently falling outwards and others staggering back, it appeals also to our Anglo-Saxon sense of humour. In Pevsner's words, 'as it comes into sight – happily reeling, disorderly, but no offence meant – it seems at first unbelievable, and then a huge joke'.

There are other characteristics too that we can recognize as specifically English. The complete asymmetry of the design, so that it appears to have grown organically, would be bound to appeal to a race always suspicious of the 'grand idea', whether in politics or in architecture. The robust naïvety of the carving has the charm we associate with the amateur, rather than the deadness of the professional. Above all, the house asserts its individuality – one might say eccentricity – with the simple self-confidence of a country squire, unabashed by his first encounter with the more sophisticated fashions of the court.

But there may be one further, subconscious, reason why our hearts are stirred at this first sight of Little Moreton rising from the dark waters of the moat: the way in which the long continuous windows of the gallery on the top floor of the south range remind us of the rows of cabin windows overhanging the aft of a Tudor man-o-war. Built at a time when the techniques of house-building and ship-building were closely allied, Little Moreton takes us back to the sturdy little craft that left the estuaries of the Dee and the Mersey, as much as Plymouth Sound and the Solent, on their way to the New World or the East Indies: the 'hearts of oak' on which our island-empire was founded.

The owners of Little Moreton were, appropriately, involved in overseas trade, and among the family papers there are still letters from William Moreton, the son of the builder of the south range, written to his father from Java in 1619, reporting that he and his cousin Matthew were there trading in silks with the King of Bantam. Later, in 1633, he was abroad again, this time on a tobacco plantation at Accomack in Virginia. It cannot be said that the Moretons ever achieved great distinction outside the county of their origin, but if we owe the house to their gradual rise in prosperity in the fifteenth and sixteenth centuries, its survival, hardly touched since 1600, is due to their subsequent decline. Royalists in the Civil War, and Tories under the Hanoverians, like so many other Cheshire squires they seemed committed to the losing side, too conservative to alter their old home even if they had had the means.

Derived from the Old Norse *mor*, meaning marshland, and *tun*, meaning farm, Little Moreton is still a rural, agricultural place, despite the proximity of the Potteries to the south. Dairy herds graze in the water-meadows, and the rich smell of manure hits you as the road passes timber-framed barns and middens. Although three miles away from its local parish church at Astbury, a manor house must have existed here as early as 1216, when it formed part of the dowry of Lettice de Moreton on her marriage to Sir Gralam de Lostock. Their third son, Geoffrey, reverted to his mother's name on inheriting the property and was the founder of a long dynasty of local landowners, many of whom served as mayors of Congleton and collected taxes for the king. However, it was between about 1450 and 1580 – the exact period covered by the building of the house – that they doubled

The south range, with the long gallery on the top floor. Built about 1570–80, it is more lightly framed than the sturdy west wing of 1480.

the size of their estate, buying up land which had been depopulated by the Black Death, or which was Church or monastic property sold in the wake of the Reformation. By the end of Elizabeth I's reign the family owned an estate of 1360 acres including two profitable water mills; not as big an estate as those of neighbours like the Breretons of Brereton, or the Leghs of Lyme, who could afford to rebuild their mansions in stone,

but still providing a substantial endowment for a large manor house.

Timber was the most popular building material in England from Roman times until the late seventeenth century. Gregory King, writing in 1688, estimated that the total area of woodland in England at that time was about three million acres, a million less than in 1500 due to the reckless felling of forests for houses, ship-building and

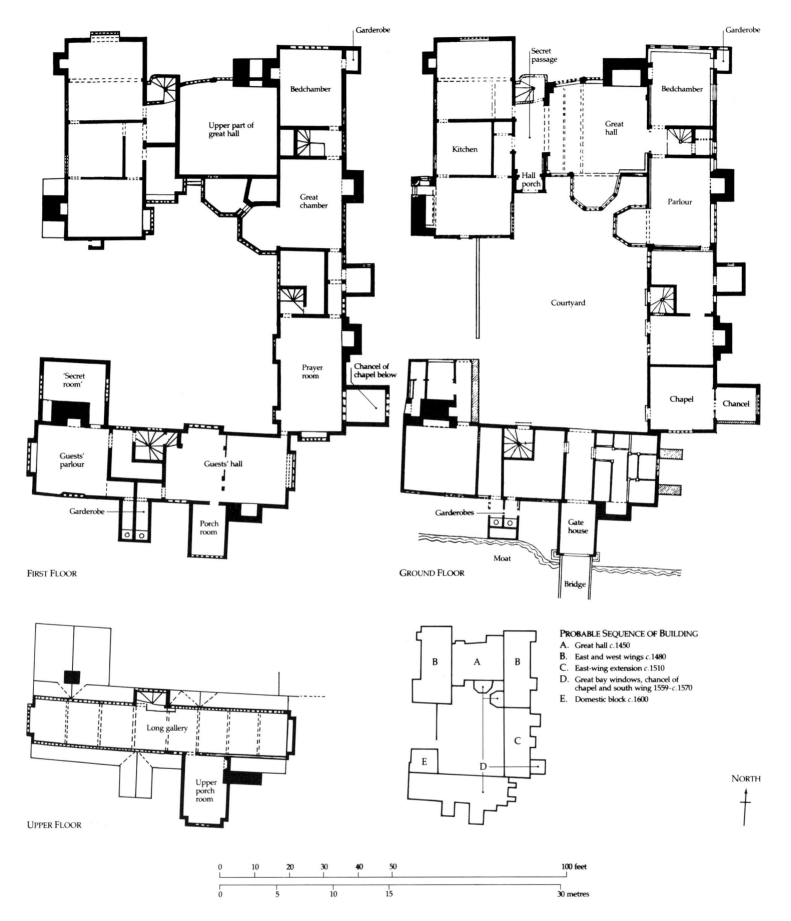

FIRST FLOOR

GROUND FLOOR

Garderobe

Bedchamber

Upper part of
great hall

Great
chamber

Prayer
room

Chancel of
chapel below

'Secret
room'

Guests'
parlour

Guests' hall

Garderobe

Porch
room

Garderobe

Secret
passage

Kitchen

Hall
porch

Great
hall

Bedchamber

Parlour

Courtyard

Chapel

Chancel

Garderobes

Gate
house

Moat

Bridge

Long gallery

Upper
porch
room

UPPER FLOOR

PROBABLE SEQUENCE OF BUILDING

A. Great hall c.1450
B. East and west wings c.1480
C. East-wing extension c.1510
D. Great bay windows, chancel of
   chapel and south wing 1559–c.1570
E. Domestic block c.1600

NORTH

```
0    10   20   30   40   50              100 feet
0         5         10        15          30 metres
```

fuel for iron-smelting. In Britain, unlike other countries in Europe, practically all the trees were hardwoods, and among these the oak was far and away the most numerous, as well as the most suitable for structural purposes. Today, we tend to underestimate the number of timber buildings in Britain, as so many of them are clad in later layers of plaster, tiling or render. But even castles, built of stone for defensive reasons, had substantial timber

elements (as can be seen at Stokesay in Shropshire); and at Bodiam the loss of so much of the interior living quarters was probably due more to the decay of untreated timber than to the thoroughness of the Parliamentary troops.

Apart from the stone plinth on which Little Moreton stands, the greenish-grey sandstone slates from Mow Cop used on the roofs, the great brick chimneystacks and a few later brick buttresses, the house is entirely built of timber, and it is a sobering thought that acorns from the trees used by the fifteenth- and sixteenth-century carpenters could have grown into the great oaks now seen in neighbouring fields and spinneys. Recent scientific analysis of a sixteenth-century Suffolk farmhouse, considerably smaller than Little Moreton, suggests that over 300 separate trees were felled and used for it. Admittedly only a few of these needed to be very large – for important members like tie-beams, posts and wall-plates – but the scale of the undertaking was still formidable, especially when the trees had to be extracted from the middle of a forest by ox-cart, or floated down-river in batches. It is also worth remembering that virtually all the timbers we see at Little Moreton, inside and out, are structural, and that if we took away the white plaster (or wattle-and-daub) infills, the house would still stand just as securely, like a child's matchstick model on a giant scale. As with model-making, many of the main elements of a house like this were also prefabricated – hence the carpenter's marks on each piece, instructing the workmen on site how to put them together. This meant that buildings could be moved in their entirety, as they have continued to be – in the case of Agecroft Hall, Lancashire, as far away as Richmond, Virginia.

The black-and-white chequerboard pattern of Little Moreton adds to its toy-like appearance. Like the traditional harlequin costume of the clown, it is something we have come to expect of timber buildings in the west, from Cumbria and the Welsh marches down to Somerset and Devon. However, pure white lime-wash was an expensive luxury in the fifteenth and sixteenth centuries, and the soft ochres still used in East Anglia are far more likely to have been prevalent at that date. The timbers themselves may have needed more protection from rain here than in the east, but again blackening probably only caught on with the advent of tar and pitch in the late eighteenth and early nineteenth centuries.

Even if their overall effect was less strident, these materials, allied to the natural conservatism of provincial craftsmen (always slow to abandon old and tried techniques), give Little Moreton a misleading appearance of unity. But although it took at least four succeeding generations of Moretons to build it, and it was not finished until well into the reign of Elizabeth I, the house belongs to an entirely medieval tradition in its planning as well as its structure. A few touches of Renaissance decoration can be found here and there, especially in some of the plasterwork, but they are never more than a veneer. To compare Little Moreton with its near-contemporary, Hardwick, would be like comparing Lutyens's Arts and Crafts style with the International Modern of Mies van der Rohe.

The great hall on the north side of the courtyard appears to be the oldest part of the building, probably erected by Sir Richard Moreton as early as 1450. As usual in this part of the world the roof is supported by massive 'crucks', or pairs of curved timbers, joined by a collar or tie-beam at the top to form an arch. Assembled on the ground, these would be raised on an appointed feast day by large teams of men, often comprising the whole population of

the village, when the owner would be responsible for providing the drink: a custom still followed until recently in places like Vermont, and immortalized by Hollywood in the barn-raising scene from *Seven Brides for Seven Brothers*. At this date the hall would have had an open fire in a central hearth, placed beneath a vent or louvre high up in the rafters, between the crucks.

As first built, Sir Richard's hall seems to have had a screens passage at the east end and a dais at the west. But in about 1480 his son Ralph reversed this arrangement – building a new service wing, with kitchen, buttery and pantry, on the west, and new living quarters on the east, so that the house then formed quite a regular H-shape. At the same time a large brick chimneystack was added on the north, not only providing a fireplace at the new dais end of the hall but also incorporating flues for the two chambers (one above the other) at the north-east corner of the house. Ralph Moreton's new porch, still the main entrance to the house, has typically late Gothic decoration, with twisted columns each side, and two curious little rows of Perpendicular colonettes above. Between these are quatrefoils (rather like four-leaf clovers – and possibly also considered symbols of good luck) carved out of solid oak, and anticipating the more elaborate patterns of the sixteenth-century carpenters. By contrast, the bold herringbone timbers on his west wing are simpler and more solidly built, looking back to medieval precedents like the fourteenth-century church at nearby Lower Peover. The same herringbone framing can be found on the south wall of the present withdrawing room, proving that the east wing once ended there.

Inside the hall, two great moulded posts or 'speres' can be seen on the west wall, framing what was originally a minstrels' gallery above the screens passage. However, the screen itself has gone, probably because it was free-standing and movable – like the wonderfully carved example at Rufford Old Hall in Lancashire. A newel staircase at the far end of the screens passage led up not only to the minstrels' gallery but also to two chambers above the buttery and pantry, both equipped with chimneypieces, and one with a double garderobe or lavatory flue. It is likely that the room between them once formed the upper part of a two-storey kitchen.

If we cannot be certain about the exact date of Ralph Moreton's work, or whether any of it can be attributed to his son William (who died in 1526), we know exactly who to thank for the extravagant transformation of their modest manor house later in the sixteenth century. The main evidence is literally in front of our eyes, for above the upper lights of the two bay windows, in the north-east corner of the courtyard, runs the inscription 'God is Al in Al Thing. This windous whire made by William Moreton in the yeare of our Lorde MDLIX' – and above one of the lower lights 'Richard Dale carpeder made thies windous by the grac of God'. Given the anonymity of so many mason and carpenter architects at this date, this proud 'signature' is of unique value, but it is not all we have, for on the second William Moreton's death four years later, in 1563, his will particularly requested his son John to complete the work at Little Moreton 'according to

The inscription above the great bay windows in the courtyard tells us that the windows were made for William Moreton in 1559.

the devyse thereof devysed betwixt me and Richard Dale the head wright and workman off the same frame'.

Hardly anything is known of Richard Dale, though his son, another Richard, is recorded working at Congleton church and building a fine new porch at Nantwich grammar school in 1612. An inventory of his goods taken in 1637 shows that he was a travelling craftsman, who also farmed to supplement his income. Masons and carpenters were of course the architects of the Middle Ages, capable of envisaging a building and expressing their ideas on the drawing-board as much as surveyors in later times. At the same time, the processes of design and construction were much more closely linked than they are now. Far more

was left to be worked out on the spot than we would consider normal – or wise – and major houses and churches were often begun with no very clear idea as to how they would be completed. A good example of this is the famous gallery on the top floor of the south range of Little Moreton, which many have considered a later addition, breaking through the roofline of the floor below as it does. But there are no signs of roof-trusses having been removed, and structurally the building seems all of a piece, so it is much more likely to have been an afterthought, carried out while the building work was still in progress.

Before looking at the south range in more detail,

A riot of black-and-white chequerboard patterns and leaded lights give Little Moreton its higgledy-piggledy toy-like charm.

however, we should return to Richard Dale's great bay windows in the courtyard and see what he did to remodel the great hall range of the old house and the living quarters to its east. The two bays, formed like huge five-sided lanterns, would have been impossible to build in stone, and exploit the potential of timber-framing to the full. Indeed, in their fantasy and structural daring they seem to look back to Henry VIII's palace of Nonsuch in Surrey, perhaps the largest and most celebrated timber-framed building of its time. Contemporaries must have been particularly amazed by their walls of glass at a time when this was still a very expensive commodity. It was not until the time of James I that the ordinary smallholder expected to have glass in his windows, and in 1567 those at Alnwick Castle were still considered so precious that they were lifted out and stored away when the owner was not in residence. Staffordshire, Shropshire and Cheshire were early centres of production, however, and by 1589 could boast nearly half of the fifteen glass factories in England. It is even possible that William Moreton had a financial stake in one of them.

Above all, it is the many different glazing patterns of the windows that give Little Moreton its sixteenth-century character. *A Booke of Sundry Draughtes, principally serving for glaziers,* published in 1615, contains over a hundred designs of similar geometrical complexity, but loose sheets of engraved ornament would certainly have been available to craftsmen at an earlier date. Displaying a remarkable variety even in the same window, these leaded lights show the same kind of intricacy found in Elizabethan knot-gardens and embroidery. The individual pieces of glass used are very small, but this is because of the weakness of the lead strips or 'cames' which hold them in place, not because larger panes were difficult to obtain. Thus Charles Cotton, celebrating the newly introduced sashes at Chatsworth in 1681, wrote of the earlier Elizabethan windows:

> The glazier's work before substantial was
> I must confess, thrice as much lead as glass,
> Which in the sun's meridian cast a light
> As it had been within an hour of night.

Battered by gales over their long history, these old leaded lights now have an attractive unevenness, with the panes reflecting light at slightly different angles, while from inside there are tints of green, yellow and faint purple caused by slight metallic impurities, from copper, iron and manganese respectively.

Apart from their glazing, Richard Dale's bays are remarkable for the projection of the upper windows – so far that they actually meet, connected by a kind of bridge on horizontal struts. 'Jettying', as this is generally called (from the same derivation as 'jutting out') was one of the favourite devices of the medieval carpenter-architect, and the ancestor of the modern cantilever. All kinds of theories have been put forward to explain it. Some have seen it as an urban phenomenon, allowing owners of restricted plots to encroach legally over streets or alleyways. In the famous Shambles at York, for instance, the upper storeys practically touch, and neighbours on opposite sides of the

One of the huge carved brackets in the guests' hall. Surprisingly, these are not structurally necessary, but were purely decorative features added in the seventeenth century.

road can lean out of their attic windows and shake hands. On the other hand, much earlier farmhouses of the 'Wealden' type in Kent are built along the same lines, and arguments that jettying had a defensive purpose, or a load-bearing one (enabling heavy pieces of furniture to stand round the walls of the upper rooms, supported by the walls below), seem equally unconvincing. A more likely suggestion is that jettying was primarily decorative, always appearing on façades that were intended for show, while at the same time giving added space and emphasis to the rooms on the upper floors – reflecting their increasing importance in terms of use.

A noteworthy feature of the jettying at Little Moreton is the way in which the projecting beam-ends are concealed behind a rounded coving – very much a regional peculiarity. This coving is found all over the house, and on all three floors of the south range, some of it painted with black-and-white quatrefoils during the nineteenth century, though perhaps following traces of earlier decoration. Like the other flat panels between the timbers, these coved sections are now mostly made of plaster on laths, but these could be later replacements for the more usual sixteenth-century technique of wattle-and-daub: a basketwork mat made of reeds, which was then covered with a thick layer of mud or clay (possibly dug from the moat), and painted with lime-wash after it had hardened.

One of William Moreton's main objectives in building the bay windows in the courtyard was to light a new room which he created at the same time in the upper part of the great hall, on a level with the old minstrels' gallery. A drawing of the hall made by J. S. Cotman in 1807 shows

NORTH

Little Moreton Hall

1 Great hall
2 Parlour
3 Bedchamber
4 Long gallery

that this mid-way floor had already been removed by that date, but the sawn-off remnants of the beams which supported it are still visible halfway up the east or dais end wall. The old opening from the minstrels' gallery was also partitioned off, and a small gallery created behind it, above the screens passage – giving access to the two chambers in the west wing.

To understand how the family used all this part of the house in the late sixteenth century, we have to forget the somewhat misleading names which have been given to the rooms since. Thus the so-called withdrawing room, approached from the dais end of the hall and lit by the lower half of Richard Dale's right-hand bay, was almost certainly the parlour. The great chamber would have been immediately above this, approached by the adjoining newel stair and distinguished by a larger window recess. The new room created above the hall probably served as the withdrawing room, while what is now called the parlour in the north-east corner of the house was a bedchamber, with another immediately above it – both equipped with garderobes.

William Moreton's alterations tell us much about the diminishing importance of the great hall in the Elizabethan period, especially in smaller houses where the number of household retainers was few. Only the lesser ranks would normally have dined here at this date, though the long oak refectory table, probably made by Richard Dale and his carvers, and one of the most elaborate of its kind to survive, kept up the appearance of 'state'. This was, after all, the room that family and guests still passed through to reach their living quarters, and the place where rents would be collected and manor courts held.

Two other surviving pieces of furniture can be identified in an inventory dated 1601: 'one cuborde of boxes', a large oak cabinet with numerous drawers, which may have stood in William Moreton's bedchamber; and 'the great rounde table in the parlour' valued at ten shillings. This must have been made specially to fit Richard Dale's bay window recess, and its octagonal base, beautifully carved with fluted supports and shaped aprons, once again suggests his hand.

As originally built in the 1480s, both the upper rooms in the east wing had open timber roofs – as the north chamber in the west wing still does. To increase the chances of warmth and comfort William Moreton inserted ceilings below these old rafters, and then to compensate for their lack of height lowered the floors. His new ceiling in the parlour below, therefore, only just clears the tops of the windows on the east wall. Its heavy moulded beams, arranged in square panels, are identical in section to the ones he inserted in the great hall, and the panelling here must be of the same date.

One puzzle is the plaster chimneypiece here, with the arms of Elizabeth I in the overmantel. As we shall see, in larger houses like Hardwick one would normally expect to see the royal arms set up in the great chamber on the upper floor, which in the event of a royal visit would become the first room in the sovereign's own suite of apartments. However, in a lesser house like Little

The wolf's-head crest and initials of William Moreton, from a stained-glass fragment in the parlour.

Moreton the parlour could have been considered a more 'public' room than the great chamber, and the arms could be set up here as a symbol both of loyalty and of authority – demonstrating that the lord of the manor acted as the Queen's representative, perhaps even dispensing justice here as the local magistrate. Both the overmantel and the panelling would probably have been painted in bright colours, giving a very different impression from the room's present dark and sombre tones.

The windows in the parlour contain some heraldic stained glass quarries, including one typically Elizabethan conceit: a punning device representing the name Moreton, with a barrel, or 'tun', below a wolf's head, standing for the Old English *maw* – the jaws of a voracious beast. 'Devices' of this sort would be enamelled on jewels, painted in the background of portraits, or stamped on the bindings of books, as marks of the wit and ingenuity of an educated gentleman's mind.

The ground-floor bedchamber to the north (now wrongly called the parlour) is chiefly remarkable for its elaborate painted decoration, only discovered in 1976 behind the Georgian panelling. Scenes from the story of Susannah and the Elders, with blackletter 'captions' between them, run round the frieze, rather in the manner of a strip cartoon – and the *trompe-l'oeil* panelling below includes vivid reds and greens, graining and marbling. The initials J.M. for John Moreton, who died in 1598, and the wolf's head crest can be seen in the arabesque border immediately below the frieze.

Biblical scenes of this sort, taken from the Old Testament and the Apocrypha, were especially popular with Puritans at the end of the sixteenth century; similar examples have recently been found in a chamber at Canons Ashby in Northamptonshire, painted for Sir Erasmus Dryden in the 1580s. Instead of favourite Catholic subjects like the Dance of Death, the Last Judgement and the suffering and ordeals of Christ and the saints, they tended to choose stories which stressed freedom of choice and the moral power of the individual: in this case the young Daniel, who interceded on Susannah's behalf and had her voyeuristic judges condemned to death.

The same team of painters must have been responsible for decorating the chapel at the southern end of the east wing, again with old-fashioned arabesque bands, here used to frame blackletter texts taken from the Tyndale Bible. Derived from the 'anticke work' of Henry VIII's Italian painters at Hampton Court and Nonsuch, these grotesques are now confined to the chancel walls, although the artist James West, who visited Little Moreton in 1847, recorded that they were also painted on the ceiling beams.

As we have seen, the original 1480s' house was H-shaped, but the southward extension of the east wing was probably added in the early part of the sixteenth century by William Moreton I – best known for his feud with Thomas Rode of nearby Odd Rode in 1513, 'concerning which of theym should sit highest in churche and foremost goe in procession'. Since the parish church of Astbury lay over three miles away, it is likely that there was a chapel for daily prayers at Little Moreton from the earliest times. However, its present site may only have been determined by the second William Moreton, who appears to have added the chancel about 1560, and who remodelled what is now called the Prayer Room above the nave – putting in a ceiling below its open timber roof, a new bay window overlooking the courtyard, and a long internal window or 'squint' placed immediately above the chapel screen and looking down on to the altar. As at Bodiam, and in later country houses right up to the end of the eighteenth century, members of the family would generally have watched the services from this gallery, invisible to their household retainers gathered below.

William Moreton's will of 1563 suggests that his building work on the house was then at a halfway stage, and it is tempting to think that he had started the south range, which his son John then completed, adding the

James West's watercolour, made in 1847, shows the chancel decorated with biblical texts which are framed by arabesques.

long gallery perched precariously on the top as an afterthought. However, this range may also incorporate elements of an earlier gatehouse building, for the twisted columns and trailing vine-leaf mouldings which flank the main portal are very much in the same spirit as the porch

The painted panelling, which was fashionable in the late sixteenth century, in the bedchamber next to the parlour.

of the great hall range beyond – thought to be of the 1480s. Richard Dale's hand is recognizable in much of the other carving, although, as with the bay windows in the courtyard, it looks back to early Tudor precedents once again. The two little helmeted figures guarding the portal on the courtyard side are for instance comparable with those at that other celebrated timber-framed house, Paycocke's at Coggeshall in Essex, which dates from about 1500. Distant echoes of the Roman Lares and Penates, the household gods placed at the entrance to the villa, they also symbolize the function of the gatehouse, with the porter's lodge under the arch acting as a guard chamber.

The patterns used in the timber-framing of the south range begin with a simple herringbone on the ground floor (again like Ralph Moreton's work of the 1480s), becoming more ornamental, and more original, the higher they climb. The double row of arches with trefoil heads above the main gate are like those on Richard Dale's bay windows, but the large quatrefoils running all round like a frieze to the first floor are 'cusped' (given projecting points between the foils) for added richness; the gallery has a different pattern again, which can be read as a series of catherine wheels intersected by squares. Fireworks are certainly a good analogy for the sheer ostentation of the carpenter's work, but Elizabethan textile and costume design often displays the same kind of 'busyness'. Geometry, as an expression of reason, was one of the most fashionable of Renaissance pursuits, and, as we shall see, provided the key to the interior of the Long Gallery as much as to its exterior.

Apart from the gallery itself, the south range seems largely to have been built for the entertainment of guests, who would arrive with their own retainers and who could therefore eat and sleep in an almost entirely separate suite of rooms. Elaborate courtesy calls would be made from one part of the house to another during these visits, but eating separately avoided difficult problems of precedence at a time when men of different rank would seldom eat at the same table. The ground-floor room at the west end was probably the kitchen, and food would have been brought up the spiral staircase nearby, to the guests' hall on the first floor. This room, more like a second great chamber than a hall, has heavy moulded ceiling beams similar to the ones that Richard Dale installed in the parlour in 1559. Like all the other rooms on this level it has a floor of lime and ash, worked together while moist and then rammed down on to a bedding of straw and laths till it set hard. This type of lime-ash flooring was relatively fire-resistant, an important consideration in a timber-framed building, especially in rooms with fireplaces – and even where there were floorboards, a similar mix was often used below as an infill between the joists.

The room above the kitchen – now called the guests' parlour – is more likely to have been a bedchamber, with another over the porch, later described as the 'Bridge Chamber'. Two very elaborate garderobes or lavatories (complete with their original wooden seats) lie between these rooms, in a little gabled projection that sticks out to the left of the gatehouse. Their flues, and those of two further latrines below, issued straight out into the moat,

One end of the long gallery showing the open timber roof. Daylight pours in through the almost continuous windows on all four sides of the gallery.

The figure of Destiny (right) above the east window in the Long Gallery was copied from the frontispiece (left) of Robert Recorde's Castle of Knowledge.

and it is possible that, like a near-contemporary example at Canons Ashby, they were washed down with rainwater brought through pipes from the gutters on either side. Important bedchambers were not always supplied with garderobes, however. An instance of this is the room off the gallery above the 'Bridge Chamber', which has the most elaborate plaster chimneypiece in the house, with figures of Justice and Mercy flanking a central panel with the Moreton arms. In an inventory of 1654 it contained a curtained bed, a cupboard, a chest, a green chair and a stool.

The long gallery itself measures 68 feet in length, and is flooded with daylight from almost continuous windows on all four sides. The great oak floorboards rise and fall like a sea-swell, and here, high above the surrounding rooftops, with the creak of the timber window-frames buffeted by the wind, you feel you could be on the bridge of a galleon, sailing proudly across the Cheshire plain. The massive weight of the roof is supported by nine huge arch-braced trusses, whose 'collars' come only just below the ridge line and would have given a clear view from one end to the other. Unfortunately cross-beams had to be inserted in the late seventeenth century to counteract signs of movement, and a flat ceiling may also have been inserted below them. But that has long since gone, and it is still possible to appreciate the beauty of the original proportions.

Between the purlins (the main horizontal timbers of the roof) the braces are curved and cusped like the cogs of gigantic wheels, giving a natural sense of rhythm as you walk up and down. So it may even be by deliberate association that the plasterwork decoration in the gables at each end also deals with wheels and spheres. Above the east window the figure of Destiny holds an astrolabe aloft in one hand and clasps a pair of dividers in the other – illustrating the text 'The Sp[h]eare of Destinye whose Rule is Knowledge' – while above the west window a blindfolded Fate holds a string attached to the hub of her wheel – 'The Wheel of Fortune whose Rule is Ignorance'.

Both figures are copied from the title page of *The Castle of Knowledge*, a treatise on the sphere published by the mathematician Robert Recorde in 1556; and a further verse explains their meaning more clearly:

> *Though spiteful Fortune turned her wheele*
> *To staye the Sphere of Uranye,*
> *Yet dooth this Sphere resist that wheele,*
> *And fleeth all fortunes villanye*
> *Though earthe do honour Fortunes balle,*
> *And bytells blynde hyr wheele advance,*
> *The heavens to fortune are not thralle,*
> *These Spheres surmount al fortunes chance.*

As with the painted decoration in the east wing and the choice of biblical texts in the chapel, the message here is clearly the power of knowledge over superstition – and of individual striving over the blind acceptance of fate. Opposed to Calvinist theories of predestination as much as to Catholic ideas of purgatory, it represents the dawn of humanism in the Protestant north.

It might seem strange to adopt intellectual and improving sentiments of this kind in the decoration of a room that was primarily intended for daily exercise and indoor sport. On the other hand the long gallery was in many ways the heir to the medieval cloister, and it is common to hear of political negotiations, religious arguments and the teaching of the young taking place here. An early seventeenth-century tennis ball found behind one of the panels shows that games could certainly be played, but there was equal opportunity to sit and talk – at least by 1654, when the inventory listed 'one sofa, Two gt. Blow Chaires, ffive lesser chaires blow' and no fewer than sixteen 'blow stooles'. A meeting place for family and visitors, for different sexes, different generations and different ranks of society, the gallery is likely to have had a more varied use than any other interior at Little Moreton. Crowded with the shades of Elizabethan and Jacobean Moretons, it still speaks to us in the language of Shakespeare, Marlowe and Jonson.

Hardwick Hall

D E R B Y S H I R E

HARDWICK is one of the wonders of the Elizabethan age. Like François Premier's Chambord, or the great Farnese villa of Caprarola, it is a Renaissance hunting lodge on a gigantic scale, a symbol of a new era, confident and outward-looking. No one who has seen it can forget their first view from the wooded valley below as the setting sun strikes the vast gridiron windows of the west front, and the huge building seems on fire.

If its size and monumental symmetry are a source of wonder to us, who are used to the tower blocks of Manhattan, how much more it must have amazed Bess of Hardwick's contemporaries, who knew only the rambling courtyard houses of the period, like Knole and Audley End, impressing more by the acreage they cover than by any of their façades. Who, they must have asked themselves, did she think she was, this daughter of a modest Derbyshire squire, who had married four husbands each grander than the last, and had outlived them all? And what could have driven her to start building this extraordinary palace at the then advanced age of sixty-three, crowning its towers with her initials and coronet (ES for Elizabeth, Countess of Shrewsbury) so that none should doubt the identity of its creator?

Born in 1527, Elizabeth was the youngest child of John Hardwick, the owner of a few hundred acres and a small manor house that still forms the core of the Old Hall at Hardwick. At least six generations of the family had lived here, but none had risen above the ranks of minor gentry, and the bequest of £26 13s 4d, which the child received on her father's death in 1528, was all she could call her own until in 1543 she married a slightly more prosperous cousin and neighbour, Robert Barlow. The young couple both seem to have been upper servants in a great household – that of the Zouche family in London; this was a normal practice at this time (and even later, as we saw at Knole), not involving menial duties, and comparable with the ladies-in-waiting and equerries still employed by the sovereign today. Barlow died after only a few months, however, and Bess, with a widow's

jointure of about £66 a year, seems afterwards to have become gentlewoman to the Marchioness of Dorset, Lady Jane Grey's mother. Here, in cultivated surroundings on the fringes of the court, she would have picked up the education and taste for luxury expressed in her later buildings.

Real advancement in status finally came in 1547 when she attracted the notice of the elderly Sir William Cavendish, a government official who had been one of the commissioners for the Dissolution of the Monasteries, and who afterwards bought the lucrative post of Treasurer of the Chamber. Though married twice before, Cavendish had no male heirs, so the three sons Bess bore him before his death in 1557 were to inherit the great estates he had amassed: the two younger ones, who had children of their own, becoming ancestors of the Dukes of Devonshire, Newcastle and Portland. Bess's third husband, Sir William St Loe, represented another step up, for he came from an old-established West Country dynasty and was a leading courtier. However, he in turn died in 1565, leaving her much of his property – to the outrage of his family – and two years later she made her final and most spectacular match, with George Talbot, 6th Earl of Shrewsbury.

The head of one of the grandest and most powerful families in England, Lord Shrewsbury had also built up a huge web of landed estates in the Midlands, exploiting their coal and lead mines, and becoming a shipowner and ironmaster as well as a farmer on an enormous scale. It has been said that his marriage with Bess was like the merger between two corporate giants, a contract guaranteed by two other simultaneous matches: his daughter with her eldest son, Henry Cavendish; and his second son with her daughter, Mary. By this time, Bess's character had become clear to her contemporaries. In Mark Girouard's words, she was 'capable, managing, acquisitive, a businesswoman, a money-maker, a land-amasser . . . she was capricious, rash, emotional, fond of intrigue and gossip, easily moved to tears, the best of company when things were going her way and spitting

*The indomitable Bess of Hardwick, '. . . a business-woman,
a money-maker, a land-amasser, a builder of great houses'.*

with spite and fury when crossed'. The flaming red hair
shown in Rowland Lockey's portrait of her, still at
Hardwick, indicated a notorious temper, as her new
husband was soon to discover.

In 1569 the Earl was entrusted with the guardianship
of Mary, Queen of Scots, and this was one of the indirect
causes of his quarrel with Bess, for in 1574 she allowed her
daughter, Elizabeth Cavendish, to become involved with
Mary's brother-in-law, Charles Stuart, Earl of Lennox.
The young couple were hurriedly married before the birth
of their daughter, Arabella, but the news was greeted with
fury by Queen Elizabeth I (since Stuart's progeny would
have a strong claim to the throne after her death), and by
Lord Shrewsbury (who saw Bess risking his good relations
with the Queen for her own family ambitions). There were
also quarrels about Chatsworth, which Sir William
Cavendish had bought in 1549 and which Bess was now
remodelling on a palatial scale with funds that the
Earl insisted were his own. By 1577 the couple were
mostly living apart, and by 1584 the marriage had broken
down completely.

The collapse of the Shrewsbury marriage and the row
over Arabella Stuart (whose parents both died within
a few years) were to have very important consequences
for the future of Hardwick. Because of constant legal

wrangles over Chatsworth, which the Earl claimed to have
acquired through his marriage contract, Bess was forced
to return to her birthplace, which was her undisputed
property, and in 1585 started to transform the little manor
there into a very large house. In 1590, before this
was completed, her husband died, leaving her in control
of all her lands and with a huge widow's jointure.
But instead of returning to the enlargement of Chatsworth
– which she saw would go to her hated eldest son,
Henry, who had sided with his stepfather – she
immediately determined to build a colossal new house
next door to the Old Hall at Hardwick. Not only would
this be a worthy seat for her favourite second son,
William (later 1st Earl of Devonshire), it would also be
on a scale suitable for the reception of Arabella –
the grand-daughter she may yet have expected to see
on the throne.

Bess's papers do not reveal the name of her architect,
but it is almost certain that he was Robert Smythson,
designer of Wollaton Hall, near Nottingham, who had
already worked for the Shrewsburys at Worksop in the
relatively amicable first years of their marriage. Several
drawings by Smythson relate to the new Hardwick;
many of the craftsmen employed here had previously
worked for him at Wollaton, including Thomas Accres,
the marble carver, and John and Christopher Rodes,
the stonemasons. However, in contrast to the richness
of the exterior decoration at Wollaton, a fruit cake of
Mannerist detail taken from French and Flemish pattern
books, the walls of Hardwick are plain almost to austerity
It is the great gridiron windows, looking back to the
structural feats of the Perpendicular cathedral builders,
that were intended to take the breath away – united with
the Renaissance symmetry of the whole building.
Of course, this symmetry is something of an illusion.
Some of the windows are false, with chimneystacks
immediately behind them. Others light rooms on two
different storeys, particularly in the corner towers
with their mezzanine floors. But from the exterior the
illusion is complete.

'Hardwick Hall, more glass than wall . . .' goes the old
Derbyshire rhyme, and at a time when glass was still a
very expensive commodity, the large proportion of
window to wall must have seemed an amazing
extravagance. However, there was more to it than sheer
ostentation. Together with Lord Shrewsbury, Bess had
been among the pioneers of lead mining and glass
manufacture in Derbyshire, and her immense wealth was
based on the development of industry as much as on
agriculture. The huge expanse of leaded lights, and the
roof entirely covered with lead to promenade and watch
the progress of the hunt below, proclaim the origins of a
great entrepreneurial fortune, and make Hardwick one of
the earliest monuments of the Industrial Revolution,
two centuries before its time.

The key to Hardwick's revolutionary design –
its compactness and verticality, its prodigal use of space
and its remarkable silhouette (the six towers aligning
themselves in different formations as you walk round the
house) – is its original concept as an overgrown lodge.

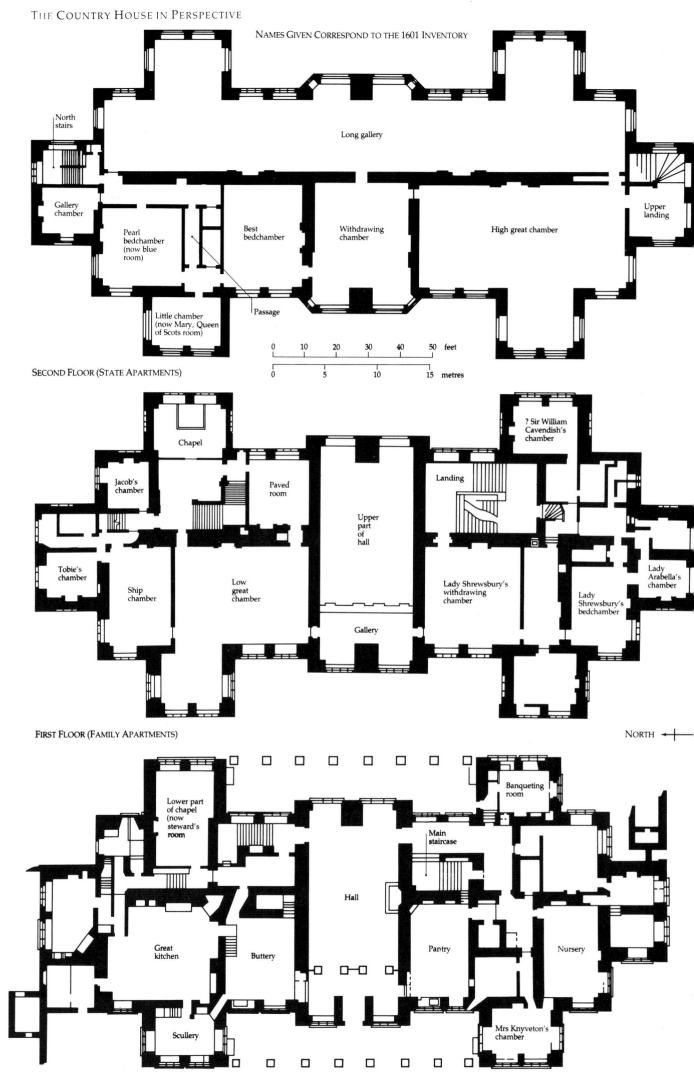

NAMES GIVEN CORRESPOND TO THE 1601 INVENTORY

North stairs

Long gallery

Gallery chamber

Pearl bedchamber (now blue room)

Best bedchamber

Withdrawing chamber

High great chamber

Upper landing

Little chamber (now Mary, Queen of Scots room)

Passage

| 0 | 10 | 20 | 30 | 40 | 50 | feet |

| 0 | 5 | 10 | 15 | metres |

SECOND FLOOR (STATE APARTMENTS)

Chapel

? Sir William Cavendish's chamber

Jacob's chamber

Paved room

Landing

Upper part of hall

Tobie's chamber

Ship chamber

Low great chamber

Lady Shrewsbury's withdrawing chamber

Lady Arabella's chamber

Lady Shrewsbury's bedchamber

Gallery

FIRST FLOOR (FAMILY APARTMENTS)

NORTH

Lower part of chapel (now steward's room)

Banqueting room

Main staircase

Hall

Great kitchen

Buttery

Pantry

Nursery

Scullery

Mrs Knyveton's chamber

GROUND FLOOR (HALL, KITCHEN AND OFFICES)

The Elizabethan love of emblems and devices was often expressed in such buildings. Sometimes they were literally full of meaning, like Sir Thomas Tresham's Lyveden New Bield, illustrating the symbols of the Passion, or his Triangular Lodge at Rushton, a pun on the first three letters of his name, which he also used to illustrate the Trinity. Sometimes they were more in the nature of visual puzzles or conceits like Lord Burghley's cross-shaped hunting lodge at Wothorpe with its corner towers, or, on a much larger scale, Sir John Pakington's X-shaped lodge at Westwood in Worcestershire. Buildings like this were the equivalent of the rebuses and acrostics of contemporary literature. Pleasing by their ingenuity, they could afford to be more experimental than the great courtyard house that generally remained a family's chief seat.

Hardwick could afford to be experimental in just this way, and for one special reason: the continued existence of the Old Hall just a hundred yards to the south-west. This rambling, asymmetrical building, incorporating parts of the old manor house where Bess had spent her childhood, is now a ruin. But it was still being completed while work on the new house got underway, and it continued to be fully lived in and maintained until at least the mid-eighteenth century. So it was here that the lower orders of the Countess's vast retinue would have been housed, together with those of visiting dignitaries.

Robert Smythson was thus called on to provide a progression of great rooms of state, but without providing endless retainers' quarters to support them. The comparatively modest size of the great hall, and its novel site, are a reflection of this. Instead of the usual medieval arrangement of a hall placed lengthwise along the main front, and entered from one end by means of a screens passage (like those at Little Moreton and Knole), Smythson placed the room at right-angles to the façade, on the central east–west axis of the house. The idea, derived from his earlier designs for much smaller hunting lodges, permitted the symmetry and compactness of the rest of the house, but also demonstrated the declining role of the great hall even in the biggest Elizabethan houses. Gone were the days when the entire household would have dined here: instead, this was where the household servants of middling importance would have been fed, while their inferiors (and outdoor servants) probably used the equivalent room in the old manor across the road.

At the same time Smythson's great hall retained its symbolic importance as the grand entrance to the new house, with the plasterer Abraham Smith's gigantic version of the Hardwick coat-of-arms above the chimneypiece, supported by life-size Cavendish stags, announcing its owner's presence in unmistakable terms. At any moment too, the company might rise to their feet as the indomitable old lady, dressed in deepest black, passed across the gallery at the western end of the room, on her way from the Low Great Chamber on the north, where she usually dined, to her drawing room and bedchamber on the south.

Compared with earlier timber screens (and also later ones, like that at Knole) the fluted stone Doric columns supporting this gallery are in a remarkably pure Italian Renaissance style, based on engravings by Sebastiano Serlio – and probably designed by Smythson himself rather than the mason William Griffin, who carved them. Echoing the effect of the colonnade outside, the screen is also remarkable for being so open, although thick woollen or leather curtains could have been hung behind the pillars in winter to prevent draughts. Under the gallery at either end are hatches and doors opening into the pantry on one side and the buttery on the other: a variation on the usual screens passage arrangement. On feast days, it would of course still be possible to have a band of musicians in the gallery itself, for the entertainment of those dining both in the hall and in the Low Great Chamber.

The hall was also important as the beginning of the great processional route that leads us from the front door, up the interminable stone staircase, becoming progressively lighter and more open in its ascent, until we emerge breathless and awestruck in the brilliant splendour of the High Great Chamber on the top floor. Never before had the 'picturesque' potential of the staircase been so fully exploited in English architecture; nor was it to be excelled until the theatricality of Vanbrugh's Castle Howard. The idea of the procession has a purely religious connotation today, and indeed the same kind of ritual significance was attached to the ceremonial of courtiers' lives in the sixteenth century. Not only would the distinguished guest arriving in the hall be taken with great solemnity up the stairs to be received in state in the High Great Chamber, preceded by an entourage of attendants in strict ascending order of seniority, but the food for the succeeding banquet would also be brought up by the same route, from the buttery next to the hall, preceded by the beadle with his mace, the footmen, butlers, servers, and even the ubiquitous musicians, to announce its arrival.

On the landing halfway up the stairs, these processions would have passed an imposing doorcase with a plaster overdoor incorporating the head and torso of a giant warrior in armour. This intimidating figure was appropriate, for sentries would always have been on guard here, at the entrance to Bess of Hardwick's private apartments occupying the whole of the first floor. As with so many Elizabethan and Jacobean houses, the great

The Old Hall, which Bess began to remodel in 1585. She lived there until the New Hall was ready for occupation in 1597.

The door on the landing of the great staircase, leading to Bess's private apartments, would always have been guarded by sentries.

'rooms of state', used for formal occasions and for entertaining, lay above, on the second floor, giving wider views over the surrounding landscape and being more remote from the smells of the kitchen and the everyday bustle of the ground floor, always the domain of the lower orders. At Hardwick, the relative importance of the three floors is plainly indicated by the exterior: two panes high on the ground, three panes on the first, and four on the second. In Frank Lloyd Wright's famous phrase, 'form follows function'.

All the same, it is impossible to guess at the cyclopean scale of the High Great Chamber until the great panelled door at the top of the staircase swings open to reveal this most famous of Elizabethan interiors. The room glows with the faded colours of old tapestries; linen curtains stir at the vast mullion windows; and shafts of sunlight fall on the rush matting on the floor. But the great magic of the room is the painted plasterwork frieze all round the walls above the tapestries: a vision of an enchanted forest in which Diana and her companions rest from the hunt; Venus chastises a mischievous Cupid; and birds and beasts frolic through sylvan glades. The masterpiece of Bess's plasterer, Abraham Smith, it culminates in the Tudor royal arms above Thomas Accres's marble and alabaster chimneypiece.

To some degree, all great houses at this date were built in the expectation of a royal visit, when the great chamber would become the sovereign's own room. In that eventuality the royal arms, and the choice of Diana in the frieze (the goddess most usually identified with Elizabeth), would have made her feel at home, as would 'a looking glass paynted about with the Armes of England', and a series of portraits, presumably hanging

either side of the bay window, representing her father Henry VIII, her brother Edward VI, her sister Queen Mary, and other early sixteenth-century celebrities like the Emperor Charles V, the Duke of Alba and Cardinal Wolsey.

These expressions of loyalty must have seemed somewhat strained when, in 1603, Queen Elizabeth's special envoy, Sir Henry Brouncker, was sent to Hardwick to investigate the potentially treasonable marriage plans of Bess's grand-daughter Arabella Stuart. On such an occasion, one of the canopies listed in the Wardrobe in 1601 would doubtless have been erected over a dais in the centre of the north wall, opposite the door from the staircase. Sitting under it, and behind a 'long table of white wood' covered with a 'fayre long carpet of silk needlework', the Countess would have dined in the semi-regal fashion demanded by her power and wealth, or sat surrounded by members of her family and high-ranking visitors to watch masques and other entertainments. In September 1600, for instance, the Queen's Players came to Hardwick, and almost certainly performed here or in the Long Gallery next door.

Curiously, the proportions of both these great rooms are due not simply to the fertile imagination of Robert Smythson, but to the two magnificent sets of tapestries that cover their walls. The eight Brussels hangings here, illustrating the *Story of Ulysses*, were bought in 1587, four years before the building was begun, and the High Great Chamber was clearly planned to take them, since they exactly fill the space between the dado and the frieze. The huge walnut table in the centre of the bay window was already here in 1601, and may also pre-date the house. Inlaid with musical instruments, playing boards, cards and other devices in marquetry, it would doubtless have been used for just those purposes: a stand for music played by minstrels during the feast, and a gaming table for the courtiers afterwards. The arms in the centre appear to celebrate the three Talbot weddings of 1567, and in the centre is the beautiful verse:

> *The redolent smele of Aeglantyne*
> *We stagges exault to the deveyne.*

The Hardwick family crest is a stag wearing a collar of eglantines, or briar roses, but the symbol (one of chastity) was also used by Queen Elizabeth, and this may have given Bess an added incentive to use it. The present canopy (only recently re-installed by the National Trust), *en suite* with the two armchairs that stand below it, and the large number of 'farthingale' chairs and stools round the walls, seem to have been made for Christian Bruce, the 2nd Earl of Devonshire's widow, in 1635 – though their frames were renewed and their embroideries remounted on brown velvet in the nineteenth century.

The Long Gallery, entered from the High Great Chamber at the southern end through a low door screened by great loops of tapestry, provides a still more astounding spectacle. As the 6th Duke wrote in the nineteenth century, visitors 'begin to get weary and to think they have done, and to want their luncheon; but they are awakened when the tapestry . . . is lifted up, and they find themselves in this stupendous and original apartment'. One hundred and sixty-six feet long, filling the whole eastern half of the house on this floor, it served as a place for exercise in winter and in bad weather; as a room where important visitors could be received, including the unfortunate Sir Henry Brouncker on his delicate mission in 1603; and as a court where, in the role of the sovereign's representative, Bess would receive pleas and administer justice over much of the county.

Thus the two monumental chimneypieces, inlaid with different-coloured marbles by Thomas Accres, incorporate allegorical statues of Justice and Mercy. The canopy in the centre of the gallery, between the windows, is the tester of a splendid state bed made for Chatsworth in the 1690s. But it occupies the same position as an earlier canopy and couch, again dating from the 1630s, recorded here in the late eighteenth century.

The thirteen Flemish tapestries of the *Story of Gideon* were woven for Sir Christopher Hatton in 1578, presumably for his great house at Holdenby in Northamptonshire, and were bought by Bess from his heirs in 1592. Like those in the High Great Chamber, they are unusually large (19 feet in height) and must have dictated the proportions of the room – which was only completed five years later – for they fit the walls perfectly, without having been cut, even in the two great eastward-projecting bays. A mixture of thirty-seven royal and family portraits are listed in the room in 1601; Bess probably hung them on the window walls, leaving the tapestry uncovered. It was either her son or grandson who began to hang pictures against them in the early seventeenth century, and the tradition has continued to this day: a wonderfully profligate idea, shocking to the

One of the bays in the long gallery, from a watercolour by David Cox painted for the 6th Duke of Devonshire.

textile expert, but pleasing to those who appreciate the layer-on-layer of taste that the old house represents.

The portraits now form a pantheon of celebrated historical figures. Greatly augmented by the 5th and 6th Dukes (though not quite as crowded as in their day), they range from a celebrated full-length of Queen Elizabeth herself, attributed to Nicholas Hilliard, to the crabbed visage of the philosopher Thomas Hobbes, who was tutor to the 2nd and 3rd Earls, and died at Hardwick in 1679 at the age of ninety-one. Above them is the original painted frieze which John Ballechouse (or 'John Painter' as he is usually called in the accounts) carried out in 1597. Thought to have been a Fleming by birth, Ballechouse could have been the source of many of the Netherlandish engravings used by the craftsmen at Hardwick: actual prints by Peter de Coster of Antwerp are pasted on to the panelling in the bay of the High Great Chamber, with painted decoration round them, while the figures of Venus (as Spring) and Ceres (as Summer) in the plaster frieze above come from engravings by Crispin van de Passe, after Martin de Vos.

In 1601 the Long Gallery was sparsely furnished, with two square inlaid tables covered with carpets in the bay windows, various chairs, stools and forms, two mirrors (still a great rarity), a little ivory table and a firescreen. However, a sense of colour and richness must have been given by the eighteen large embroidered cushion covers provided for the window seats. Most of these still survive elsewhere in the house, and can be identified from their descriptions in the inventory, whether mythological subjects like the story of Diana and Actaeon, biblical scenes like the Sacrifice of Isaac, genre like the 'fancie of a fowler', or 'hunting the hare', or purely decorative motifs like the 'platt of Chatesworth house', or one with a pattern of 'Straweberries and wormes'. Some of the finer covers may have been the work of professional embroiderers in Bess's employ – two of whom are mentioned as having chambers in the house at an early date – and some may also have been imported, like the fine *Judgement of Solomon* which appears to be French. But most would have been made by her own gentlewomen, and under her immediate supervision. Discourse was one of the chief objects of exercise or recreation in the gallery, and many private conferences must have taken place in these window seats, as well as conversations inspired by the different scenes and characters depicted here, in tapestry, in needlework and in painting.

A constant source of amazement at Hardwick is the way in which works of art were brought from all over the globe, even at this early date, to furnish Bess's rooms. Apart from the French embroideries and Flemish tapestries here, the two brass chandeliers in the bay windows are thought to be German of about 1600; the carpets on the tables below include a Turkish 'Star Ushak', almost certainly one of those listed in the 1601 inventory – and quite possibly brought back by Henry Cavendish, Bess's eldest son, after a visit to Constantinople in 1589; and there is even mention of Chinese porcelain in the shape of a 'purs-land Cup with a Cover trymmed with Silver and guilt waying fourtene

Hardwick Hall

1 Hall
2 Staircase
   (with door to Bess of Hardwick's private apartments)
3 High great chamber
4 Long gallery
5 Withdrawing chamber
6 Best bedchamber (now green velvet room)
7 Pearl bedchamber (now blue room)

NORTH

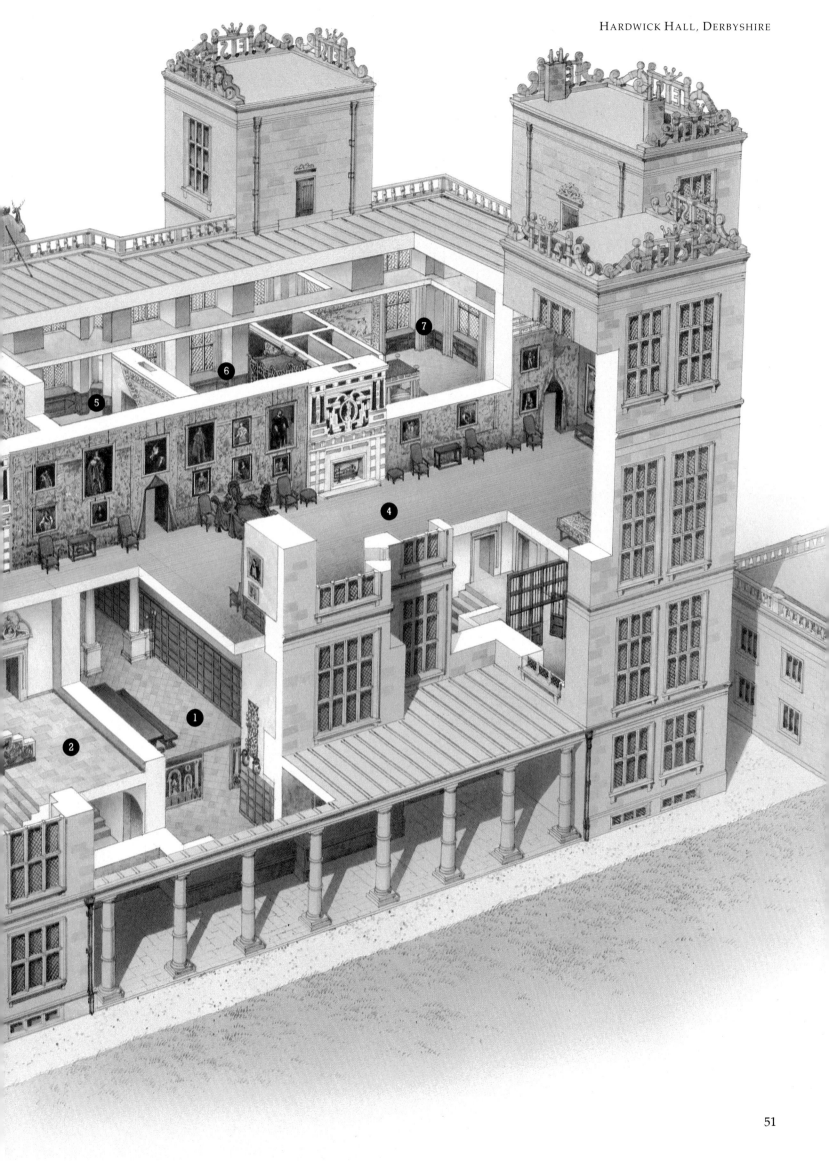

ounces'. A fine blue-and-white ewer and cover with silver-gilt mounts dated 1589 does survive in the house, but it is possible that this was simply an inspired purchase by the 6th Duke of Devonshire in the nineteenth century.

The central door opposite the canopy, and between the two chimneypieces, leads through to the Withdrawing Room, where, on state occasions, Bess would have retired after dining in the High Great Chamber or witnessing some great entertainment in the Long Gallery. The ceiling here was originally as high as in the two preceding rooms, and was only lowered in the eighteenth century to provide more servants' rooms above and to increase the chances of keeping warm. In Bess's day warmth must also have been a consideration, for the room was supplied with two sets of hangings – a set of Flemish tapestries of the story of Abraham for the summer, and a thicker set of patchwork appliqué hangings representing classical heroines and their accompanying Virtues (a theme with obvious attractions for the lady of the house) apparently hung on top of them in the winter. These patchwork hangings, thought to have been made for Chatsworth in the 1570s and now shown in the hall and on the chapel landing, are fascinating in that they are made of pieces of velvet, cloth of gold and figured silk, many of them cut out of medieval copes and chasubles. Pagan as their message is, with the figures of Penelope and Lucretia, Zenobia and Artemesia, they symbolize the effects of the English Reformation with sudden clarity, suggesting that houses like Hardwick were the new cathedrals of a more secular age. Perhaps, like the marvellous iron lock on the High Great Chamber door, decorated with Perpendicular tracery, the vestments came from monasteries which Sir William Cavendish had helped dissolve in the 1530s.

As in 1601, the Withdrawing Room contains one of the most remarkable pieces of furniture at Hardwick. The famous 'sea-dog' table in the centre is described in the inventory as 'a drawing table Carved and guilt standing uppon sea doges inlayde with marble stones and wood' – the word 'drawing' referring to the sliding leaves that can be drawn out from under the top. Once again the table may be French in origin (or made by French craftsmen working in England), for it is very close to an engraving by Jacques Androuet du Cerceau – and a pair of 'french stooles set with marble stones' are also listed in the High Great Chamber. The sea-dogs, perhaps inspired by the talbots, or dogs, of the Shrewsbury arms, are in fact chimeras, the fastest creatures in the world, and the fact that they rest on the backs of tortoises, the slowest, must illustrate the Latin motto *Festina lente* (make haste slowly) – one of those punning tags so dear to the Renaissance mind.

A richly carved walnut cabinet, also in the style of Du Cerceau, is less easy to identify in the inventory, though a 'cubberd with tills [drawers] carved and guilt' was in this room in 1601. The square table in the bay, with a chess board and playing cards in marquetry on the top, is more typically English, and the only survivor of a number of similar inlaid tables described in the house at that date. The members of Bess's household must have

been fond of gambling at draughts, cards and other games, standing round these tables placed in Smythson's deep bay windows.

The Withdrawing Room also contains (as in 1601) one of the few pictures with a non-religious subject in Bess of Hardwick's collection: a painting of the return of Ulysses to Penelope. Perhaps she even identified herself with the heroine, who also appeared in the patchwork hangings here, and in the Ulysses tapestries in the High Great Chamber – representing the faithful and virtuous wife fond of spinning (or, in Bess's case, embroidery).

Beyond the Withdrawing Room lay the Best Bedchamber in 1601, now called the Green Velvet Room after the splendid eighteenth-century state bed brought from Londesborough in Yorkshire. Here too there was originally a set of patchwork hangings: this time showing the Virtues with their Contraries – Faith with a cringing turbanned Mahomet; Hope with the despairing Judas; and Temperance with a drunken Sardanapalus. However, these are now shown elsewhere in the house, and their place has been taken by the four *Story of Abraham* tapestries, once in the Withdrawing Room. The overmantel with its figure of Chastity, the doorcase to the Withdrawing Room and the panelling between them, are all of alabaster, blackstone and other Derbyshire marbles, no doubt dug from Bess's own quarries; they were put up by Thomas Accres in 1599, perhaps once again using an engraving by Serlio as a model.

The bed described in the 1601 inventory was of the utmost splendour, with a gilt frame and a 'fayre lardge sparver', or tester, suspended from the ceiling. This was hung with a double valance of cloth of gold and cloth of silver, besides 'sondrie Coulers of velvet imbrodered fayre with divers armes with portalls and pictures, and with a deep gold frenge'. Its six curtains were of blue and red satin striped with gold and silver, and it was provided with white-ground Turkey foot-carpets on all three sides: a great rarity at a time when most carpets were used as covers for tables. Now that the colours of faded tapestry and needlework, worn paint and discoloured varnish have produced a wonderfully mellow and romantic tone to the rooms at Hardwick – a magic that is lost on few visitors – it is good to be reminded of the vibrant, even garish, effect they may have had in Bess's day.

Behind the Best Bedchamber lay a servant's chamber, wardrobe and closet (none of them apparently day-lit) and a 'Little Chamber' now called Mary Queen of Scots' Room, after some panelling that bears her insignia, probably brought from Chatsworth at a later date. Although Mary was executed four years before the building was begun, the tradition that she had been a prisoner here made Hardwick a place of pilgrimage in the eighteenth century, and this antiquarian interest did much to save it from later 'improvements'. In 1601, the Little Chamber contained a field-bed with rich hangings and a quilt of 'India Stuff imbrodered with beastes' – perhaps one of the first pieces of Chinese embroidered silk to reach England. The room very much belonged to the Best Bedchamber, and was probably used both as a dressing room and as a warmer, more comfortable place to sleep after the ceremonial

The fireplace with its plasterwork overmantel is the only Elizabethan feature that remains from the Low Great Chamber (now the dining room). The walls are hung with eighteenth- and nineteenth-century portraits, and the panelling dates from the time of the 6th Duke.

retirement to bed, or *couchée*, had been performed next door. To discover a taste for exotic Oriental items already emerging here is of particular interest, providing a foretaste of the chinoiserie dressing rooms and closets found a century later.

The Pearl Bedchamber, the last of the state rooms on the second floor, is now called the Blue Room after its bed, which dates from about 1630. Originally it was furnished almost as magnificently as the Best Bedchamber, the bed itself having curtains of 'black velvet imbrodered wth silver golde and pearls with sivines [raspberries] and woodbines fringed with golde, silver and black silk'. On the other hand, the appearance of 'my ladies and Sir William Cavendishes Armes' on the backcloth suggest that this was an old state bed brought over from Chatsworth. The alabaster bas-relief of *The Marriage of Tobias* over the chimneypiece is also thought to have come from Chatsworth, although Bess surely commissioned it – for the story (with its many marriages) was another that she was fond of applying to herself.

Another smaller bedroom called the Gallery Chamber lies next door, sharing the tower with part of the north staircase – this room would probably have been occupied by an upper servant or high household official of the visiting guest – together with four more bedchambers in the turrets on the roof. These were surprisingly well

equipped, with fireplaces and plasterwork overmantels as well as tapestries or leather or cloth hangings. Of the two remaining towers, the one on the north contained the upper part of the north stair, giving access to the leads, while the other on the south (above the upper landing of the main staircase) was a banqueting house, with the Countess's arms carved over the door. Here on a fine summer's day a dessert course of sweetmeats, fruit and wine could be served. It is easy to imagine Bess and her ladies taking the air after dinner (then usually served at about eleven in the morning), and watching the departure of the menfolk to hunt stag in the thickly wooded deer park below. Two other little banqueting houses still survive in the north and south orchards, and a third lay on the ground floor, at the southern end of the east colonnade.

Descending from the rooms of state in the upper storey to the family rooms on the floor below, we are immediately conscious of a change of scale and of character. Lower-ceilinged and less formally arranged, these interiors have undergone greater changes than the ones above. But, seen through the eyes of the 1601 inventory, they give a wonderfully complete picture of Bess's everyday life when she was not entertaining – and when the key had been turned in the lock of the High Great Chamber door, sealing off those vast treasure-filled apartments from the rest of the house.

Imagining ourselves grand enough to be ushered into the old lady's presence (a frightening prospect even in retrospect), we should retrace our steps down the main staircase and pass the sentries on the middle landing, guarding the door to 'My Lady's Withdrawing Chamber' and doubtless holding the 'three holberdes' mentioned in the inventory. In Bess's lifetime, this essentially private room would have been open only to members of her immediate family and most favoured attendants, while beyond it lay the inner sanctum of her own bedchamber and that of Lady Arabella Stuart, the all-important grand-daughter who was to be used as a pawn in the fulfilment of her dynastic ambitions. The six pieces of Flemish tapestry forming a frieze above the panelling were another of Bess's acquisitions from the heirs of Sir Christopher Hatton, and it is amusing to find her arms simply painted on canvas and sewn on top of his in the borders. Yet again, these tapestries must have dictated the dimensions of the room.

The inventory shows that in 1601 Bess's withdrawing chamber had a cluttered arrangement of furniture, with little attempt to produce the sort of consistent scheme fashionable by the end of the century: practically none of the seats, forms and stools were upholstered in the same material, from the 'Chare of black lether guilded' complete with footstool (probably intended for the Countess's own use) to the 'Little Chare of wrought cloth of gold', made either for Arabella at an earlier date, or for one of William Cavendish's children. Two other 'chares for Children' are listed here, proving that they were not always confined to the nursery on the ground floor (below Bess's bedchamber) – and it is thus appropriate to find a portrait of Arabella as a child still hanging here. Painted in 1577, when she was nearly two, it shows her richly dressed in the most fashionable costume of the day. Another rare survival is a small *verre-eglomisé* panel with the Hardwick achievement in richly glowing colours, described as 'a glass with my ladies arms', and listed here in 1601. Apart from some other early portraits and needlework cushion covers, the room now has a comfortable country-house mixture of furniture arranged by a later dowager, Evelyn, Duchess of Devonshire, who appropriately used this as her private sitting room until 1956, when the National Trust took over the house.

Warmth has always been one of the greatest problems at Hardwick. There was, after all, a price to pay for the vast expanse of Smythson's gridiron windows. So Bess's bedchamber, in the south-west corner of the house, not only had red cloth curtains for the two windows, but also 'three Coverletes to hang before a windowe', 'a Coverlett to hang before a Dore', and 'a counterpoynt of tapestrie before another dore'. Her bed, with two linen-covered quilts, three pairs of fustian blankets and six Spanish blankets, sounds like something out of *The Princess and the Pea*. It also had two sets of curtains – one of scarlet woollen cloth trimmed with silver and gold lace, and the other of purple bays – while there were no fewer than eight 'fledges' or mats on the floor round the bed to overcome the problem of cold feet.

The bedchamber also doubled up as a study at this date, and it was here that Bess kept the only six books listed in the house – Calvin's commentary on Job, Solomon's proverbs, a book of meditation and three other unspecified volumes – together with chests and coffers for her papers, and 'three Deskes covered with lether', the kind of portable writing boxes with sloping lids that could be placed on a table. Her jewel coffer also stood here, and a list of its contents drawn up in her own hand in 1593 gives a vivid idea of her wealth, with its lists of diamonds, rubies, emeralds and pearls.

One curious feature of the inventory is that it lists 'My Ladie Arbells bedsted' in Bess's bedchamber, despite the fact that Arabella had her own chamber (also with a bed) in the adjoining room in the south tower. By the time the house was completed in 1599 she was already twenty-four, so this can hardly have been a relic of her childhood. But whether this second bed stemmed from Bess's strict guardianship of the child, or from some more practical consideration – like warmth in winter – is hard to say. The two rooms also shared an unlit 'Inner Room' equipped with two close stools: box-like seats with hinged lids containing pewter basins, that had now superseded the old-fashioned garderobes, or latrines. Bess's own stool was 'covered with blewe cloth sticht with white, with red and black silk fringe', but there were no back stairs, and the fact that the servants had to carry these pans up and down the two main staircases explains why the inventory also lists 'perfuming pans', 'sweet bays' and pomander cases.

Other family chambers at this end of the house included those of Bess's favourite son, William Cavendish. Her half-sister Jane Knyveton's room was on the floor below, and adjoining the nursery, suggesting that she was given responsibility for William's eleven-year-old son and eight-year-old daughter. A few upper servants and gentlewomen were also given small chambers here, though most had quarters in the Old Hall. The lower servants slept almost anywhere – on landings, outside chamber doors, by the fire in the hall, in the kitchen or scullery: in fact wherever they were most likely to be needed.

For the main meal of the day Bess would leave her apartments on the south side of the house and cross the 'tarrass' or gallery above the hall screen to reach the Low Great Chamber – still used as the main dining room at Hardwick up to the 1950s. In most other houses of the period this room would have been called the parlour and situated on the ground floor, below the great chamber. But because of the extra 'state' floor at Hardwick it assumed a higher position and a more dignified name. In 1601 it was furnished as one might expect, to cater for all sorts of functions – sitting, eating, recreation such as embroidery, music or card games, and as a common room for the upper servants. In a letter of March 1603, Lady Arabella refers to a group of them gossiping in it and 'taking the advantage of the fire to warm them by'. The walls were originally hung with tapestries of the *Story of David*, but there were also twelve portraits: of Queen Elizabeth, Bess herself, Lord Shrewsbury, Lord Burghley,

The kitchen, with its stewing hearths on the left, and copper pans – all engraved with the Devonshire crest – on the right.

Arabella, with her father and grandmother, four generations of Cavendishes, and (rather surprisingly listed in the middle of them) 'The Virgin Marie' – perhaps positioned by the door to the Chapel landing.

In the late seventeenth century the Low Great Chamber was slightly reduced in size, in order to enlarge the bedchamber beyond it – one of three at this end of the house, probably intended for guests who did not merit the full 'state room' treatment on the floor above. But it was the 6th Duke who installed the panelling brought from the Old Hall. He records that, as a boy, he turned the bay window here into 'a kind of menagerie: a fishing net nailed up under the curtain confined the rabbits, hedgehogs, squirrels, guinea pigs, and white mice, that were the joy of my life . . . a tree stood in the middle for the unhappy birds – caught by John Hall the gamekeeper – to perch on, and an owl made its melancholy hooting in one of the corners'. In the time of Evelyn, Duchess of Devonshire, the bay was much used for the repair of tapestries and embroideries, probably reverting to one of its original uses in Bess's day.

The Little Dining Chamber adjoining (now called the Paved Room) seems to have been an afterthought. Originally intended to be the first-floor landing of the north staircase, matching that on the south, it has a stone floor instead of the lime-cement found elsewhere, always covered with a sweet-smelling rush matting that is one of Hardwick's trademarks. It was also very simply furnished in 1601, with only one chair and fifteen stools, a long table covered with a Turkey carpet, and 'waynscott rownde about'. This suggests that it may have been used as a dining room for the upper servants, although it could also have served on occasion as a more intimate 'winter parlour' for the Countess and her family.

The ingenuity of Robert Smythson's planning at Hardwick is nowhere more evident than in his handling of the chapel and kitchen, on either side of the north staircase. Like the great hall, the chapel originally rose through two storeys, with a gallery at first-floor level, divided off from the staircase behind and with the surviving oak screen at its front. As at Little Moreton, household servants would have sat in the lower part for daily prayers, while Bess and her family upstairs remained invisible to all but the chaplain at the altar, or in the pulpit. In the late eighteenth century the 5th Duke, perhaps rather unfortunately, ceiled off the lower chapel to make a steward's room and brought the altar, communion rails and pulpit up to first-floor level.

The four wall hangings, crudely painted with scenes from the Acts of the Apostles, may be those for which John Ballechouse was paid in 1599–1600. A cheap alternative to tapestry, quite common at this period, they are now of exceptional rarity. An early sixteenth-century Flemish *Madonna and Child* may also be one of 'too pictures of Our Lady the Virgin Marie and the three Kinges', which hung here, with 'the salutation of the Virgin Marie by the Angle'. Despite her copy of Calvin, the Countess was evidently no Puritan. One of her daughters became a Catholic, and another was also suspected of recusancy.

The kitchen, which in earlier times would have been housed in a separate building, was conveniently placed in the north-west corner of the house – near the great hall where the servants would have eaten, and immediately below the Low Great Chamber where the family dined. Food at this date was still cooked at huge open fires, however, and to give a chance for the smoke and heat to rise, Smythson sank the floor into a half-basement, thus increasing its height. The windows placed round the upper part could thus extract the fumes, while preventing the menials working here and in the adjoining scullery from overlooking the forecourt. Later additions include the charcoal-burning 'stewing hearths' installed below the windows in the eighteenth century (and ancestors of the Victorian range), as well as the unrivalled *batterie de cuisine* of copper pots and pans – each piece stamped with a D under a ducal coronet and the name of the house, in order to keep them separate from kitchen equipment in other Devonshire houses.

A serving hatch connected the kitchen with the original 'surveying place' or serving room, later amalgamated with the buttery. Both these rooms were of course at a higher level, and that left space for the beer and wine cellars below, approached by their own small staircase. In 1601 the former contained thirty-three hogsheads and the latter twenty-one: enough to satisfy a whole army of retainers and gentlefolk respectively – not to mention the little band of resident craftsmen who were busy up to the day of Bess's death putting the finishing touches to her great house. Nearly four centuries later, as we wend our way back through the park to the Hardwick Inn, built in that very year, 1608 – and by the same John Ballechouse whose painted decoration can be seen in the High Great Chamber and the Long Gallery – we should surely drink a bumper ourselves, in her honour, and in theirs.

Belton House

L I N C O L N S H I R E

FACED WITH the impossible task of choosing the one archetypal English country house – a single building that might stand for all the others, not too big or too small, not too early or too late – you might well end up by choosing Belton. Indeed the horrible new road-sign symbol for a country house, apparently designed for those who cannot read by those who cannot draw, has the same kind of pediment and symmetrical flanking wings, reduced to their barest outlines.

Simple it may at first appear, but Belton has a kind of balanced perfection that is the result of endless refinement. Like one of Thomas Tompion's clocks, made at the same date, it is a piece of working machinery that is at one with its beautifully proportioned case and its restrained decoration. Begun in the last year of Charles II's life, it is also the culmination of a type established at the very beginning of his reign: a type that will always be associated in our minds with the Restoration.

There is little wonder that, with this sense of balance and understatement, Belton should in the past have been attributed to Sir Christopher Wren. Like Wren's City churches, it has that lucidity of expression and appeal to reason which we see in the writings of Isaac Newton and the early deliberations of the Royal Society. On the other hand, Wren was too deeply occupied with public buildings to have played much part in the design of country houses, and the dominant influence in this field was his friend and fellow-architect, Sir Roger Pratt.

First at Coleshill in Berkshire in the 1650s, and then at Horseheath in Cambridgeshire and Kingston Lacy in Dorset, both of 1663–5, Pratt established what he called the 'double-pile' house – a compact rectangular block with sets of rooms back to back – as the model for practically all the gentlemen's seats built in England until the arrival of William and Mary. Courtyard houses like Knole, Audley End and Castle Ashby, which had continued to be built up to the Civil War, were now, in his own words, 'fit only for a large family, and a great purse'. But 'as to the double pile, it seems of all others to be the

most useful . . . for that we have there much room in a little compass'. One other important building designed by Pratt, Clarendon House in Piccadilly, of 1664–7, was a slight variant on his earlier designs in having short wings flanking the main block – and this, described by John Evelyn as 'without hyperbolies, the best contriv'd, the most usefull, gracefull, and magnificent house in England', was to be still more influential, seen by every visitor to London and the court.

Clarendon House was demolished as early as 1683, following the fall of Charles II's great minister. But there is no doubt that Belton was its posthumous child, nor that its begetter was a member of Pratt's immediate circle: just as he recommended, 'an ingenious gentleman who has seen much of that kind abroad and been somewhat versed in the best authors of Architecture'. Thanks to one vital document, we can also be fairly sure of his identity, for in a letter to Lady Bridgeman of Castle Bromwich, in February 1690 (only a short time after Belton had been completed), her architect Captain William Winde suggests she employ the plasterer Edward Goudge, 'now looked on as the beste master in Ingland in his profession, as his work at Coombe, Hamsted, & Sir John Brownloe's will evidence'. Combe Abbey in Warwickshire and Hampstead Marshall in Berkshire were both houses built by Winde for the Earl of Craven, and indeed the latter's designs for Combe were also closely based on Clarendon House. So it seems virtually certain that he drew up the designs for Belton, too, for Sir John Brownlow.

Like the Bankes family of Kingston Lacy, and the Bridgemans of Castle Bromwich, the Brownlows of Belton made their fortune as lawyers in London, before going on to acquire a country estate and establish themselves as landed gentry. Richard Brownlow, Chief Prothonotary of the Court of Common Pleas, started to make acquisitions in the county in 1598, much to the annoyance of local magnates like the Earl of Lincoln, who described him as 'a villayne . . . that purchased land every day from under his nose, and . . . would purchase Sempringham House

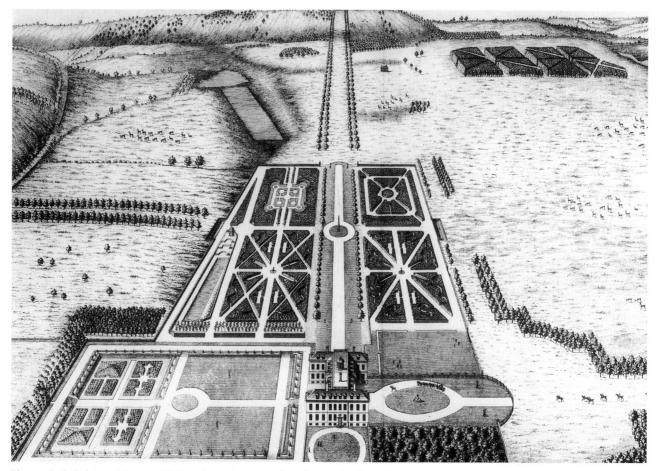

Thomas Badeslade's aerial view of Belton shows the park and gardens in the time of Lord Tyrconnel.

[the Earl's own seat] if were suffered'.

The reversion of the manor of Belton was acquired by the Prothonotary in 1609 from the Pakenhams, another old family on the decline, who were further impoverished by having to entertain James I there in 1617, and finally sold up two years later. Even after this date, however, the old manor house next to the parish church (on the site of Wyatville's orangery) was rarely occupied, for both Richard and his eldest son (always known in the family as 'Old' Sir John Brownlow) preferred their London mansion in Holborn, and another at Enfield in Middlesex.

'Old' Sir John married an heiress, Alice Pulteney, but the couple were childless, and by 1675 he was lamenting that he had 'only two kinsmen left of my name and blood'. He also expressed his 'earnest desire' that a marriage be arranged between the eldest of them, his great-nephew 'Young' Sir John, and his great-niece, Alice Sherard, 'in case they shall affect one the other'. To the infinite joy of the old man, the young cousins did affect each other, and the following year, when they were both sixteen, they married. Three years later, on their great-uncle's death, they inherited Belton with the then prodigious income of £9000 a year, as well as about £20,000 of ready money. They immediately bought a London house in the new and fashionable Southampton Square, Bloomsbury, and within a year or two – still in their early twenties – started to think about rebuilding the old manor house at Belton.

The golden Ancaster stone began to be dug from Samuel Marsh's quarries at Heydour, only about five miles away, in 1684, while finer, and paler-coloured,

ashlar for the keystones and quoins was brought from Ketton in Northamptonshire. Many second-hand materials also came from the old manor, and the demolition of another house owned by the Brownlows at Kingston. In March 1685, the steward finally noted that he 'Gave the Mason to drinck att Laying the first ston of the new house, 5s.'.

The master mason William Stanton, who was in overall charge of the work at Belton, received nearly £5000 over the next two years; his professionalism must account for the amazing speed with which the house was built, and for the precision and quality of the craftsmanship, inside and out. A warden of the Masons' Company in 1681 and 1684, and Master in 1688 and 1689, he may later have designed houses in his own right, including Denham in Buckinghamshire, which bears a distinct resemblance to Belton. Stanton's second-in-command was John Thompson, who worked on several of Wren's City churches and on St Paul's, while among the other master craftsmen were the joiner John Sturges, who worked for Talman at Chatsworth (as well as designing Lyndon Hall in Rutland), and the carpenter Edward Willcox, who afterwards worked for Winde at Castle Bromwich.

It is highly unlikely that this high-powered team needed much supervision. So William Winde may have done little more than furnish the original drawings, leaving Stanton and his men to work out the details. The far more amateur design of the stable block to the west suggests that that was entirely entrusted to the master mason. However, Winde's skilful planning of the house, fulfilling almost every one of Roger Pratt's precepts for the building

A painting of Belton House, ascribed to Henry Bugg, Sir John Brownlow's porter, who stands in front of the gates holding a mace.

of a gentleman's seat, is a constant source of pleasure, closely integrated as it is with the exterior elevations.

In what ways did Belton differ from the Elizabethan E-and H-shaped plans, already seen developing at Hardwick? To begin with, the disposition of the rooms back to back in the central core allowed them to be just as well lit, better warmed, and more convenient of access than in the old 'single-pile' ranges – yet all placed under one, more easily constructed, roof. We can see the process actually happening at Ham House in Surrey in the previous decade: the Duchess of Lauderdale thickening out the single-pile main block of her father's Jacobean house by the addition of a new great parlour on the central axis (beyond the old hall), flanked by apartments for herself and her husband.

Another obvious benefit of the 'double-pile' was the regularity of the whole design. At Hardwick the symmetry of the façades was only skin-deep, and at Ham the old great hall was still entered off-centre, but here at Belton the layout could not be clearer or more balanced. On the ground floor, the two-storey chapel was originally paired by a two-storey kitchen in the corresponding north wing – probably also provided with a gallery at first-floor level – while the shorter south wings contained bedchambers and closets. The hall and 'Great Parlour' were placed on the central axis, with the great chamber (or 'Great Dining Room') above the hall, and the state bedchamber and dressing room above the Great Parlour. On this upper floor, all four wings contained 'apartments' consisting of bedchamber and closet (or closets) – though one was to be used as nurseries. The only asymmetrical feature of the whole plan was the placing of the great

staircase to one side of the hall – instead of combining them as Roger Pratt had done at Coleshill.

The exterior of the house expresses the functions of the rooms admirably and the fact that it looks like a giant-size model may be revealing, for Pratt always recommended the making of a preliminary scale model in wood – and Winde may well have followed his advice. The wings form separate 'pavilions' containing the apartments, while the main rooms on the central axis (sometimes call the 'state centre') break forward from the rest and are dignified not only by wider-spaced windows, but by a broad pediment with the arms of the Brownlows prominently carved in its tympanum. Another gentleman architect of the period, the lawyer Roger North, pointed out that the pediment was a sign of rank in classical times: a status symbol 'which few Romans were allowed, being a piece of state and was called *fastigium domus*, than which nothing is more proper or agreeable'.

Another important indication of function was the use of expensive new sash windows for the two main floors, but old-fashioned mullion-and-transom frames for the servants' quarters in the basement and garrets. This is clearly seen in a naïve, but wonderfully evocative, painting of Belton, traditionally by 'Young' Sir John's porter, Henry Bugg, who stands, (larger than lifesize) outside the forecourt gates, holding the silver-tipped staff which still hangs below the picture frame. Sashes were first introduced on a large scale at Chatsworth between 1676 and 1680, but the idea does not seem to have caught on until they were installed at Whitehall Palace in 1685. Sir John and his architect were therefore in the forefront of fashion, assuming that the picture shows the original arrangement and not an afterthought. Bugg also shows a pair of *oeil-de-boeuf* windows and carved stone garlands flanking the arms in the south pediment, as still found on the north front. Giving a much richer decorative effect, these may have Dutch precedents, like the engravings of Philips Vingboons – especially when we remember that Winde had spent most of the Civil War as a Royalist soldier in Holland.

We have to return to Roger Pratt, however, for the idea of the balustraded platform on the roof, reached by a staircase within the central cupola: 'some masterly framed, not babling turret . . . furnished with seats within . . . chiefly to be made use of either when the weather is windy or wet'. On a sunny day, by contrast, 'Young' Sir John and his wife could walk on the leads and survey

the formal lines of their parterres and avenues spread out below, while the gilded ball supporting the weathervane acted as a beacon, seen by approaching visitors from almost as far away as Grantham. The original platform and cupola were swept away by James Wyatt in the late eighteenth century, but were fortunately reinstated in the 1870s by the 3rd Earl Brownlow, exactly as they had been.

One of the 'rules of building' most strongly urged by Roger Pratt was that the ground floor should be raised, and approached by a flight of steps, not only to add 'height and majesty' to the house and improve its views, but also to supply 'a very good storey' below '. . . sufficient to keep the servants from encumbering the upper parts of the building by their appearing, or lodging'. In this apparently innocuous statement lies the

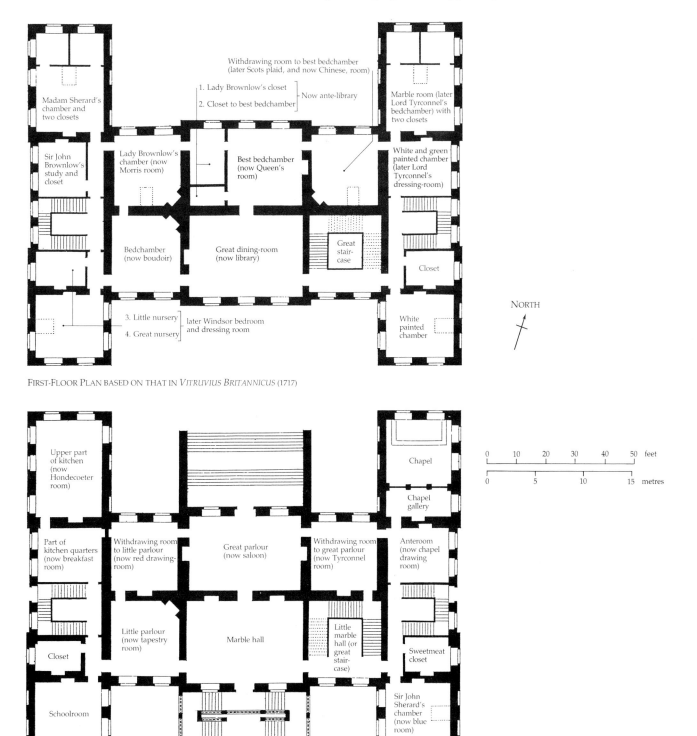

FIRST-FLOOR PLAN BASED ON THAT IN *VITRUVIUS BRITANNICUS* (1717)

GROUND FLOOR PLAN BASED ON THAT IN *VITRUVIUS BRITANNICUS* (1717)

key to the immense social upheaval of the seventeenth century, and the great divide between houses built before and after the Civil War. A comparatively *nouveau riche* family like the Brownlows had no need of a vast household retinue like Bess of Hardwick or the 1st Earl of Dorset, consisting of poor relations, dependants and lesser gentry, bound by feudal ties and fulfilling largely ceremonial functions. Servants were not only less numerous, they were also of lower status than in the past, including many more women to ensure the smooth running of the house. So instead of occupying rooms on the principal floors, they could be banished to eat and sleep in basements and attics respectively.

The crucial development here was the back stairs, hailed by Roger North as one of the most important inventions of his day. At Belton both the east and west staircases rise the whole height of the house, from the kitchen, buttery, larder, still house and servants' hall in the basement, to their garret bedrooms lit by dormers in the roof. The west stair, positioned next to the porter's lodge, and the back door of the house must have been the one generally used by servants, for it was sparsely furnished, containing only a 'Pendulum Clocke' (to ensure their punctuality) in the inventory of 1688. However, the east stair, with thirty-seven pictures in gilt frames, and some silver-gilt sconces, must have been used by servants as well as members of the family, since it offered convenient access to the closets and dressing rooms of some of the principal apartments. The 'backstairs intrigue' resulting from such mixed use can well be imagined. By contrast, the great staircase rising only between the two main floors would have been out of bounds to servants. As Mark Girouard has put it, 'gentry walking up the stairs no longer met their last night's faeces coming down'.

Belton is by no means the untouched Restoration house that many would have us believe. In fact, almost every generation of Brownlows and Custs has left its mark. But thanks to their conservatism, and the respect almost always shown for the work of their ancestors, it is still possible to walk round the house and imagine how each room must have looked, and worked, in the late seventeenth century. Three valuable inventories – one of 1688 (made just after the house was completed); one of 1698 (made after 'Young' Sir John's death); and one of 1737 (in the time of his nephew, Viscount Tyrconnel) – make this a particularly rewarding exercise.

The Marble Hall, the obvious place to begin, takes its name from the black-and-white marble floor which William Stanton laid here and in the adjoining great staircase in 1687, for the then large sum of £100. At first sight, the grained panelling also gives an authentic seventeenth-century feel, so it comes as a surprise to find that it was installed by Wyatville in 1811, and that he also brought the spectacular wood carvings above the two chimneypieces from other rooms.

Originally the hall would have been more purely architectural in emphasis, forming a natural transition between exterior and interior. The panelling is likely to have been bolder, with broken pediments over the doors (decorated with busts by 1737), and either painted stone colour or marbled – which would have given more point to the room's name.

No longer a place for the household to eat, the hall had become more a ceremonial entry to the house and a waiting room for visitors – hence the 'twelve high back chairs' standing round the walls. A touch of pomp was provided by no fewer than twenty-eight half-length pictures of kings and queens, from William the Conqueror to William III, hung on the walls. The kind of series previously found in Elizabethan or Jacobean long galleries, this would have been seen not only as an expression of loyalty, but also as a statement of dynastic continuity, complementing the rather shorter run of family portraits in the Great Parlour beyond and the Great Dining Room above.

The Great Parlour (renamed the saloon in the late eighteenth century), lies on the central axis overlooking the garden to the north. The room retains its original oak panelling with great segmental pediments over the doors very much in the manner of William Winde's interiors at Combe Abbey. At Knole, as we have seen, the parlour was where the upper household officials like the steward and chaplain ate. But with the disappearance of these officials (or their removal to servants' quarters below) the parlour was upgraded, and at the same time made into two rooms. Thus the Great Parlour at Belton is the equivalent of Bess of Hardwick's Low Great Chamber at Hardwick, where Sir John and his wife would dine in some state when a number of guests were staying; while the Little Parlour, to the west of the Marble Hall, was the equivalent of her Paved Parlour, placed next door to the staircase to the kitchen, and used as an everyday eating room when not entertaining.

The room still contains the 'four verie large Pictures'

'Young' Sir John Brownlow and his wife, Alice Sherard, painted by John Riley around the time building began at Belton.

A carving in the Marble Hall, attributed to Grinling Gibbons, surrounds Soest's portrait of 'Old' Sir John Brownlow.

listed here in 1688, flanking the door to the Marble Hall: Riley's portraits of 'Young' Sir John (heavily double-chinned at the age of only twenty-six), his wife Alice, and his brother and sister-in-law, the parents of Lord Tyrconnel. Two more portraits, of Sir John's daughters, Jane (who married the Duke of Ancaster) and Margaret (who died from smallpox on the eve of her wedding), were painted by Henry Tilson in 1689–90, and were probably always intended to hang above the chimney-pieces at either end of the room, surrounded by more magnificent garlands of dead game, fruit and flowers in carved limewood.

Some mystery surrounds these superb trophies – so suitable as decoration for an eating room. There is a bill dated March 1688 from the carver Edmund Carpenter, evidently describing the one at the east end of the room, together with another 'don wth varieties of fish and sheals' for the 'wth drawing roome to the greate Parlor' (but now in the Marble Hall). However, the remaining pair of surrounds – one in the Hall, and one in the Great Parlour – are of still higher quality, with positively three-dimensional woodcock, mallard and other gamebirds. Despite the absence of documentation these can surely be attributed to Grinling Gibbons, the only craftsman capable of such bravura. Gibbons often worked alongside lesser carvers, like John Selden at Petworth,

and Jonathan Maine and Thomas Young at Burghley. But it is still puzzling that 'Young' Sir John should have commissioned work by two such different hands for the same room, and the present arrangement may be due to the Victorian restorer W. G. Rogers, who was the author of much other carving in the house in the same style.

In 1698, the Great Parlour contained 'two large seeing glasses – all japanned' on the piers between the windows, with matching tables and candlestands below them: the standard set of furniture found in Baroque state rooms up to the 1730s, whether ebonized, veneered in marquetry, gilded or even plated in silver. There were three red silk window curtains and twenty-four 'Dutch chairs' placed round the walls – giving some idea of the numbers of diners who might be entertained here. On such occasions three or four separate tables would be brought in from elsewhere, and the chairs set round them rather like in a modern restaurant.

The Little Parlour, west of the Marble Hall, was originally panelled, but has been known as the Tapestry Room since about 1880, when it was remodelled by the 3rd Earl Brownlow. However, the early inventories show that it was more comfortable and informal than the Great Parlour, as befitted an everyday family dining room. Besides two sideboards, two oval tables, two caned armchairs (for the squire and his wife) and fifteen single chairs (for the rest), there was a 'large fine birde Cage with three Lofts', a 'lesser bird cage', a child's chair, three red velvet cushions, and a pendulum clock in an inlaid case. The corner chimneypiece would have helped warm the parlour by bringing the hearth out from the wall, while also making it easier to share a flue with the fire-places in the two next-door rooms.

Both parlours had withdrawing rooms adjoining them, each very richly furnished. The one next to the Little Parlour was described as the 'White Varnished Drawing Room' in 1698 – at a time when white was still the most expensive and ostentatious paint colour to choose. It had another carved overmantel by Edmund Carpenter, described in his bill as 'a rich Chimny Peece wth birds fruit & flowers' with 'a very rich large frees for the same Chimny', and costing £32 as opposed to £18 for the one in the Great Parlour. Unfortunately this was removed during Wyatville's complete remodelling of the room in the 1820s – since when it has always been known as the Red Drawing Room. But the carvings may well have been reused in the Chapel Gallery.

As originally furnished in 1688, the room was supplied with a gilded pier glass, pier table and candlestands, ten gilded armchairs and five pictures in gilded frames. It also had two tapestries, probably belonging to the Mortlake set of the *Story of Diogenes* now in the Tapestry Room, with later borders added at the instigation of Lord Tyrconnel. Tapestries or woven hangings would never at this date have been hung in an eating room, where they were thought to retain the smell of food. But they were immensely popular in withdrawing rooms and bed-chambers, giving added insulation and warmth.

One fascinating item variously described in the inventories as a 'glass screen', a mirror 'in the doorstead',

Belton House

1 Marble hall
2 Great parlour (now saloon)
3 Little parlour (now tapestry room)
4 Withdrawing room
5 Little marble hall (and great staircase)
6 Sir John Sherard's chamber
  (now blue room)
7 Chapel
8 Boudoir
9 Great nursery (now Windsor bedroom)

One of the 'Two pieces of Dutch hangeings', which were set into the panelling of the walls of the Chapel Drawing Room.

and 'a glass door in six plates' seems to have been installed on the west wall. In the seventeenth and eighteenth centuries, the adjoining room formed part of the upper kitchen quarters and there can have been no necessity for a way through – so this is likely to have been a false door, mirrored like the one in Talman's Great Dining Room at Chatsworth to give the impression of a still longer enfilade.

Retracing our steps through the Great Parlour on this same enfilade, we reach its own withdrawing chamber, also called the Green Damask Drawing Room by 1698. In many houses at this date the state bedchamber was on the ground floor, and indeed 'Young' Sir John's nephew, Lord Tyrconnel, used this room for precisely that purpose in the early eighteenth century. But we have to remember that these functions could be interchangeable: Sir Roger Pratt specifically mentions 'the With-drawing-room [next to the Great Parlour] with its conveniences like a bedchamber, and so to be used in time of need'. In 1698 the room had 'two pieces of green damask hangings', with ten cane chairs upholstered to match, green silk window curtains, and a japanned pierglass, pier table and candlestands like those in the Great Parlour. The third of Edmund Carpenter's documented overmantels was made for this room, and although the major part was removed to the Marble Hall in the nineteenth century (and replaced by garlands attributed to W. G. Rogers), the panel immediately above the fireplace is undoubtedly the 'frees for the same Chimny wth y^r cipher' (in other words Sir John's monogram). Argument has raged about the date of the painted floor here. This could well be a rare survival from Lord Tyrconnel's day – when the room contained a crimson damask bed and wall hangings – but is more likely to date from the 1880s when the 3rd Earl Brownlow first called this the Tyrconnel Room, and filled it with many of his ancestor's acquisitions.

The last room, at the east end of the ground-floor enfilade, giving access to the chapel gallery, was called simply the Ante Room in 1698, though it had more the character of a state dressing room – particularly after Lord Tyrconnel made its neighbour into his best bedchamber. The two chinoiserie tapestries were specially made for the room by John Vanderbank in 1691 with 'Indian figures according to ye pattern of the Queens wch are at Kensington', and the taste for the exotic Orient encouraged by Queen Mary (and the English and Dutch East India Companies) was continued by lacquer and japanned furniture, including, by 1737, a cabinet with twenty-two pieces of porcelain on it, 'two large blue and white jars', a 'large china punch bowl', an 'India tea table', and whole tea and coffee services, each with six cups and 'all of enamelled china'. The fashionable, and still very expensive, pastime of drinking tea was quite a ritual; it is easy to imagine Lady Brownlow and her successor, Lady Tyrconnel, entertaining favoured guests here, in a setting that would have seemed particularly opulent. The blue-green marbled decoration of the woodwork is now known to date from 1772, but could easily be a repetition of an earlier scheme, since this was called the 'Blue Dressing Room' in 1737.

The two-storey chapel, in the north-east wing, is one of the least altered seventeenth-century interiors at Belton, with the family gallery at the south end overlooking the pews for the household and servants below. No expense was spared on the decoration here, and very large amounts were paid to William Stanton for the marble paving and to Edward Goudge for the spectacular plasterwork ceiling. The reason why Goudge was employed here and on the great staircase, rather than on any of the main state rooms, can again be found in Roger Pratt's notes in which he says that 'ceilings in plaster which are cast in squares, ovals, etc. with mouldings after a masterly way, I take to be done only . . . for rooms of the greatest height viz. 20 or 30 ft., and where the divisions will fall out to be large'. The wreaths of fruit and flowers, and panels with winged cherubs' heads, are modelled in such high relief that they must have needed wooden armatures, and this explains the joiner Edward Willcox's bill for '. . . Cutting and putting up brackets in ye Chapel & staircase ceiling for ye frett work'.

The huge reredos with its great segmental pediment supported by Corinthian columns must have been designed by William Winde, and can be paralleled in some of Wren's City churches. But the quality of the wood carving is noticeably poorer than in the gallery festoons, which would be seen by the family at closer quarters. The nineteenth-century marbling may again be a repetition of an earlier decorative scheme.

In 1688, the room in the south-east wing was called 'Sir John Sherrard's Chamber over the Still House', and since Sir John was Lady Brownlow's grandfather, the young couple were again taking Pratt's advice – to 'have one bedchamber at least upon the first floor for those who are sick, weak, old etc.'. Rather surprisingly, the little room between this chamber and the east staircase cannot have belonged, for it was called the Sweetmeat Closet in 1698 and the Little Breakfast Room in 1737. The bedchamber is now called the Blue Room after the spectacular bed with its flying canopy (otherwise known as an 'angel-tester') reaching right up to the ceiling. Probably made in the first decade of the eighteenth century, this is very much in the style of the Huguenot upholsterer Francis Lapiere, and may well be the bed listed in the Tyrconnel Room in 1737, then covered with crimson damask. It was re-upholstered in blue in 1813, and the window curtains of blue 'tabouret' (now faded to a rather different colour) also go back that far.

The corresponding chamber in the south-west wing was the School Room in 1698 – appropriately, as it lay immediately below the nurseries – and it is easy to imagine Sir John's five little girls at their studies here.

The room was later turned into a library by Lord Tyrconnel, and is still a book-lined study.

The great staircase, otherwise known as the Little Marble Hall, still preserves Stanton's black-and-white marble floor and Goudge's plaster cornice and ceiling, incorporating the greyhound crest of the Brownlows. However, the plasterwork panels on the walls date from the 1740s, and the staircase itself was reconstructed by Wyatville in 1813. The walls were originally densely covered with pictures – forty-four of them in 1698, when the room also contained a billiard table with sticks and balls, and a chamber organ. Evidently this ceremonial way from the Marble Hall to the Great Dining Room was also

The huge reredos of twin columns with Corinthian capitals surmounted by a great segmental pediment is of wood, painted to imitate marble.

used for recreation, like an earlier long gallery.

The old medieval idea of a first-floor great chamber died hard in England, and indeed one can still be found at a house like Beningbrough in Yorkshire, only completed in 1716. However, these 'Great Dining Rooms' or 'Saloons' as they came to be called (after the Italian *salone*) were increasingly used only on special occasions, and remained sparsely furnished at other times. When a great banquet was held here, however, it must have presented a very different spectacle, with great buffet tables brought in and piled with all the family silver and gold plate and one long trestle table probably put up in the old-fashioned manner, covered with the best white linen damask.

One such occasion must surely have been William III's visit to Belton in October 1695, when he was 'mighty nobly entertained at Sir John Brownley's' according to the diarist, De La Pryme. 'Sir John killed twelve fat oxen and 60 sheep besides other victuals for his entertainment . . . the King was exceeding merry and drank freely which was the occasion that when he came to Lincoln he could eat nothing but a mess of milk'. Notwithstanding this over-indulgence, the monarch obviously enjoyed himself, as De La Pryme also records that 'he has sent up for him [Sir John] to London to honour him the more and to requite him for his kindnesses'.

In Lord Tyrconnel's day, the Great Dining Room was hung with six full-length portraits (including his own by Jervas, and his wife's by Seeman), but it was still sparsely furnished and not often used. However, in 1778 it obtained a new lease of life when the 1st Lord Brownlow commissioned James Wyatt to turn it into a fashionable Neo-Classical drawing room. Extra height was obtained by raising the floor levels of the garrets above, and a fine new barrel-vaulted ceiling with delicate plasterwork was inserted. The chimneypiece was also moved from the west

The state bed in the Blue Room, made about 1700 but re-upholstered with blue silk damask in 1813.

to the long south wall, in place of the original door to 'Young' Sir John's best bedchamber. A final chapter to the room's history came in 1877 when the bookcases were brought up from Wyatville's library (created in the upper part of the kitchen in 1813).

As we have seen, the 'best bedchamber' and its closet were originally given a prominent position in the pedimented section of the house immediately above the Great Parlour: a legacy from the days when the family still lived on the upper floor, and the servants occupied the rooms below. In the early eighteenth century, Lord Tyrconnel made a new state bedchamber downstairs and turned this into a drawing room. However, a hundred years later the wheel of taste was to turn full circle, when the 1st Earl Brownlow's wife became lady-in-waiting to Queen Adelaide. In 1844 the Queen announced that she wished to stay at Belton, and the old 'best bedchamber' was refurnished in her honour. The panelling, mostly of the seventeenth century, was unfortunately stripped of its paint in 1939.

Rather curiously, the closet which so obviously goes with the Queen's room, divided from it by the thinnest of partitions, is listed in the early inventories as belonging to Lady Brownlow's room on the other side. The answer probably is that the best bedchamber was only used very occasionally by the most distinguished guests, and that for the rest of the time Alice Brownlow treated it as her own preserve. To make matters more complicated there was also an inner 'cabinet' partitioned off at its southern end, and this *was* associated with the best bedchamber in 1698. The two rooms were probably made into one in 1778, when Wyatt opened a new door from here into his 'Great Drawing Room'. This in turn became the Ante-Library in 1877 (with rich marbled decoration added in 1884), but even now the alcove section at the southern end still reveals the proportions of the old 'cabinet'.

Besides its closet on one side, in 1688 the best bedchamber also had its own drawing room on the other – really more a dressing room in eighteenth-century terminology. By 1698 this was called the 'Scots Plaid Room' with 'one piece plaid hanging' and a bed, possibly matching it. After various transmutations in the eighteenth century, it finally became the Chinese Room in 1830, decorated with bamboo-grained woodwork and Chinese painted wallpaper, probably for Lady Sophia Cust, the 1st Earl's eldest daughter.

Another of Sir Roger Pratt's pieces of advice to builders was that the guests' apartments should be separated from those of the family, and the early inventories of Belton seem to bear this out – with the former grouped on the east, and the latter on the west. Thus the second-best guest's chamber was the one above the chapel (with two closets partitioned off its northern end), called the Velvet Room in 1688, and the Marble Room ten years later. The third-best would have been the 'White Painted Chamber' above the present Blue Room (with one closet). Lord Tyrconnel changed all this in the early eighteenth century, taking the suite above the chapel for himself. A small adjoining room (previously called the 'White and Green Painted Chamber') became his dressing room,

Belton, seen here from the south-east, is based on Sir Roger Pratt's 'double-pile' house – a compact block with sets of rooms back-to-back.

and it was here that he kept the great walnut bureau-bookcase with mirror-glass doors now in the Blue Room.

The family rooms, on the west side of the house before his time, included the chamber over the kitchen (with its two closets) occupied by Lady Brownlow's mother, Margaret Sherard. This was conveniently close to her daughter, who, as we have seen, slept in the room to the west of the 'best bedchamber'. The great and little nursery in the south-west wing (now called the Windsor Bedroom and Dressing Room) were also very close by, and these were furnished with great concern for the comfort of the little girls and their attendants. The youngest was to marry her cousin, Lord Tyrconnel, and to continue living in the house where she grew up; her sisters, thanks to their large dowries, became Duchess of Ancaster, Countess of Exeter and Lady Guilford, in ascending order of age. Sadly, however, the Tyrconnels had no children of their own, and by 1737 the great nursery had become the 'Black Room' – possibly because it had been used as a mourning chamber on her death, and still contained some black-painted furniture.

The room next to the nurseries and immediately above the Little Parlour (now called the Boudoir), was another bedchamber, probably occupied by a member of the family in 1698. However, by 1737 it contained only three tapestries and may have been used as an adjunct to the Great Dining Room next door. In 1776 James Wyatt completely redecorated it as a dressing room for Frances Bankes, wife of the 1st Lord Brownlow, who occupied the same bedchamber to the north that had belonged to 'Young' Sir John's wife so many years before.

Like Wyatt's 'Great Drawing Room', remodelled at the same time, it has a sumptuous Neo-Classical ceiling, apparently by a little-known plasterer called Utterton, and a marble chimneypiece attributed to the sculptor William Tyler – although the plaster wall panels and overmantel mirror are additions of 1875, by George Jackson & Sons.

Lady Brownlow's own room, called the 'Blue and White Painted Chamber' in 1698, was later called the 'Best Wrought Room' after its embroidered bed hangings – and it is not too fanciful to think that these might have been of her own making. Her husband is not given a room of his own in the early inventories, and it is quite likely that he shared hers, though having his own dressing room and closet immediately adjoining on the west. Here, with his 'screwtore' or writing desk, his iron chest for valuables, his globes and books and caned armchair, he could settle down to his studies, while keeping a close watch on the comings and goings in the service courtyard below.

In July 1697, Narcissus Luttrell reported that 'Sir John Brownlow member of Parliament for Grantham . . . last week shot himself at Mr Freakes [his uncle's house] in Dorsetshire, but the reason not known.' Suicide hardly seems likely for a man with so few financial or family problems; and if it had been proved, he would not have been able to take his place in the family vault in Belton church, or be commemorated there by William Stanton's splendid monument. So it seems more likely that he died by accident, and we can only regret that the builder of one of the most perfect houses of its kind in England lived such a short time to enjoy it.

Petworth House

W E S T   S U S S E X

WHEN WE THINK OF PETWORTH, it is usually through Turner's eyes: the long, low, silvery-coloured façade seen from across the lake as if floating on a bank of mist, the silence broken in our imagination only by the barking of a deer, or the beating wings of a duck among the reeds. Then there is that other vision, no less romantic, of a vast concourse of people seated at tables on the greensward for one of the annual feasts given by Turner's patron, the 3rd Earl of Egremont. Banners wave, bands play, and on the hill above the house the artist, Witherington, shows the old man on horseback doffing his hat to a group of tenants' wives.

Both these images belong to the golden age of Petworth, when it was an open house for artists, sculptors and their families, entertained by one who, in Burke's words, 'delighted to reign in the dispensation of happiness'. Liberal, unconventional, generous to a fault, the 3rd Earl will always be the man who comes first to mind as we walk across the park at close of day and see the welcoming lights in the windows, or stroll through the state rooms overwhelmed by the mixture of splendour and comfort, the great works of art of every age crammed on to the walls in such profusion.

Yet, like so many of the greatest collectors, Lord Egremont was not a great builder. Apart from the North Gallery, notable more for the pictures and sculpture it contains than for its architecture, his only real contribution to the building was the removal of some of its more Baroque decoration: the squared dome that originally gave it a much stronger central emphasis; the separate mansard roofs that gave the end 'pavilions' so much more prominence; and the series of statues and urns that once crowned the parapet. Doubtless he would have considered all these features – fortunately known to us from an early painting of the house at Belvoir – pompous and pretentious, quite apart from being old-fashioned. A Whig, who as a young man had come under the influence of Charles James Fox, he abhorred ceremony of any kind – including, it seems, the ceremony

of marriage, since he only went through with it after the birth of his children, and then left his wife within a year. Thoroughly patrician at heart, he liked to maintain what we would now call a 'low profile' in everyday life, shabbily dressed and always accompanied by a pack of small dogs as he made his rounds of the house, checking that his guests were happily occupied.

It would, in fact, be hard to imagine two characters more unlike than the 3rd Earl and his great-grandfather, Charles Seymour, 6th Duke of Somerset, the real creator of Petworth as we know it today. The 'Proud Duke' was obsessed by his lineage, as the nickname given him by his descendants suggests. Never for a moment did he forget that his ancestors, the Norman St Mauros, had been Welsh marcher barons under Edward I, and that later Seymours had accompanied the Black Prince to Gascony, helped Henry VI to the throne, and had finally provided Henry VIII with a wife – and England with a Protestant heir. But a sense of grievance was allied with this family pride. The 1st Duke, Jane Seymour's brother, ruled England as Lord Protector for his nephew Edward VI, but was executed in 1552 and his honours declared forfeit until the Restoration. His great-grandson (eventually 2nd Duke) had to go into exile after marrying a potential heir to the throne, Arabella Stuart – whom we have already met at Hardwick – without her cousin James I's permission. Above all, the family estates were so reduced that they would hardly have supported a dukedom had the 2nd Duke's younger brother, Lord Seymour of Trowbridge, not married a Wiltshire heiress, Frances Prinne.

Added to all this, the Proud Duke may have suffered from a complex as the younger son of a younger branch, not expected to succeed until the untimely death of his elder brother in 1678. Burke's *Peerage*, usually so reticent about such matters, records the circumstances with some exactness: '. . . this nobleman [the 5th Duke] during his travels in Italy, having, in company with some French gentlemen, visited the church of the Augustinians at

Fête in Petworth Park, W.F. Witherington's painting of one of the 3rd Earl of Egremont's annual feasts.

Lerice, and there offered rudeness to ladies of the family of Botti, of that place, was shot to death by Horatio Botti, the husband of one of those ladies, at the door of his inn'.

After this ignominious episode, the new Duke must have been determined to restore both the honour and the fortunes of his family with a spectacular dynastic alliance, and this he achieved four years later with his marriage to Lady Elizabeth Percy, only daughter of the 11th and last Earl of Northumberland – probably the greatest heiress of her day. Lady Elizabeth, whose dowry included Petworth, had also had her troubles. Though not quite sixteen, this was her third marriage in three years: her first husband, Lord Ogle, died after only a year in 1680, while the second, Thomas Thynne, was killed in the following year by her lover, Count Charles Königsmarck. After these excitements she must have been ready to

The west front of Petworth before the 3rd Earl removed the square central dome and the statues and urns on the parapet.

settle down to the security of an arranged match and, as Duchess of Somerset, soon became a pillar of the establishment, counting both Queen Mary and Queen Anne among her closest friends. Indeed, it was she who was appointed Mistress of the Robes after Queen Anne's famous quarrel with the Duchess of Marlborough.

The Proud Duke was one of the noblemen who invited William and Mary to take the throne in 1688, and must have seen this as doubly appropriate: first because his family had been staunch supporters of the Protestant Succession since the Lord Protector's day, and second because his own dynastic alliance mirrored theirs. However, a sense of grievance remained, for he was not given one of the highest offices of state, which he considered his due. In later years the diarist Jeremiah Milles describes him spending most of his time at Petworth 'in a grand retirement peculier and agreable only to himself. He comes down to breakfast at 8 of ye clock in ye morning in his full dress with his blue ribbon [the Order of the Garter]; after breakfast, he goes into his offices, scolds and bullys his servants and steward till dinner time; then very formally hands his Duchess downstairs. His table, tho' spread in a grand manner as if company was expected consists of his own family ye Duchess and his 2 daughters; and when he has a mind to be gracious the chaplain is admitted. He treats all his county neighbours, and indeed everybody else, with such uncommon pride and distance, yt none of them visit him'. Added to all this, Milles found, like other visitors, that the Duke 'studiously concealed' the artists of most of his pictures 'out of an unusual and ridiculous whimsy'.

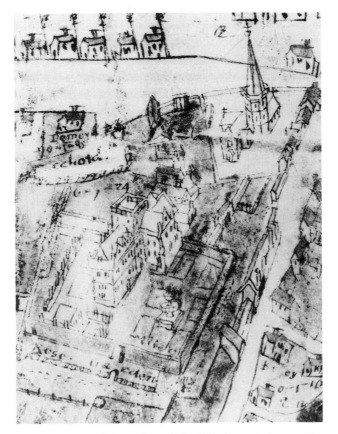

Treswell's survey of Petworth, made in 1610, shows the house and church in the time of the 9th Earl of Northumberland.

While it would be easy to dismiss the Proud Duke as a figure of fun, he was also a cultivated man, who as Chancellor of Cambridge University helped found the University Press in 1696 and gave huge endowments to Trinity, St Katharine's Hall and other colleges. Moreover, the rebuilding of Petworth, his most splendid monument, might have taken a very different – and less interesting – course had it not been for the peculiarities of his character, the royal connections of which he was so conscious, and the style of life he felt he must maintain.

In one respect Petworth is different from almost all other English country houses. Instead of standing at the centre of its park in splendid isolation, its huge bulk dominates, but at the same time turns its back on, the little market town – rather like a French château, with the church and village huddled up behind its show front. Apart from castle towns like Arundel and Warwick, only Cirencester Park in Gloucestershire has the same feel. At the same time there is an extraordinary contrast between the decorative unity of the long west front, French again in inspiration, and the jumble of old buildings behind on the east, with windows of every shape and size and date punched through massive walls, part brick, part rough stonework, part ashlar, supported by huge buttresses. In this patchwork of different styles and abandonment of symmetry lies the key to Petworth's architectural development, for unlike the Brownlows of Belton who had bought another family's seat and had no compunction in tearing it down and building on another site, the Proud Duke wished to demonstrate the continuity of his wife's family inheritance. The old Percy house, and above all its fourteenth-century chapel, was a link with the past which must be preserved at all costs.

Petworth had been acquired by the Percy family in 1150 though the earliest reference to a building here occurs in 1309 when Henry, Lord Percy, obtained a licence to crenellate an existing manor. However, this 'castle' (as it continued to be called until the mid-sixteenth century) was of only modest size compared with the Percy's northern fortresses like Alnwick and Warkworth, and as their southern estates never produced more than about one-sixth the revenues of their northern ones, it seems rarely to have been visited by the first five Earls of Northumberland.

It was more by accident than choice that Petworth became the chief seat of the family after 1576. Because of their immense power in the north and their Catholicism, the family were in more or less constant trouble from their attainder for treason in 1537 to the execution of the 7th Earl at York in 1572. On being summoned to the Lords in 1576, his brother, the 8th Earl, was consequently required to live in the south, and took up residence at Petworth. Over the next six years he spent nearly £3000 there, on what must have been a virtual rebuilding. The appearance of the house as he left it can be judged from the sketch on Ralph Treswell's map of 1610: almost cruciform in shape with a large square tower at the west end of the chapel, a wing with three gables projecting further westwards beyond it, and a shorter but thicker wing to the south. The large buttresses at the ends of this wing are remarkably similar to those still on the east front, and the very thick walls in this part of the house also suggest an early origin.

The 9th Earl of Northumberland, known because of his interest in science and alchemy as the 'Wizard Earl', succeeded in 1585 after his father's mysterious death in the Tower of London, where he was himself to spend fifteen years on suspicion of complicity in the Gunpowder Plot. The prodigious width of the 9th Earl's interests included architecture, and, having already rebuilt Syon in Middlesex to his own designs, he drew up a vastly ambitious scheme for a new house at Petworth while still in the Tower in 1615. This new house was to have been built on the hillside north-west of the present building, which Treswell shows cut into terraces or 'rampiers' already by 1610, and with descending courtyards to the south of it. These courtyards would have been flanked by a new stable quadrangle on the west, which the Wizard Earl actually built after his release from the Tower in 1621, and by the old house (converted into offices and servants' quarters) on the east. In preparation for this grand design, he seems to have altered the latter by lowering or demolishing the tower, and extending the west and south ranges, probably intending to make it another quadrangle balancing the stables. A painting now at Syon clearly shows the relationship between them, and to what extent the scheme was achieved by the time of his death in 1632. More concrete evidence of his work can also be found in the long tunnel-vaulted cellar under the present rooms on the west front, stretching from the Marble Hall to the White Library – and showing how far he enlarged his father's house. An ornate cast-iron fireback

*The old Percy house
as it might have looked
around 1610, based
on Treswell's survey.*

in the Carved Room, bearing his initials and crest
and the date 1622, also suggests a date for this work.

Where the Wizard Earl had failed to make Petworth the
palace he had dreamt of, the Proud Duke succeeded in the
final decade of the seventeenth century at least in giving
the main front of the house a palatial (and for the first time
symmetrical) appearance. Palace is certainly the key word,
for the Duke aimed to build on a royal scale. Did his arms
not include the leopards and lilies of the royal standard,
specially granted by Henry VIII, together with the unicorn
supporter balancing the Seymour bull? Did his wife's
ancestors not also share the royal blood, as well as being
virtually independent princes in the north? There is still an
over-lifesize feel to the rooms at Petworth, more like the
interiors of Wren's Hampton Court than any other
subject's house until the building of the Duke of
Marlborough's Blenheim and Lord Carlisle's Castle
Howard. An inventory made in the early 1690s, lists an
amazing amount of rooms still devoted to upper
household officials such as the steward, chaplain,
comptroller, butler and master of the horse, apparently on
the first floor of the house. So it is likely that the Duke was

also perpetuating the old quasi-royal lifestyle practised at
Knole before the Civil War.

The initial inspiration for the design may itself have
been a royal commission, for there is a distinct
resemblance between the central squared dome shown
in the Belvoir painting and Wren's designs for
Winchester Palace, made in 1682–3, and half completed
by the time of Charles II's death. It can be no accident,
either, that many of the workmen employed at Petworth
were master craftsmen in the King's Office of Works,
several of them previously employed at Winchester:
men like Samuel Foulkes the mason (and supervisor at
Petworth), Edward Dee the bricklayer, John Hunt the
glazier, and of course the 'Master Sculptor' Grinling
Gibbons. John Scarborough, clerk of the works at
Winchester from 1682 to 1696, was also employed on
measuring work here in 1690. It is significant too that
the Duke's contract with the joiner Thomas Larkin of
St Martin-in-the-Fields, signed in December 1686, should
specify 'Waintscott with Ballections [bolection mouldings]
. . . according to the worke in his Maties Great and new
Gallerye at Whitehall, and window shutters and compass

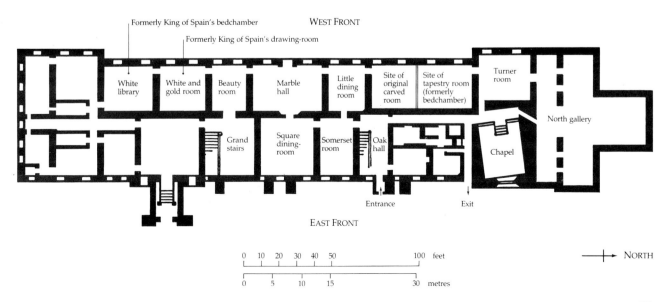

Formerly King of Spain's bedchamber   WEST FRONT

Formerly King of Spain's drawing-room

White library | White and gold room | Beauty room | Marble hall | Little dining room | Site of original carved room | Site of tapestry room (formerly bedchamber) | Turner room

Grand stairs | Square dining-room | Somerset room | Oak hall | Chapel | North gallery

Entrance   Exit

EAST FRONT

0 10 20 30 40 50   100 feet

0 5 10 15   30 metres

NORTH

[segmental] pedim^t over the doores as those in the newest lodgings in Whitehall'.

At this early date, however, the Proud Duke seems only to have been remodelling the 9th Earl's existing building, and new work did not begin seriously until the Duchess came into her full inheritance in 1688, at the age of twenty-one. New quarries were opened in the park in that year and £381 spent on building, rising to £1536 in 1689, back to £980 in 1691 and down to £300 in 1692 (the total for 1690 is not recorded, but must also have been over £1000 to judge by the number of surviving bills). The first evidence for work on the west front is a payment to Foulkes 'towards the frontice-peece in the new Buildings' in the winter of 1689–90, when the carver John Selden was also paid for the 'keystones with carved winges' (the angel's wings from the Seymour coat-of-arms), which are such a notable feature of the façade. The dome was slated in August of that year, though 'three gable heads att ye South end of ye house' (evidently part of the 9th Earl's building) were not taken down until July 1691, and the 'old hall' not until 1692. Presumably the work was more or less complete by 1693, when William III visited Petworth.

Despite this wealth of documentation, the designer of the west front remains a mystery. As early as 1832, the county historian Dallaway recorded the tradition that the architect of Petworth was 'Pouget, a Frenchman, who gave the designs for Montagu House' – an attribution evidently based on Colen Campbell's description of that building in the first volume of *Vitruvius Britannicus*, published in 1715. Montagu House in Bloomsbury (on the site now occupied by the British Museum) was rebuilt by Ralph, Duke of Montagu, in 1686–8 after a serious fire; it was, to judge from Campbell's engraving, very closely related to the west front of Petworth, particularly its central squared dome, crowned by a balustraded platform and with statues on the parapet below. Another dome of the same sort still exists on the stable block at Ralph Montagu's other house, Boughton in Northamptonshire, and the relationship between these three francophile buildings is made even closer by the fact that Montagu (several times ambassador to Louis XIV) was married to the widowed Countess of Northumberland, the Proud Duke's mother-in-law.

Practically nothing is known of the mysterious Pouget, though two or three drawings signed '*Boujet fecit*' have come to light, seeming to confirm Campbell's verdict. On the other hand, there is evidence that a far less shadowy figure, William III's Huguenot designer-in-chief, Daniel Marot, was also involved with this whole group of houses. Marot, who was trained under Jean Berain, Louis XIV's chief *dessinateur*, before leaving France at the Revocation of the Edict of Nantes, is known to have been summoned to England soon after William and Mary's accession to design the parterre at Hampton Court, the Delft-tiled dairy, and probably the entire interior of the Queen's Water Gallery apartments (destroyed after her death). He also designed a series of elaborate painted panels for Montagu House, while at the same time the north front of Boughton, with its open arcade, is almost

identical to an engraving in his father's book, the *Petit Marot*, later republished in his own *Oeuvres*. There are numerous parallels between Daniel Marot's known work and the west front of Petworth – perhaps most notably the busts on tapering plinths above the

The extravagantly baroque Marble Hall was probably designed by William III's Huguenot architect, Daniel Marot.

ground-floor windows of the end 'pavilions', which recall his design for a chimneypiece at De Voorst in Holland, or the bracketed frieze of the central section, with magnificent hunting trophies carved over the windows, reminiscent of engravings in his *Seconde Livre*

d'Architecture. Reminders that Petworth was conceived as a glorified hunting lodge, these trophies also recall the frieze of the Salon de la Guerre at Versailles, begun in 1679, just at the moment the young Marot joined Berain's *atelier*.

Louis Laguerre's mural on the Grand Staircase. The Duchess of Somerset rides in a triumphal chariot attended by her children.

Detail of Laguerre's painting, showing the plan of the house in the time of the 6th Duke of Somerset.

On the other hand it has been pointed out that Marot was usually working in collaboration with William III's Dutch architect, Jacob Roman, at this period: for instance at Het Loo, the King's own hunting palace in Gelderland; at Zeist, built for his cousin William of Nassau-Odijk; and at De Voorst itself, built for his favourite, the Earl of Albemarle. Roman was in England in 1690, when he almost certainly designed the King's Gallery façade and Clock Court at Kensington Palace. These are more austere in style than Petworth; but, knowing the Proud Duke's anxiety to be a member of William III's inner circle, it remains a possibility that he consulted the King's two *chefs des dessins* – just as in France some of Louis XIV's close relations (and mistresses) were allowed to consult Hardouin-Mansart and Berain.

One of the chief problems with such attributions is that at this date an architect was seldom responsible for supervising the job from start to finish, but merely gave a design which was executed (often with major differences) by the workmen on the spot. As he himself would be paid out of the patron's private purse, his name rarely occurs in the main series of building accounts. No mention of Roman has yet been found among the Petworth papers, but there is one imprecise record of 'twenty Pounds which was paid to Mr. Maro' in September 1693, and one other tantalizing scrap of information implying that Daniel Marot actually came to the house: a note in the flyleaf of the Proud Duke's library catalogue recording that 'Monsr Marot' borrowed a copy of the essays of Montaigne.

Unfortunately the year is not given, but from its placing it seems to belong with entries of either 1690 or 1693.

The room where Marot's presence seems unmistakable is the Marble Hall, occupying the central three bays of the west front and strikingly similar to the Trèveszaal in the Binnenhof Palace at The Hague, which he designed for the States-General in 1696–8. The huge bracketed frieze, the chimneypieces at either end with round-topped overmantel frames breaking into the segmental pediments (rather like reredoses in a church), and the giant acanthus mouldings round the doors, have a theatricality worthy of a Baroque stage designer – another of Marot's chief roles at the court of William and Mary.

As a waiting place for servants and visitors, and as an introduction to a family's rank and status, it was still usual for a hall to be prominently decorated with its owner's coat-of-arms. So the great cartouche above each chimneypiece, encircled by the Proud Duke's Garter and flanked by an almost life-size bull and unicorn, would have brought the message home in no uncertain terms. While the rest of the room is likely to have been painted in stone colours, these might have been picked out in bright heraldic colours.

Always called the 'Hall of State' in the accounts, the room was created in 1692 with carving by John Selden, joinery by Thomas Larkin, the 'dove-coloured' bolection-moulded chimneypieces by Nicholas Mitchell, and the beautiful marble paving by a 'Mr. Stroud'.

There may originally have been a more elaborate plasterwork ceiling, to judge by payments to Daniel Lance and Edward Goudge (whose work we have encountered at Belton), but a serious fire damaged this part of the house in 1714 and it could have been lost then. The fact that John Madgwick was paid for 'beateing down pte of the wall in the hall of state for the neeces' shows that the very thick inside wall here was part of the earlier house; and that also explains the wide recess framing the door in the centre, splayed to give an impression of still greater depth.

Theatricality, as in this piece of false perspective, was a quality eminently suitable for country houses at a time when a great nobleman's life was still played out with the kind of ritual we now associate more with religious ceremonies. Axial vistas were a favourite concept of the Baroque period, and by the early 1690s, when Petworth was being rebuilt, no house was complete without its enfilade of doors stretching out on either side of the central hall, and the great dining room or saloon on the floor above. This alignment was intended not only to impress by its length and diminishing perspective but to form an ideal setting for the formal processions that preceded a great man's *levée* in the morning, his dinner in the afternoon, and his *couchée* at night. Romeyn de Hooghe's engraving of Het Loo in William and Mary's day shows a procession of food crossing the forecourt from the kitchen wing towards the main block – solemn bewigged figures in twos and threes bearing what appear to be stuffed peacocks, joints and puddings as well as tureens and napkins. The same must have happened at Petworth, since the great kitchen lay in a separate block to the east, along with the other domestic offices.

Trying to work out how the main rooms in the house were originally used is a much more difficult matter than at Belton, since we have only a fragmentary inventory of the early 1690s, evidently made before the building was finished, and then nothing until the full one taken on the death of the Proud Duke's only son in 1750. However, it is clear that in the early inventory the Duke's and Duchess's apartments lay on the ground floor, perhaps flanking the 'state centre' like William and Mary's balancing apartments at Het Loo. The Duke's adjoined the main staircase, so was probably on the right as you look at the west front today, beyond a lobby (now known as the Beauty Room) which led to the stairs from the Marble Hall. The Duchess's would then have been on the left, beyond a 'little parlour' (still known as the Little Dining Room) and a withdrawing room (the southern half of the present Carved Room).

The 'great parlour' was a huge room beyond the hall, as at Belton, but not on axis with it, probably because it was a survival from the earlier house: it was split up to form the present Square Dining Room and Somerset Room in the 1790s. The 'great dining room' or saloon lay above the hall, and could have been two storeys high as it lay below the dome. Unfortunately we know very little about its appearance, as it had already been split up into bedchambers and dressing rooms by 1750. It may have been badly damaged in the fire of 1714, but would surely

have been reconstructed afterwards, since Laguerre's great painted staircase of that date was conceived as a ceremonial approach to it: an ascent to Olympus, suggesting to the Proud Duke and his guests that they were leaving the world of mere mortals below, to sup like gods above.

Here, the solid architecture of the west front and the Marble Hall melt into illusionism, as the painter creates vistas through impossibly ornate Composite columns, building up from stone colours and *grisailles* below to an explosion of colour in the ceiling. The lower scenes depict the story of Prometheus, thought to be an allusion to the fire, but also a good mythological persona for the Duke himself. Not only was his crest a phoenix rising from the flames, but he could well have seen himself being released by Hercules – William III's usual *alter ego*. Above the first flight of stairs, the Duchess of Somerset is shown riding in her chariot, apparently representing Ceres, attended by the Three Graces – and her very English-looking spaniel – while on the upper landing are the Muses, once again appropriate as they were supposed to live on the slopes of Mount Parnassus, halfway between the mortal world and the divine. Above, in the ceiling, the gods themselves assemble in a whirlpool of fluttering draperies and writhing limbs, billowing clouds and fitful sunbursts.

The huge doorcase at the top of the stairs must have led into an ante-room, in which the procession would turn at right-angles to enter the great dining room. Beyond that lay 'the great drawing room above stairs' as it is called in one of the Duke's letters to his agent, and beyond that again the main state apartment consisting of bedchamber, dressing room, closet and servant's room.

To judge by the inventory made in the early 1690s, the house was already quite richly furnished – with silver andirons and hearth furniture (like those which still survive at Knole and Ham) in the withdrawing room on the ground floor, red gilt leather hangings in the dining room of the Duke's apartment, a 'striped Indian damask Angill bed' lined with yellow taffeta in the Duchess's bedchamber, and a great deal of tapestry, much of it inherited, since it bore the Percy crescent – a 'half-moon and garter at the Corners'.

The 1750 inventory describes much else probably acquired later in that decade and in the early eighteenth century, in particular the vast quantity of Chinese porcelain and lacquer and japanned cabinets that are still in the house. The surviving bills show that the Duchess was buying from many of the same English and Dutch dealers as her friend, Queen Mary, and details like the glass panels over the door and chimney of her closet, 'both ornamented with carved work & 45 pieces of China', recall Daniel Marot's engraved designs for porcelain rooms in the 1690s. The drawing room to the state apartment on the ground floor (now the White and Gold Room) also had twelve pieces of china over the chimneypiece, twenty-two on the tops of two 'India Cabinets', and two large jars on mahogany pedestals – made for the house in several different patterns. The Oriental theme was continued by 'India Damask Hangings' on the walls, and 'India Brocade' covers to the seat furniture,

Petworth House

1 Marble hall
2 Beauty room
3 Grand stairs
4 Square dining-room
5 Somerset room
6 Little dining-room
7 Carved room
8 Turner room
9 North gallery
10 Chapel

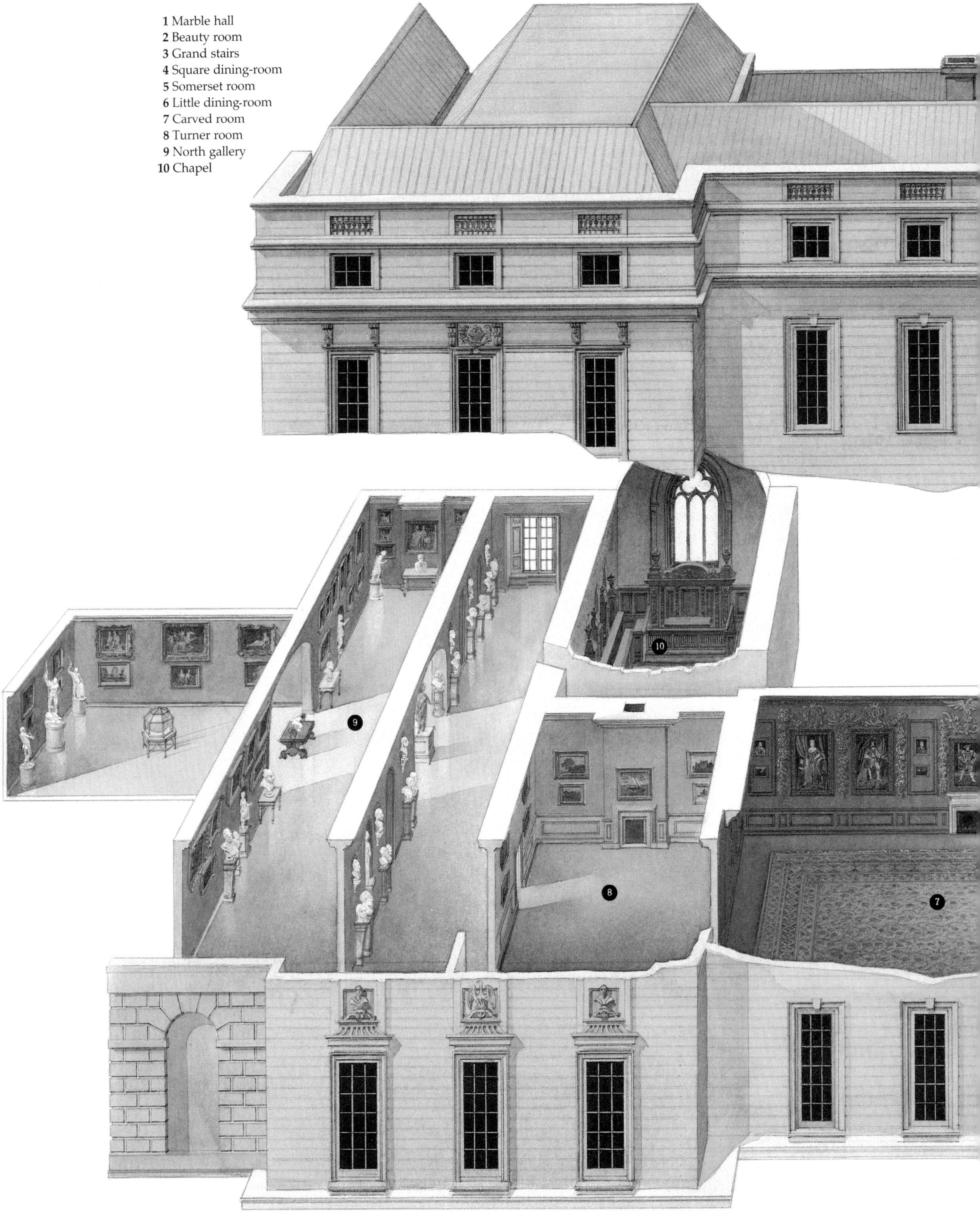

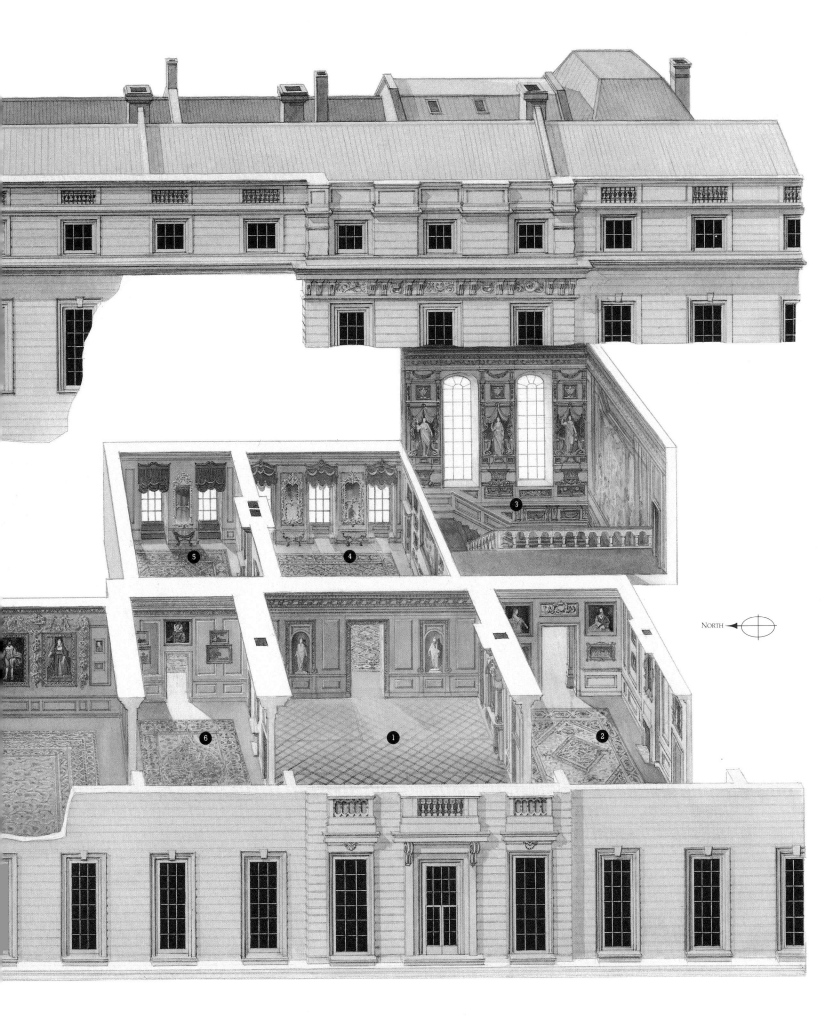

NORTH

and it is no surprise to find a tea service also listed, as in the Chapel Drawing Room at Belton.

Other exotic items listed include metal-inlaid (Boulle) bureaus used as dressing tables in some of the bedrooms, a silver chandelier with eight branches in the Tapestry Room (the northern half of the present Carved Room), and six tall panels of mirror glass apparently set into the walls of the Dining Room (now the Beauty Room), with portraits arranged in between.

Of all the Proud Duke's legacies, however, it is the wood carvings by Grinling Gibbons and John Selden that take the palm. As at Belton (though again on an infinitely grander scale) these seem to have been intended for parlours and withdrawing rooms, and it was only in 1794–5 that the 3rd Earl gathered most of them together in a large new Carved Room, created by amalgamating two smaller interiors. Selden, who seems to have been a local man – the equivalent of Samuel Watson at Chatsworth – was almost Gibbons's equal in skill, as can be seen from his overmantel surround of 1689–90 'made with ffowles, ffishes and flowers', and appropriately intended for the dining room (presumably the little parlour rather than the great one).

However, Gibbons's pair of double picture frames either side of the chimneypiece, and his great pendants at either end of the same wall, are in a class of their own: in Horace Walpole's words, 'the most superb monument of his skill' and 'worthy of the Grecian age of Cameos'. On the left the garlands frame the portraits of the Proud Duke and his wife by Riley and Clostermans, with his Star of the Garter hanging from the angel's wings of the Seymour arms. The ducal coronets above are held aloft by palms so thinly cut that they seem to defy the medium, while lower down hang a pair of classical vases carved almost in the round, perhaps a tribute to the Duke's patronage of the arts. On the right the Duke's grand-parents, Lord and Lady Seymour of Trowbridge, are given a hardly less sumptuous setting: putti with trumpets sounding their praises, sheafs of musical instruments, songbirds and baskets of flowers.

The scale of these great set-pieces must have been even more telling as originally arranged, in a withdrawing room occupying only the southern half of the present Carved Room. This was the first room of an 'apartment', leading to a tapestry-hung bedchamber and a dressing room beyond (now the Turner Room). From here a door led into an open arcade (now part of the North Gallery), looking over the main parterre to the orangery. As we have seen, this suite of rooms may originally have been occupied by the Duchess – and again there is a parallel with Queen Mary, whose apartments at Het Loo and Hampton Court were specially arranged to give access to the gardens that were her passion. However, the Duchess probably moved to another apartment upstairs in the early eighteenth century. By 1750, the bedchamber had become simply the 'Tapestry Room', once again equipped for making tea, while the dressing room had become a picture cabinet, hung with sixty paintings of different sizes.

While it is a pity that the inventories do not give us greater insights into the use of the main rooms, we do have one fascinating document that explains, better than any other, how a Baroque house like Petworth actually worked. This is an account of a visit made by the King of Spain (later the Emperor Charles VI) on 28 December 1703, on his way to stay with Queen Anne at Windsor. The writer, who was in the retinue of the Queen's husband, Prince George of Denmark, recounts how the Prince arrived from London the day before the King, who was coming from Portsmouth, but how 'the magnificence of the Duke of Somerset's house (though it is not near finished), the exceeding rich furniture, fine pictures, carvings &c. made next day short enough to his Highness, who would not eat till the king's arrival'. Quite a lot of building activity is recorded at the house in 1702–3, including the creation of a new apartment for the Duke on the first floor near the chapel – possibly in connection with this visit. At all events, the King was given the ground-floor apartment to the right of the Marble Hall (which may previously have been the Duke's), and these rooms continued to be known as the King of Spain's

Portraits of the 6th Duke of Somerset, and his wife, Elizabeth Percy with their son, Algernon Seymour. Petworth was acquired by the 'Proud Duke' through his marriage to Elizabeth, the daughter and heiress of the 11th Earl of Northumberland.

The gigantic proscenium, which frames the family pew in the chapel,
is carved and painted to look like curtains of crimson and gold brocade.

Drawing Room and Bedchamber until the 3rd Earl's day, when they were renamed the White and Gold Room and White Library.

On the King's arrival, the Prince took over the role of host, being of a higher rank than the Duke, and having greeted him at the door of the Marble Hall 'waited on him directly to his own apartment, and there left him about half an hour, after which he sent to visit him, and was received at the door of his bed-chamber by his Catholic Majesty, and seated in an arm-chair opposite to his own'. The formality of this scene recalls the famous Gobelins tapestry of Louis XIV receiving the Papal Nuncio in his bedchamber, with the bed behind him acting as a symbol of authority just as potent as the canopy of state that developed from it. At Petworth, the bed was probably the one still in the room in 1750, of 'Indian green and white Sattin laced with broad & narrow Silver Lace, & 34 Silver Tassels'.

Our informant continues: '. . . the ceremony was short, and the Prince had not been long retired to his quarters [on the first floor], before the King sent to return the visit, and was received at the top of the stairs, and conducted to the Prince's bed-chamber. After he had been there a little while, he signified to the Duke of Somerset his desire of seeing my Lady Duchess; whereupon the Prince, the two Dukes, &c. [the Duke of Marlborough was also present] waited upon him at her Grace's apartments [back on the ground floor].' He then recounts that the Duchess 'came forward several rooms, even to the bottom of the stairs to meet the King, and making a very low obeisance, she received a kiss from him, as also the two young ladies, her daughters . . . After that, he accompanied her to a little drawing room [probably the Carved Room, in its original guise], where he staid three or four minutes, and then was carried by the Prince to see the house.'

After this exhausting social round, all involving solemn processions with officials bearing emblems of their office, and probably watched by scores of spectators, the participants gathered for supper – almost certainly in the great dining room above the Marble Hall – 'served up with so much splendor and profusion, yet with so much decency and order that I must needs say I never saw the like'. Interestingly, 'the table where they supped was an oval and very large; the King sat about the middle of it, and the Prince almost at the end'. What a world of difference lies between this scene and Thomas Phillips's painting of the Allied Sovereigns arriving at Petworth in 1814, windswept and disorganized, to be greeted by the 3rd Earl and his (illegitimate) family – the Tsar's bearded Russian coachmen adding an appropriately bizarre touch.

Today, as we have seen, it is the mixture of grandeur and informality that gives Petworth its particular character and charm. It is doubtful whether the Proud Duke would even recognize many of his rooms today, enriched as they are by his grandson's Old Masters and antique sculpture, and softened and humanized by his great-grandson's notions of Regency comfort. Yet there is one room where his shade surely lingers: the old Percy chapel at the north-east corner of the house.

Apart from its early fourteenth-century window arcades and its rare fifteenth-century eagle lectern, everything here is due to the Proud Duke and his wife: the plaster-work ceiling by Edward Goudge; the stalls with their original graining, marbling and gilding; the reredos and communion rail; and the family pew like a gigantic opera box at the west end, with carved wooden 'curtains' held up in great festoons and painted to look like crimson and gold brocade. Everywhere there is heraldry – carved, painted or in stained glass; and everywhere there are the Seymour wings – from the marvellously expressive cherubs' heads on the stalls, looking towards the altar as if caught in a 'rushing, mighty wind', to the life-size angels bearing the arms of the Duke and Duchess high above their gallery. Here, if anywhere, we still feel their presence, framed in the wide proscenium arch, and with seraphs either side trumpeting their glory to posterity.

Stourhead

W I L T S H I R E

And blest is he, who tir'd with his affairs,
Far from all noise, all vain applause, prepares
To go, and underneath some silent shade,
Which neither cares nor anxious thoughts invade,
Does for a while, himself alone possess;
Changing the Town for Rural happiness
. . . To ev'ry part he may his care extend,
And these delights all others so transcend,
That we the City now no more respect,
Or the vain honours of the Court affect
But to cool Streams, to aged Groves retire,
And th'unmixed pleasures of the fields desire.

THESE LINES, translated by John Evelyn from a Latin poem by René Rapin (consciously evoking Virgil's *Georgics*), could have been written about the Hoares of Stourhead, goldsmiths and bankers, who took time off from the City to create a house and garden that echoed Italy – but that came to symbolize a very British idea of Elysium.

The gulf that divides Petworth from Stourhead, the Baroque palace from the Palladian villa, is not merely one of scale, nor of social condition. It is a fundamental change of direction in thinking. Colen Campbell's architecture looked forward to the end of the 'power house' as a centre of absolute rule, just as the second Henry Hoare's architecture spelt the end of regimented parterres and avenues. Both were founded on new principles of 'natural liberty', and both foreshadowed the cultured informality of the Regency period when Sir Richard Colt Hoare gave them their finishing touches. Instead of swinging backwards and forwards with the barometer of fashion, the work of these three generations resulted in a corporate work of art that is one of the supreme expressions of eighteenth-century taste.

Now that the woodlands have grown up as a barrier between the house and garden, there is a mistaken tendency to see them as quite separate entities. But it is their interdependence that makes Stourhead such an endlessly satisfying place. The same restrained architecture, based on antique precedents and harmonic proportions, can be found indoors as well as out: in the perfect cube of Campbell's entrance hall as in the perfect circle of Flitcroft's Pantheon. The same idealized views of classical landscape, after Claude and Poussin, hanging on the walls of Colt Hoare's picture gallery, can be seen brought to life on the walk encircling the lake. The same poets and philosophers whose works crowd the bookshelves of his library are behind the literary references and inscriptions found throughout his grandfather's garden.

This was a period, in Christopher Hussey's words, when 'the relation of all the arts to one another, through the pictorial appreciation of nature, was so close that poetry, painting, gardening, architecture and the art of travel may be said to have been fused into the single "art of landscape" '. So in a book devoted largely to the architecture and planning of the country house, this is a moment too when the description of timber and stone, bricks and mortar, is not enough, and the building has to be seen in its wider setting.

In this respect, nature can hardly have dealt Stourhead a better hand. At the south-west extremity of Salisbury Plain, a wide, smooth chalk ridge extends for several miles before the land suddenly falls in narrow valleys, formed by the heads of three rivers, the Brue, the Wylye and the Stour. The little village of Stourton shelters in one of these combes, and here, just above it, lay the ancient castle of the Stourtons, lords 'of the River Stouer from its fountains to the sea'. The six springs that rise in the parish were indeed featured (with the river) on the family's arms: 'sable, a bend or, between six fountaines'. Their castle was a massive pile, built round two main courtyards, and probably adjoining the present stable yard. However, it was ransacked by Parliamentary troops in the Civil War, and may never have been occupied thereafter, for the Stourtons were in constant trouble as Catholics, and finally followed James II into exile.

In 1717 the estate was acquired by trustees of the Hoare family, and in 1720 (the year in which the 13th Lord Stourton died in Paris) Henry Hoare, second son of the founder of the bank, took on sole ownership, demolished the remains of the old castle, and began to build a new house on higher ground to the north-west. The new owner's pedigree was scarcely a match for the old: his father, Sir Richard Hoare, Lord Mayor of London in 1712, was the son of a successful horse dealer. However, he had been apprenticed to a goldsmith at the age of seventeen, and by 1672 he was in business on his own at the sign of the Golden Bottle, Cheapside – later moving to Fleet Street, where the firm has flourished ever since. This was at a time when goldsmiths had developed a system of accepting money as well as plate on trust, and lending it out again at high interest in the form of promissory notes, the origin of the modern banknote. Huge fortunes were to be made in this way, particularly through loans to the government, which financed Charles II's Dutch and William III's French wars.

Unlike the Brownlows of Belton, however, who had wished to make the transition from the professional classes to the landed gentry in the previous century, the Hoares never wanted to give up their interest in the bank, nor to establish a political and territorial power-base in the shires. The evidence is that they acquired the land first as an investment, and second as a country retreat not far away from Henry's cousin and brother-in-law, William Benson – one of the chief inspirers of the house and garden that were to follow. In the uncertainty

surrounding the Bank of England in the 1690s, and the period leading up to the South Sea Bubble of 1720, the shrewder members of the financial community like the Childs, the Duncombes and the Hoares (all closely associated at this period) saw the need to spread their assets and to buy land as an alternative to shares. So the formal gardens of Wanstead in Essex, the semi-formal terraces of Duncombe and Rievaulx in Yorkshire, and the informal landscape of Stourhead, had to some extent common origins.

William Benson's own introduction to Wiltshire had come in similar circumstances, for his father, a wealthy iron merchant who became Sheriff of London in 1706, settled £5,000 on him specifically to purchase land in the county when he married in 1707. The following year Benson took a lease of Amesbury Abbey (designed by John Webb about 1660, but then thought to be the work of Inigo Jones); and very soon afterwards he built himself a house a few miles away at Wilbury, clearly based on the upper storeys of Amesbury – but with real claims to be the first eighteenth-century Palladian villa.

Perhaps rather unfairly, William Benson has gone down to history as the villain who supplanted the octogenarian Wren as Surveyor in 1718, and then, in Hawksmoor's words, 'got more in one year (for confusing the King's Works) than Sr. Chris. Wren did in 40 years for his honest endeavours'. However, his connections with Colen Campbell, who served as his deputy and who published Wilbury in the first volume of *Vitruvius Britannicus* (1715), show that he was a key figure in the early years of the

Henry Hoare I, holding a plan of Colen Campbell's villa, from a portrait by Michael Dahl.

Palladian movement. He was also keenly interested in gardening and hydraulics, designing some 'curious waterworks' for George I's gardens at Herrenhausen in Hanover in 1716. In addition he was 'Master of the most refined Parts of Literature', according to Campbell, and in 1737 erected a monument to Milton in Westminster Abbey, with a bust of the poet by Rysbrack.

In all these spheres, Benson was undoubtedly the *eminence grise* of Stourhead, advising first his brother-in-law and then his nephew.

The diminutive size of Wilbury, not unlike Colen Campbell's later Ebberston in Yorkshire, shows that they were never intended to be country houses in their own right. In fact they were more like the hunting lodges and 'stands' of an earlier period, pleasure pavilions where a landowner could stay for a night or two away from his main house. Instead of having a purely sporting purpose, however, Roger North wrote in 1698 that 'a villa is quasy a lodge, for the sake of a garden, to retire to enjoy and sleep, without pretence of entertainment of many persons'. The very fact that Henry Hoare's new house was built on a fresh site, away from the old seat of the Stourtons, shows that it was never intended to be a proper country seat; and the fact that it was set high to enjoy the best views, and re-christened Stourhead – in reference to the sources of the river – suggests that it was always intended to be a villa in Roger North's sense, built 'for the sake of a garden'. While it did not 'belong' to a greater house as Wilbury did to Amesbury, here was a place where a City banker could spend a few months in the summer, check up on the running of his farms and the planting of his woods and pleasure grounds, ride, fish and follow other country pursuits, and then, after a time of refreshment, return to his business in London.

This relatively new function – a house in the country, rather than a country house – was perfectly suited to a new architectural style, or rather the revival of an old one. The *casa di villa* which Andrea Palladio had developed for the country estates of the Venetian and Vicenzan nobility in the sixteenth century (itself based on the Roman villas described by Vitruvius) fulfilled many of the same needs. A place to retire from the heat and plague of the city in the summer months, it was also a working farm, and a centre of production for the surrounding vineyards: hence its spreading wings with barns and granaries. Inigo Jones had first seen its potential in an English context in the early seventeenth century, borrowing ideas for the Prince's Lodging at Newmarket and the Queen's House at Greenwich.

Jones's revolutionary Palladian style was too strongly identified with court circles to survive the upheaval of the Civil War, however, and it was only after another political upheaval – the rout of the Tories, and the establishment of a Whig oligarchy under a new Hanoverian dynasty in 1714 – that Lord Burlington and his circle returned to Jones, and to Palladio, for their inspiration. These new arbiters of taste saw the different forms of the Baroque as symbols of foreign absolutism – whether the Franco-Dutch style of Boughton and Petworth; the Roman 'licentiousness' of Gibbs's early work, inspired by

Borromini; or the theatricality of Vanbrugh and Hawksmoor. Instead they supported Lord Shaftesbury's call for a building programme in a new 'national taste', made in his *Letter concerning Design* of 1712. A return to the purity and balance of Jones's and Palladio's designs was to reflect Whig ideas of a balanced British constitution – set up in 1688 and re-affirmed in 1714 – and to set this country on a different course from the rest of Europe, architecturally as well as politically.

Lord Burlington, whose Grand Tour had been largely spent studying the buildings of Palladio, was the undisputed leader of this faction, but it was Colen Campbell's *Vitruvius Britannicus* that was the manifesto for the new style. Campbell's introduction to Henry Hoare could have come from Burlington himself, for the Earl was a major client of the bank. But it could equally have come through John Aislabie, Chancellor of the Exchequer in the years leading up to the South Sea Bubble, and the man who had engineered William Benson's appointment as Surveyor to the King's Works in 1718. Aislabie not only commissioned Campbell to build a new stable block and banqueting house in his garden at Studley Royal, near Ripon, but he also persuaded his brother-in-law Sir William Robinson to build a Palladian villa to Campbell's designs not far away at Newby (now called Baldersby).

Completed only a year before Stourhead, in 1721, Newby was practically its twin, the only major difference being the absence of a rusticated basement floor, and the provision of two flanking service wings now thought to be contemporary with the main block. As a former Lord Mayor of York, and MP for the city, Sir William was in rather a similar position to Henry Hoare: he needed to maintain a large town house, and therefore wanted a

The east front, with Sir Richard Colt Hoare's library and picture gallery flanking Campbell's original villa.

country retreat rather than a principal residence.

For both these villas – and for a third, designed for Aislabie himself in 1725, next to the ruins of Waverley Abbey in Yorkshire – Campbell drew inspiration from Palladio's Villa Emo at Fanzolo, built in the 1560s. Emo was a comparatively modest farmhouse compared with the famous Villa Rotonda, which he copied at Mereworth and which was afterwards the basis for Lord Burlington's Chiswick, but it was far better suited to the English climate. Instead of the latter's four porticoes casting the rooms behind into deep shade, it had only one recessed loggia on the entrance side, which in all three of his villas Campbell turned into a hall. There was of course a loss of drama here, reducing Palladio's three-dimensional columns to an 'attached' portico. So at Stourhead Campbell proposed a projecting portico with steps leading up it each side, at the same time replacing the simple Doric with the more decorative Corinthian order. But whether for reasons of economy, or because he wished his house to have a 'lower profile', Henry Hoare chose to have applied half-columns like the Robinsons at Newby – and it was only in 1838 that Campbell's original proposal was carried out by Charles Parker, a pupil of Wyatville, working for Hoare's great-grandson.

One other important modification Campbell made to Palladio's design was to conceal the roof behind a heavy balustrade at Stourhead and Newby (but not at Waverley), resulting in a more equal balance of the horizontal and vertical elements. In the *Quattro Libri*, Palladio's published works, the villa is shown without an attic storey, but in execution it was given the same square first-floor windows as appear in Campbell's three houses – suggesting that he had actually seen Emo during his time in Italy.

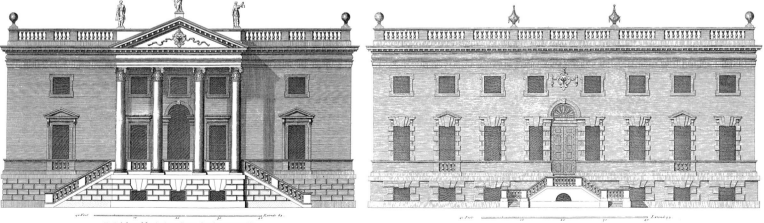

The east and south fronts, from Colen Campbell's Vitruvius Britannicus, *1725, were based on Palladio's Villa Emo at Fanzolo.*

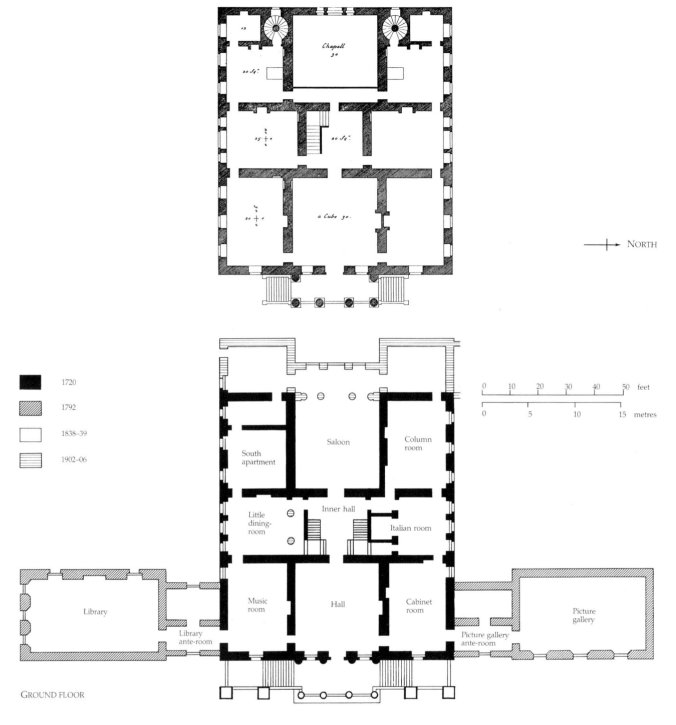

Chapell
30

20 Sq.

25 + 0   20 Sq.

20 + 0   a Cube 30.

NORTH

1720

1792

1838–39

1902–06

0   10   20   30   40   50 feet
0   5   10   15 metres

South
apartment

Saloon

Column
room

Little
dining-
room

Inner hall

Italian room

Library

Music
room

Hall

Cabinet
room

Picture
gallery

Library
ante-room

Picture gallery
ante-room

GROUND FLOOR

By contrast with the entrance side, the south elevation overlooking the garden had a more obviously English Palladian source: the south front of Wilton (less than twenty miles away, and attributed to Inigo Jones), but without its corner towers. The Venetian window employed as a central motif in a façade was one of Campbell's main contributions to the eighteenth-century Palladian canon – particularly useful, as here, where there were an even number of window bays. The heavy rustication of the window frames, based on Palladio's Palazzo Thiene in Vicenza, may have been thought specially suitable for the garden side of a house since it was supposedly natural in origin: the architectural forms struggling to 'escape' from the surrounding rocks. For the same reason, very similar door and window frames recur in Campbell's design for a 'garden room' at Hall Barn in Buckinghamshire, built for John Aislabie's stepson, Edmund Waller, and in Aislabie's own banqueting house at Studley Royal.

Stourhead and Newby were to have enormous consequences for the development of the English country house. Not only did they inspire the architects of a whole generation of smaller villas – from James Gibbs and Roger Morris, right up to James Paine, Isaac Ware and even Sir William Chambers – but they were also to some extent models for the much bigger country houses with which Campbell and his contemporaries were experimenting in the 1720s: vastly enlarged versions of the Palladian villa like Wanstead and Houghton, to reach final fruition at Holkham and Kedleston.

What was it about these early villas that was so revolutionary, and so influential? To begin with, Campbell adopted the Italian idea of the *piano nobile*, one main floor set (in Stourhead's case) above a basement for the servants, and with an attic floor containing less important family bedchambers above. These functions are clear from the outside, where the basement is rusticated, and the attic windows are far smaller and simpler than those

below. The old idea of a great dining room or saloon on the first floor was thus abandoned, and the usual practice was to bring it downstairs on axis with the hall.
The two plans of Stourhead published in the third volume of *Vitruvius Britannicus* (one 'as design'd by Mr. Campbell', and the other 'as Executed by Mr. Hoare') both show this space occupied by a chapel – with a family gallery at *piano nobile* level, and seating for the servants below in the 'rustic'. Mrs Hoare, William Benson's sister, is said to have been very pious, so this may have been her idea. But it is interesting that after her death in 1741 her son swiftly replaced the chapel with a saloon designed by Henry Flitcroft.

A second important innovation in the plan of these villas was the tripartite arrangement – in place of the old 'double pile' – with the rooms roughly forming a circuit round a central, sky-lit staircase. At Newby, which followed the plan of the Villa Emo more literally, there were twin staircases flanking a central lobby between the hall and saloon – and this model was usually preferred for larger houses like Houghton and Nostell Priory. Because of the lack of early inventories at Stourhead, and because of a disastrous fire which gutted the main block in 1902 and destroyed much of the original decoration, it is hard to be sure how the rooms were originally used. Campbell's original intention was probably to have the saloon and parlour flanking the hall, withdrawing rooms in the centre of each side, and then the two main bedchambers with dressing rooms beyond, each with a spiral staircase for the servants. In Henry Hoare's altered version, however, the right-hand withdrawing room was to become a state bedchamber with an alcove (now the Italian Room), equipped with a dressing room carved out of the adjoining parlour (now the Cabinet Room); the spiral stairs were replaced by closets, serving the other two bedrooms; and a new servants' staircase was contrived next to the main stairs (in the space that is now the sideboard alcove of the Little Dining Room).

Despite these changes, Campbell still seems to have been closely involved with the decoration of the interior. The alcove bedchamber is close to his engraved designs for a room at Compton Place, Eastbourne – with the central arch and its flanking closet doors echoing the Venetian window on the opposite wall – while the chimneypiece and overmantel in the Music Room (replicas made after the fire) are like those in the 'back parlour' of his own London house, in Brook Street.

A third break with tradition at Stourhead was the use of 'harmonic proportions' to determine the dimensions of the rooms, as well as the balanced composition of the façades. The hall, rising through the attic floor, is a 30-foot cube (and the chapel was also 30 feet square); the Music Room measures 30 by 20 feet square, like the central staircase. In Campbell's symmetrical plan, these southern rooms would also have been exactly matched by the corresponding rooms on the north. The idea that beauty could be achieved through such simple mathematical relationships can be found once again in Palladio, and goes back to one of the fundamental principles of the Italian Renaissance: the notion that man is at the centre

of an ordered universe, and that by *ratio*, or reason, the human scale can be used as a universal rule.

As we have seen, Stourhead was not originally given flanking pavilions like Newby, and early survey plans show that it had a service wing to the north, probably joined to the house only at basement level. However, in 1783, after a run on the banks caused by the Gordon Riots and the loss of the American colonies, Henry Hoare II gave the house to his grandson (later Sir Richard Colt Hoare) on the understanding that he give up his partnership. For the first time in its history it now became a permanent residence rather than a mere country retreat, and it was this which encouraged Colt Hoare in 1792 to add wings either side of the main block to house his collections of books and pictures. These pavilions could have been designed by Willey Reveley, a pupil of Chambers, who is known to have built lodges for Colt Hoare in the following year. But they are so reticent that they might equally be Hoare's own work: as he was later to write, 'the same style of architecture is faithfully kept up; and at this time, though after the short lapse of twenty years, the walls of the new buildings have so completely acquired the tints of the old, that the interval between 1720 and 1820 cannot be distinguished'.

Inside, the two rooms remain perfect examples of Regency taste, with all their original furniture supplied by the younger Thomas Chippendale. Colt Hoare was one of the leading antiquaries and archaeologists of his day, and it was in the library that he wrote his celebrated histories of ancient and modern Wiltshire. So it is appropriate that the carpet (re-woven in 1968) should

Samuel Woodforde, who painted this portrait of Sir Richard Colt Hoare and his son, described Sir Richard as 'a shy man to strangers.'

Stourhead

1 Hall
2 Music room
3 Library
4 Little dining-room
5 Saloon
6 Italian room
7 Cabinet room
8 Picture gallery

NORTH

derive from a Roman tessellated pavement, and that the simple trellis-work pattern painted on the ceiling should have had antique precedents. The intellectual mood is also sustained by Chippendale's great writing table, supplied in 1805 – its 'Therm'd legs with philosophers heads carved on ditto' – by his armchairs with Egyptian figures, based on Denon's *Voyage dans la Basse et Haute-Egypte* of 1802–3, and by the great lunettes at either end – one representing Raphael's *School of Athens* in stained glass by Francis Eginton, and the other a copy of his *Parnassus* by Samuel Woodforde.

By this date the library had become the main informal living room in most country houses, so the bookcases are ingeniously recessed into the walls rather than taking up valuable space for furniture. Humphry Repton illustrates a very similar room in his *Fragments* of 1816, with French windows leading out into a garden, and his accompanying verses could just as well apply to the Stourhead library:

> *Where guests to whim, to task or fancy true*
> *Scatter'd in groups, their different plans pursue.*
> *Here politicians eagerly relate*
> *The last day's news, or the last night's debate.*
> *Here books of poetry and books of prints*
> *Furnish aspiring artists with new hints. . . .*
> *Here, midst exotic plants, the curious maid*
> *Of Greek and Latin seems no more afraid.*

The picture gallery, by contrast, was more formally arranged, with Chippendale's furniture placed round the walls. The intention here was to show the cream of his grandfather's collection, and the Old Masters and contemporary paintings that Colt Hoare had himself acquired – massed on the walls three or four deep, as they remain. Chippendale also supplied many of the picture frames, including the magnificent gilt surrounds to the Cigoli altarpiece above the fireplace – a picture which Colt Hoare acquired in Florence in 1790 – and the two huge pictures flanking it: one by Carlo Maratta, bought by Henry Hoare II in 1758, and the other

A view of the garden by C.W. Bampfylde. The lake was created by joining a chain of ponds, and the stone bridge was built in 1762.

commissioned specially as a pendant from Anton Raphael Mengs in the following year. The key to the hanging scheme of the room, these paintings show what importance British collectors attached to the balanced, symmetrical display of their works of art. Unlike so many museum curators today, they realized that the decorative effect of the walls as a whole can radically enhance our appreciation of the individual pictures shown on them – whether masterpieces or copies.

Because so many of the Hoares were christened Henry or Richard, they have been distinguished by nicknames within the family: so the first Henry has always been known as 'the Good' for his charitable works; and his elder son and namesake 'the Magnificent' for the prodigal scale of his collecting and landscape gardening. An echo of that other great heir to a banking fortune, Lorenzo de Medici, the adjective certainly seems appropriate as we look at his heroic equestrian portrait in the hall, painted by Wootton and Dahl, and as we read his surviving correspondence – erudite, entertaining but above all Italophile.

Henry was only nineteen in 1725, when he succeeded to the business on his father's death. In early manhood he divided his time between the house above the bank in Fleet Street, and a hunting lodge at Quarley in Hampshire, leading a 'gay and dissolute style of life' (as he later admitted to his grandson), while his mother continued to live at Stourhead. However, in 1734 he bought Wilbury – only 12 miles away – from his uncle William Benson, and may already have started to plant the valley above Stourton on his regular trips over to superintend the estate. An account of the garden in the *London Chronicle* for 1757 refers to the walk on the hillside south-west of the house, 'bordered on each side by stately Scotch Firs of Mr. Hoare's own planting, about twenty-four years since'.

In March 1738, at a much more mature age than the usual Grand Tourist, he went abroad for three years, spending most of the time in Italy, and only returning in September 1741 after his mother's death. Two years later his wife died, and it may have been at this point that he decided to devote himself seriously to building and planting. In the eighteenth century, gardening was often seen as a way of recovering from affliction. In Addison's words, 'delightful scenes, whether in nature, painting, or poetry, have a kindly influence on the body, as well as the mind, and not only serve to clear and brighten the imagination, but are able to disperse grief and melancholy, and to set the animal spirits in pleasing and agreeable motions'. Sir George Lyttelton's landscape at Hagley in Worcestershire, begun about this time, also coincided with the loss of his wife, while the poet William Shenstone began the transformation of The Leasowes, a few miles away, on his mother's death in 1743. In Henry Hoare's case there was to be still greater need for distraction, when in 1751 his only surviving son died in Naples at the age of twenty-one.

Just as the circuit of rooms inside a Palladian villa like Stourhead put paid to the old idea of the enfilade, so the circuit walks invented by William Kent at Rousham in

The River God in the grotto, carved by John Cheere in 1751, is based on an etching from Salvator Rosa's Dream of Aeneas *series.*

Oxfordshire spelt the end of the old axial layouts, the straight avenues and geometrical patterns of the Baroque garden. The parallel can be taken further still, for as the century wore on, the rooms on the circuit of a house were often decorated in contrasting colours, so as to give a sequence of changing moods and associations. In the same way the walk round the garden offered a series of different views, each composed like a separate picture and each with its own theme, whether sombre or melancholy in the style of Poussin, open and *riant* (Horace Walpole's favourite adjective) in the style of Claude, or wild and rocky in the manner of Salvator Rosa – inspiring an atmosphere of Gothic alarm.

The key development here was the ha-ha, by which (as Walpole put it) Kent 'leaped the fence, and saw all Nature was a garden'. The first circuit walk at Stourhead was probably made in the 1730s with a ha-ha round the edge of Great Oar meadow south and west of the house, and incorporating Henry Hoare's straight Fir Walk. As Addison had expressed it, 'fields of corn make a pleasant prospect, and if the walks were a little taken care of that lie between them, and if the natural embroidery of the meadows were helped and improved by some small additions of art . . . a man might make a pretty landskip

of his own possessions'. However, the views over the valley below, with its chain of ponds fed by the six springs of the Stour, must have inspired more ambitious ideas, and in 1744 Henry Hoare set about realizing them.

In that year Henry Flitcroft, Lord Burlington's protégé and draughtsman, designed the first of his many garden buildings at Stourhead: a 'Venetian Seat' (with an open loggia in the form of a Venetian window) at the point where a path descended from the hillside walk to the valley, and a Temple of Ceres (later re-dedicated to Flora) below, overlooking a rectangular basin with a spring, apparently used as the village water supply. As might be expected of 'Burlington Harry', the Temple with its Tuscan portico looks like the one on the canal at Chiswick, while the river god in a pedimented grotto below was based on William Kent's cascade at Rousham.

In 1746 Henry Hoare built the obelisk at the far end of Great Oar meadow. On axis with the west front, but also aligned on the Fir Walk, it formed a crucial link between the house and the new garden that was visible from everywhere; '120 feet in height, built on the highest ground', as the *London Chronicle* put it, 'it has a Mythra, or Sun of six feet diameter, in gilded copper at the top'. Over the next eight years, his major preoccupation was the merging of the old ponds in the valley to make one great lake, culminating in the dam near the Pantheon, completed in 1754. Many of the buildings on the circuit round the lake were erected at the same time, from the grotto of 1748 to the Pantheon or Temple of Hercules itself in 1753–4.

Unlike Lord Cobham's famous gardens at Stowe, which were to a great extent political in inspiration, Henry Hoare's were almost entirely literary and philosophical. Here his mentor was probably his uncle, William Benson, who had sponsored Christopher Pitt's translation of the *Aeneid*, as well as being an admirer of Ovid and Milton. Virgil's epic about the founding of Rome is undoubtedly the *leimotiv* of the garden at Stourhead, even if there are other layers of mythology and history to unravel. The theme is first announced in the inscription above the door of the Temple of Flora, *Procul, O procul este profani* ('Begone, you who are uninitiated! Begone!'), the words spoken by the Cumaean Sybil when about to lead Aeneas into the underworld, where the future history of Rome will be revealed to him. The path itself, later descending into the grotto, thus becomes associated with Aeneas's journey, something that would have delighted eighteenth-century visitors, brought up on the classics. In a letter to his daughter, Henry Hoare writes, 'I have made the passage up from the Sousterrain serpentine and will make it easier of access facilis descensus Averno' – or, as Virgil's Sybil has it, 'Light is the descent into Avernus, but to recall thy step and issue to the upper air, there is the toll and there the task.'

The grotto itself, with a marble statue of a sleeping nymph, is also associated with the cave near Carthage, the home of the nymphs, where Aeneas and his men take refuge from the storm after their flight from Troy. Cheere's River God beyond, based on an etching from Salvator Rosa's *Dream of Aeneas* series, represents the

Tiber, pointing the way to the Pantheon (or Temple of Hercules) – just as in Virgil, Aeneas takes Tiber's advice to seek out the Arcadian king, and finds him worshipping at an altar dedicated to Hercules.

As Kenneth Woodbridge has suggested, there was almost certainly a pictorial as well as a literary symbolism in all this, for a famous picture by Claude Lorrain, *Coast View of Delos with Aeneas* (now in the National Gallery in London), shows a Pantheon, bridge and Doric portico placed in much the same way as their counterparts at Stourhead. The painting represents Aeneas, with his father Anchises and son Ascanius, standing on the terrace at Delos, the birthplace of Apollo and Diana – while he prays, 'Apollo, grant us a home of our own. We are weary. Give us a walled city which shall endure and a lineage of our blood.' In 1750, Henry Hoare's son was in Aix attempting to buy some paintings by Claude for his father, and although only copies were finally acquired for Stourhead, it was landscapes like this which lay behind the three-dimensional 'pictures' that unfolded throughout the garden. Like Aeneas, Hoare too was trying to establish his family in a place 'loved by the Gods' – and that feeling must, if anything, have been strengthened after his son's death in 1752, and the marriage of his daughter Anne to his nephew and next male heir, Richard Hoare.

This wealth of classical and Renaissance sources should not give us the impression that Henry Hoare was too serious and learned in his approach. Just as his father had built the house as a pleasure pavilion for the summer months, so the garden was to extend its sense of delight and informality. In the hot summer of 1764, for instance, he wrote: 'We dine with the Hall Doors open into the Stair Case which we never did before for the Door into the Air would let in the Heat of a Firey Furnace . . . a Souse into that delicious Bath & Grot filled with fresh Magic, is Asiatick Luxury & too much for Mortals or at least for Subjects, next I ride under the spreading Beaches just beyond the Obelisk on the Terrace where we are sure of Wind and Shade and a delightful View into the Vale. . . .' To compare such a letter with Jeremiah Milles's account of the 'Proud Duke' at Petworth, only thirty years before, is to see a revolution in manners spreading into the world of architecture, gardening and all the allied arts.

Cold baths for medicinal purposes were becoming increasingly popular at this period, with the rise of the spa towns. But it is also interesting to find that the Pantheon was originally heated by a stove, with a grille behind Rysbrack's statue of Hercules ('like a grate for Nuns in a Catholic chapel', according to Horace Walpole), so that bathers could retire there to recover, and most probably to dine, in some comfort. Early drawings and engravings of Stourhead also show large vessels on the lake, as well as figures fishing, sketching and engaged in other activities.

The last of Flitcroft's buildings in the classical style was the Temple of Apollo, built in 1765 on the hill above the southern edge of the lake, and based on the Temple of the Sun illustrated in Robert Wood's *Ruins of Balbec*. Continuing the earlier Virgilian theme of Delos (Apollo's birthplace) the temple may also have shared a more general mythological role with its neighbours round the lake. From his high eminence, the sun god's energy is responsible for the growth of grass and trees, the light and shade; while Flora causes the waters to run; and finally the man-god Hercules, in the Pantheon, represents the human labours that bring the whole to fruition.

Up to the 1760s, almost all the garden buildings at Stourhead had been classical and Palladian in inspiration, following the style of Colen Campbell's original villa. However, as time went on, Henry Hoare turned increasingly to the Gothic, not only for its inherent 'picturesque' qualities but because it provided a link between the ancient and modern worlds. So instead of moving the old medieval church and village of Stourton or concealing it, he decided it would make 'a charming Gaspard picture at that end of the water', with his five-arched bridge below (based on Palladio's bridge at Vicenza), and with the fifteenth-century Bristol Cross, which he acquired from the city in 1764, artfully placed on the rising ground between the two. Other Gothic buildings included a greenhouse nearby (no longer in existence), the Convent in the wooded valley to the north of the lake (now a private house), and finally Alfred's Tower on the escarpment above it, completed in 1772.

The cult of King Alfred was very much a political cause in the eighteenth century. Lord Cobham had included his bust in the Temple of British Worthies at Stowe thirty years earlier – representing the ideal English king, founder of our national liberties, as against the German-speaking Hanoverians. The triangular form of the tower at Stourhead is also reminiscent of Gibbs's Gothic Building at Stowe, surrounded by statues of the Saxon deities who gave their names to the days of the week. On the other hand Henry Hoare's immediate inspiration seems to have been literary: a passage praising Alfred in Voltaire's *Histoire Générale*, reminding him of the legend that the King had raised his standard on this spot (known as Kingsettle Hill) after coming out of hiding in the Isle of Athelney and challenging the Danes. Alfred may at first seem a radical departure from the classical theme of the earlier buildings. Yet, according to the twelfth-century chronicler Geoffrey of Monmouth, Aeneas was an ancestor of the British race through his grandson Brutus.

The visitor to Stourhead today may find such references elusive, but those who flocked to see Mr Hoare's latest 'improvements' in the eighteenth century would have been immediately aware of their significance. The enormous interest that the garden generated can be judged from the descriptions of contemporary diarists. In 1776, for instance, Mrs Lybbe Powys found that the village inn was full and had to go back to Mere, where the only available room had just been taken by Horace Walpole and Robert Adam. Three years later, the King of Sweden sent the artist F. M. Piper to record the garden and its buildings in the greatest detail – still the best source for its appearance at that date.

In some ways, this early tourist trade was to have an effect on the very form of the houses and gardens that were its object. The circuit walk was ideally suited to its needs, and at Stourhead, in line with other houses, there

The Stourhead landscape and the Pantheon, by Henry Flitcroft, were almost certainly inspired by the paintings of Claude Lorrain.

were two: an inner circle round the lake, to be attempted on foot, and an outer serpentine (which included the Convent and Alfred's Tower) for those on horseback or in a chaise. In some ways, these circuits directly anticipated the modern 'theme park'. By 1783, when Henry Hoare presented the house to his great-nephew Richard, the buildings on them formed a virtual encyclopaedia of architectural styles – not only Greek, Roman, Gothic and Italian Renaissance, but also including a Chinese 'umbrello', a Turkish tent, an obelisk of distinctively Egyptian form, and a 'primitive' Hermitage ('lined inside and out with old gouty knobbly oakes'), looking forward to the world of Soane and Ledoux. The surprise light effects in the hermitage, the grotto and the Temple of Apollo were likewise ancestors of the 'tunnels of love' and 'halls of mirrors' still popular today.

Colt Hoare was to weed out many of the more exotic and 'artificial' of these buildings with what was then regarded as the more refined taste of the Regency period. He also introduced greater variety of planting, with many recently imported ornamental species, where his great-uncle had largely used native hardwoods and conifers. Nevertheless Henry Hoare had decided views about planting, expressed in highly aesthetic language, as reported by Joseph Spence: '. . . the greens should be ranged in large masses as the shades are in painting, to contrast the *dark* masses with the *light* ones,

and to relieve each dark mass itself with little sprinklings of lighter greens here and there'. Much advice was in fact given him by two artist friends, Coplestone Warre Bampfylde (whose views of Stourhead still survive in the house) and William Hoare of Bath, who was not a relation, but whose daughter married one of Henry's nephews. The two combined to design the cascade in 1765 – and suggestions also came from Charles Hamilton, creator of another famous garden at Painshill in Surrey.

In the end, however, it is Henry Hoare alone who must be considered the presiding genius of the Stourhead landscape, and thus one of the most important garden designers of his age. Uniting architecture and sculpture, horticulture, silviculture and engineering within one single all-embracing vision, he deserves a place in the annals of British taste as much as professionals like Capability Brown and Humphry Repton. 'What is there in Creation,' he wrote to his nephew in 1755, 'those are the fruits of industry and application to Business, and shows what great things may be done by it, the envy of the indolent who have no claim to Temples, Grottos, Bridges, Rocks, Exotick Pines and Ice in Summer'.

House and landscape together, Stourhead represents an English ideal: that of the cultivated country squire, without ambition for great titles or offices of state, content to say, like Voltaire – *'il faut cultiver notre jardin'*.

91

Kedleston Hall

D E R B Y S H I R E

IF ANY English country house can truly be described as a 'Temple of the Arts', it is Kedleston. Shown to visitors virtually from the day it was built, it seems to greet you open-armed as you emerge from the shade of the ancient oaks along the main drive, and see it for the first time mirrored in the still waters of the lake.

A vast Corinthian portico in the centre, raised on a high podium and with broad flights of steps marching up to it on either side, aptly recalls the great public buildings of classical antiquity. Here, as on the Acropolis at Athens or the famous temple ridge at Agrigento, you feel you have come to pay tribute to the gods: to Venus atop the pediment, the embodiment of beauty and fertility, and to Ceres and Bacchus flanking her, deities of the harvest and vintage, and harbingers of hospitality to come.

Only when you catch sight of the battlemented church-tower, rising just above the roof of the right-hand wing, is there a feeling of culture-shock. Now almost buried within the fabric of the great house, the little parish church of All Saints represents a very different world – older in terms of time, but far younger in terms of philosophy – at variance with the Georgian ideals of classical perfection, but also a key to the family pride that lies at the heart of Kedleston, and to its origins way back in the early Middle Ages.

The Curzons are among the very few English families directly descended in the male line from a Norman who came over with William the Conqueror. Two villages in Normandy still bear the name of Courson, one near Coutances, the other near Lisieux, and the three popinjays of the family coat-of-arms continued to be borne by the Norman and Breton de Coursons long after their cousins had departed to England. When the family first settled at Kedleston is unclear, but it was probably before 1150, and certainly before 1198–9, during the reign of Richard Coeur de Lion, for it was then that Richard de Curzun of the senior branch, based at Croxall in Staffordshire, made a grant to Thomas de Curzun of 'all the vill of Ketelestune with the advowson of the church'.

The Norman south door of the church dates from about the middle of the twelfth century, and its unashamedly pagan decoration of wolves' heads and wild beasts takes us back to the primitive culture of the medieval forests, when strip-farming was only just beginning to change the face of the countryside. Agriculture was to be the foundation of the Curzons' fortune, and the family monuments that fill the little church, in stone, in brass and in alabaster, each one slightly grander than the last, tell a story of gradual advancement – by good marriages as much as by good fortune.

The progress from minor squire to major landowner was mostly achieved in the hundred years after 1640, however; during this period the estate grew to nearly 10,000 acres, with properties not only in Derbyshire, but also in the neighbouring counties of Staffordshire, Leicestershire and Nottinghamshire, and in London. Much of this expansion was due to Sir John Curzon, who was created a baronet in 1636, and who became the senior representative of his family when the Croxall branch died out in 1645. During the Commonwealth Sir John was on the Parliamentary side, but by the early eighteenth century the Curzons had become the great Tory family of Derbyshire, just as the Cavendishes, (Earls and Dukes of Devonshire), were the leading Whigs.

Hardly *parvenus* by our standards, the Cavendishes had come to Derbyshire from Suffolk in the sixteenth century, and had benefited hugely from the acquisition of monastic lands after the Dissolution. But memories in country circles are long, and the Curzons could claim seniority by over four hundred years, rallying to their cause the backwoods gentry with grievances against any newcomer. 'Let Curzon have what Curzon helde', that proudest of family mottoes (complete with archaic spelling) came to refer as much to their social and political standing in Derbyshire as to their actual estates.

Competition with Chatsworth, the great Cavendish seat known from an early date as the 'Palace of the Peak', was thus to be the driving force behind the creation of

The south front and the Church of All Saints, seen from the Park. A formal garden, here laid out by Charles Bridgeman in the early eighteenth century, was swept away by Robert Adam to create an unbroken expanse of lawn and parkland, separated only by the invisible ha-ha.

Kedleston. It explains some of the apparent paradoxes of its history: that it was built by a member of an old-established family rather than a *nouveau riche*; that, instead of the fruits of high political office, it depended purely on the proceeds of its own acres; and that, given the size of the estate, the colossal scale of its initial conception was never likely to be entirely realized.

There had, of course, been a manor house next to the church at Kedleston since medieval times. But the earliest pictorial record is of the neat red-brick box built by Francis Smith of Warwick for Sir Nathaniel Curzon, 2nd Baronet, about 1700, and seen in a painting attributed to Griffier. Sir John Curzon, his successor, swept away its modest walled gardens in the 1720s; in its place went a grand Baroque layout designed by the royal gardener Charles Bridgeman, with formal canals and ponds in the valley to the north, and parterres and descending terraces cut into the hillside to the south. At the same time Sir John considered an ambitious remodelling of the house, suggested by that favourite Tory architect, James Gibbs – then engaged on rebuilding All Saints' church in Derby. Nothing was achieved, perhaps because Curzon remained a bachelor, but what is of particular interest is Gibbs's surviving design for a large two-storey entrance hall, filled with copies of classical sculpture and with giant columns of the Corinthian order: all features of the Marble Hall which Adam was to create for Sir John's nephew nearly forty years later.

Unlike some other Tories who were compromised by

the Jacobite Rebellion of 1745, when Bonnie Prince Charlie marched south almost as far as Derby, Sir John's brother Nathaniel, the 3rd Baronet, contributed almost as much as his chief rival, the Duke of Devonshire, to 'defend our excellent constitution in Church & State'. It was a wise move, for his son, another Nathaniel, was about to leave Oxford to pursue a political career and, with perhaps more conviction, to take up his uncle's rebuilding schemes on an even more grandiose scale. In 1750 the young man duly married an heiress, Lady Caroline Colyear, daughter of the Earl of Portmore, and in 1756, two years before his father's death, he seems already to have been in charge of the estate, commissioning the landscape gardener William Emes to work on the garden.

For many people Kedleston embodies the ideals of the Grand Tour, the fascination that young men visiting Italy for the first time discovered in the ruins of the antique world: an appreciation of the arts of the past that was so closely allied to their classical education and, whether Whigs or Tories, to their political creeds of democracy and liberty. So it comes as another surprise to find that Nathaniel Curzon's sole recorded tour on the Continent, in 1749, took him only to France, Belgium and Holland, lasted just one month, and cost £300 including the purchases he made. Compared with Lord Burlington's two visits to Italy, or Lord Leicester's six years of European travel, it is hardly an impressive record. Yet there can be little doubt that Curzon was as imbued with the culture of the Mediterranean as they, and that he was personally responsible for the creation of Kedleston in collaboration with his architects – just as Burlington and Leicester had provided the ideas for Chiswick and Holkham, leaving professionals like Kent and Brettingham to provide the detail and bring them to reality.

Thomas Coke, 1st Earl of Leicester, was Curzon's particular hero, and it was his admiration for Holkham in Norfolk that was to influence the form of the new house at Kedleston from the outset. Barely a month after his father's death in November 1758 the new baronet summoned Lord Leicester's architect and builder, Matthew Brettingham, to Kedleston to measure up, and presumably set out as far as practicable, the outline of the

new house. The old stables and other outbuildings were quickly demolished, and the foundations for the family and kitchen pavilions were laid.

As originally planned, Kedleston was in the mainstream of the Palladian revival – the return to the rules of the Renaissance architect Andrea Palladio, first followed in England by Inigo Jones in the early seventeenth century, and then readopted a hundred years later by Lord Burlington and William Kent. Like its three most important predecessors, Houghton and Holkham in Norfolk, and Nostell Priory in Yorkshire, it was based on the unbuilt Villa Mocenigo from the second book of Palladio's *Quattro Libri*: with a central block to which four pavilions would be joined by curved (or quadrant) corridors.

Palladio's own villas in the countryside were generally working farmhouses of quite modest size, visited by their owners only for a month or two to escape the summer heat of the city *palazzo*, and with their pavilions used as barns, stables and domestic offices. By contrast, the hugely enlarged Palladian houses of the British aristocracy were always the principal family seat, built to live and entertain in for most of the year, with only occasional forays to London and Bath.

In these houses there was a natural division between the public and private apartments: at Houghton,

The entrance front of Kedleston seen from the north-east. The Church of All Saints, rather incongruously tucked into the strict classical formalities of the Palladian plan, was retained by the 1st Lord Scarsdale as a shrine to his Curzon ancestors whose tombs it contains.

Sir Robert Walpole's everyday rooms were largely on the ground floor or 'rustick', with the state rooms on the *piano nobile* above, while the two pavilions contained the stables, laundry and other offices – in the Italian fashion, if on a much bigger scale. At Holkham, however, one pavilion contained the family apartments, another was used as the 'strangers' wing' for visitors, a third was occupied by the chapel, and a fourth by the kitchen. That left the principal floor of the main block entirely free for rooms of state, where Lord Leicester's famous collections of Old Masters and antique sculpture could be displayed to their best advantage: almost a prototype of the modern museum.

Kedleston was to follow this scheme very closely, although the two southern pavilions containing the chapel and a huge 'music gallery' (instead of a strangers' wing) were never built, and guests were always housed on the top floor of the main block. The provision of a separate family wing had added advantages for Nathaniel Curzon and his family in that it could be built before the demolition of the old house, which lay on the site of the present main block. His descendants have had good cause to thank him, too, for providing what is effectively a sizeable country house in its own right, where they can live comfortably in rooms of human size, opening up the great rooms of state in the main block for special occasions or for the visitors who have flocked here ever since the builders downed their tools.

Although Matthew Brettingham supervised the construction of the family pavilion early in 1759, a still better-known Palladian architect, James Paine, arrived on the scene soon afterwards, and he was responsible for building the corresponding kitchen pavilion on the north-west, as well as starting the two northern quadrants and the eastern end of the main block. However, at this critical moment, Palladian architecture and Rococo decoration were being challenged by the new craze for Neo-Classicism among English connoisseurs. Sir Nathaniel had already toyed with the idea of interiors by James 'Athenian' Stuart when in December 1758 he was introduced to Robert Adam, the ambitious young Scottish architect who had just returned from Italy, brimming over with enthusiasm for the monuments of classical antiquity.

At this first meeting, Adam showed some of the drawings he had made in Rome, afterwards reporting to his brother James that their potential patron was 'struck all of a heap with wonder and amaze and every new drawing he saw made him grieve at his previous engagement with Brettingham. He carried me home in his chariot about three and kept me to four seeing said Brett's designs, and asking my opinion. I proposed alterations and desired he might call them his own fanceys.'

These boasts should not be taken too literally, for Adam was initially put in charge only of the buildings in the park, and its landscaping. However, by about April 1760 he had finally been given sole direction of the house as well – superseding Paine as he was later to do at Nostell, Alnwick and Syon. On the north front, which has been described as 'the grandest Palladian facade in Britain, and with few rivals anywhere in the world', he retained all the main features proposed by Brettingham and Paine, though with a more dramatic central portico and steps. The provision of skylights for the hall meant that the windows here could be replaced by niches and medallions, far more like an ancient Greek or Roman temple. The windows at the ends of the quadrants were also enlarged, increasing their sense of monumentality.

The fireworks were to come on the south front, however. Here Adam produced an entirely new design, with a central feature based on the Arch of Constantine in Rome, combined with the low stepped dome of the Pantheon. The revolutionary nature of this façade was its return to 'movement' in architecture, as expressed in the buildings of Vanbrugh and Hawksmoor: as the architect put it himself in his *Works in Architecture*, 'the rise and fall, the advance and recess with other diversity of form in the different parts of a building, so as to add greatly to the picturesque of the composition'. The forward thrust of the columns, with the entablature breaking out over them, the receding curve of the horseshoe staircase and perron, give the south front a truly Baroque exuberance. Even without the flanking pavilions he had intended, it remains one of Adam's greatest architectural achievements.

The internal planning of the main rooms at Kedleston was worked out around the central axis of the hall and saloon, two monumental interiors corresponding to the *atrium* and *vestibulum* of the Roman palace or villa – as described in eighteenth-century treatises such as Robert Castell's *Villas of the Ancients*. On the east side of this main axis are the music room, drawing room and library, representing respectively the arts of music, painting and literature; while the corresponding interiors on the west are devoted to hospitality, with the dining room, and the principal apartment (consisting of state bedchamber,

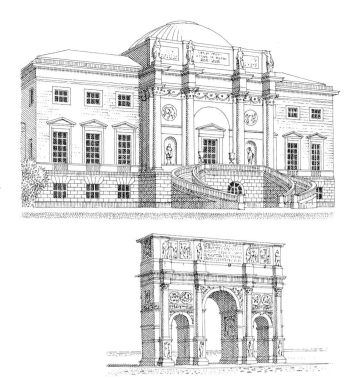

Adam based his design for the south front of the house (top) on the Arch of Constantine (below), built in AD 315, which he had drawn during his time in Rome.

dressing room and wardrobe, or closet) for important guests – in other words, rooms to satisfy your material needs on one side and your spiritual needs on the other.

As an evocation of the splendour of imperial Rome the Marble Hall at Kedleston has few rivals, at least before the wilder imaginings of Cecil B. de Mille. With no windows to distract attention from the splendours within, it is lit from above to suggest the open courtyard at the centre of the classical villa, with statues of gods and heroes in the niches where the Roman senator would have placed

Robert Adam (1728–1792) attributed to George Willison.

The Marble Hall, with its giant alabaster columns, reflects the Roman enthusiasms of Robert Adam and his patron, Lord Scarsdale. Lit from skylights above, it suggests an open courtyard at the centre of a classical villa.

Kedleston Hall

1 Hall
2 Music room
3 Family corridor
4 Family wing
5 Drawing-room
6 Library
7 Saloon
8 Dressing-room
9 State bedroom
10 State dining-room
11 Kitchen corridor
12 Kitchen wing

NORTH

The east side of the house, from a sketch made by Adam in 1759. The cut-out elevation of the house may be an earlier drawing by James Paine.

effigies of his ancestors. In the eighteenth century the room was sometimes called the Egyptian Hall, after Palladio's interpretation of a room so described by the Roman architectural theorist, Vitruvius – and, as in the hall at Holkham, this was another source for the treatment of the walls.

But, unified as the room now appears, it is in fact of two dates and by two hands, like the saloon beyond. In Adam's original plans, the decoration was to have been far more austere. The floor, of local Hopton Wood stone inlaid with Italian marble, was designed by him and laid in 1763, but the twenty great alabaster columns from the family's quarries at Ratcliffe-on-Soar in Nottinghamshire (each 25 feet high) were originally unfluted; the room

contained only two statues (the Apollo and Meleager flanking the door to the saloon); and there was no other decoration apart from the frieze with its winged lions, and the *grisaille* panels over the niches.

It was not until 1776–7, eight years after the completion of the other state rooms, that Sir Nathaniel (now 1st Lord Scarsdale) returned to complete the decoration here and in the saloon – in a noticeably lighter and more playful style. To begin with, the masons fluted the columns *in situ*, an extraordinary feat of craftsmanship. Then Joseph Rose's team of plasterers decorated the great coved ceiling with panels of military trophies and arabesques designed by Adam's chief draughtsman, George Richardson. Richardson was also

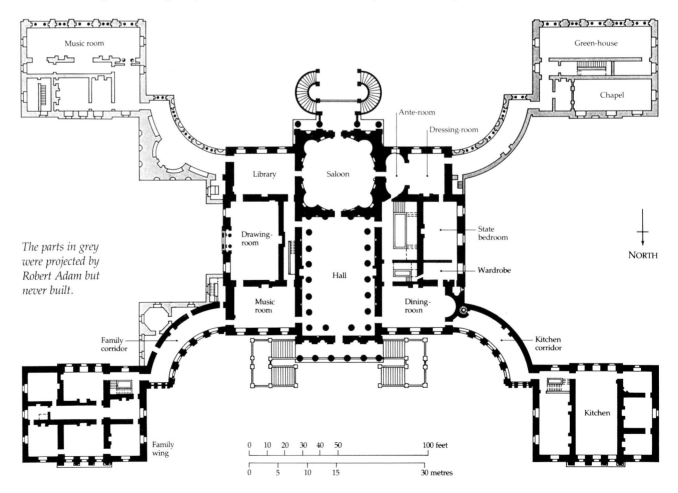

The parts in grey were projected by Robert Adam but never built.

responsible for adding the two marble chimneypieces in the centre of the side walls with their supremely elegant plaster overmantels – the inspiration for some of Charles Cameron's later work for Catherine the Great at Tsarskoe Selo. The soft pinks and greens shown on Richardson's drawings also mark a departure from the more masculine stone colours suggested by Adam, and were intended to form a transition between the architecture of the exterior and interior. The finishing touches were the stools carved by John Linnell, from an Adam design inspired by the sarcophagus of Agrippa. The iron torchères on tripod bases were similarly inspired by antique prototypes, excavated on the sites of Roman temples.

Beyond the Marble Hall the great domed saloon, rising to a height of 62 feet, was based on the Pantheon in Rome, one of the most admired buildings of classical antiquity – then as now. But details of the decoration are taken from other buildings like the Basilica of Maxentius, which Adam studied in detail during his time in Italy. Like the hall, the room was created in two stages. In the classic Roman villa plan, the saloon corresponds with the *vestibulum*, entered directly from the *atrium*, and considered sacred to the gods. So it was appropriate that Adam should conceive it as a sculpture gallery, with statues of deities placed in the four large alcoves and in niches between them. By the 1780s, however, Lord Scarsdale seems to have tired of this rather chilly arrangement; he wished to provide a more comfortable

setting for entertainments, and in particular the great county balls which were so much a part of eighteenth-century life. Accordingly, the statues were removed to the hall and staircase, the niches were walled up and replaced by elaborate wall sconces with ormolu branches, and large bronzed altars installed in the alcoves – the two on the north side incorporating cast-iron stoves. A circular carpet was woven with a pattern reflecting the coffers of the dome, and new doorcases made with scagliola pilasters by Domenico Bartoli added richness to the overall effect. At the same time John Linnell supplied a set of chairs and settees, painted green and gold, with curved backs and front rails so as to fit exactly against the walls and in the alcoves.

The four large paintings of Roman ruins over the doors are by William Hamilton, one of Adam's Scottish protégés, and in the perfection of this vast space they symbolize the way in which the English aristocracy of the eighteenth century hoped to build a new classical order based on the ruins of the old. In between them are *grisailles* of scenes from early English history by Biagio Rebecca, an expression of pride in the Curzons' ancient origins, and a suggestion that the family formed a bridge between the antique and modern worlds.

The state rooms on either side of the hall and saloon – for entertainment on the west, and recreation on the east – formed a well-planned circuit not only for guests attending the Scarsdales' great parties, but for everyday

In competition with 'Athenian' Stuart's designs for a similar recess, this is Adam's finely executed design for the dining room alcove.

The magnificent alcove in the State Dining Room was described by the Duchess of Northumberland in 1766 as 'adorn'd with a vast quantity of handsome plate judiciously dispos'd on Tables of beautiful Marble & of very pretty shapes.' These curving tables are one of Robert Adam's first designs for furniture. The huge wine-cooler was cut in 1758 from Sicilian jasper by the sculptor Richard Hayward.

Adam's design for the ceiling of the Painted Breakfasting Room, 1768. Intended to adjoin the principal apartment, the room was never built.

visitors, guided by Mrs Garnett, the 'well-drest elderly Housekeeper, a most distinct Articulator . . .', who took Boswell and Johnson round in 1777. Her portrait still hangs in the house, and shows her holding a copy of the printed Kedleston catalogue. Evidently written by Lord Scarsdale, this first appeared in 1769, and at least four further editions were published before 1800, describing the rooms and their contents very much as they remain today.

The music room to the east of the hall shows the care that Adam took with the arrangement of Lord Scarsdale's pictures. Most of them here have a musical theme, like Rosselli's *Triumph of David* over the organ, the huge Giordano *Triumph of Bacchus* on the opposite wall and the Orizzonte landscapes flanking the chimneypiece, which have figures of peasants dancing and playing bagpipes and flutes. All those in the upper row, except the Rosselli, are in fitted plasterwork frames, which means that they have never been moved, and represent the original

hanging scheme. Both the organ case (a simplified version of Adam's first design) and the chimneypiece by the Danish sculptor Michael Spang (with a central relief of *Singing at a Greek Wedding*) make use of the Ionic order, which is the architectural theme of the whole room. The kettledrums flanking the organ are listed here in early inventories, as is the magnificent harpsichord on the opposite wall, attributed to Burkat Shudi.

The drawing room was the only interior at Kedleston begun before Adam replaced Paine as Lord Scarsdale's architect. But Paine's alabaster Venetian window-surround was 'improved' by Adam, who was also responsible for the four alabaster doorcases. Spang, who again carved the chimneypiece, had proposed an elaborate painted ceiling celebrating English naval victories over the French in the Seven Years' War – but Adam disapproved of frescoed ceilings, which he thought 'tired the patience of any spectator' and instead preferred 'grotesque' ornaments which could be appreciated without neck-straining effort. Here, as elsewhere in the house, they were executed by his favourite plasterer, the Yorkshireman Joseph Rose.

The maritime theme was, however, maintained in the four great settees carved by the London cabinet-maker John Linnell. The mermaid and triton supporters recall those of George III's coronation coach, made at the same time (in 1761) and still, of course, in use today. Linnell also made a pair of charming inlaid card tables with folding tops, very much in the French taste, to stand below the pier glasses. When in use, they would have been brought out into the centre of the room, and chairs placed round them on the Exeter carpet.

The drawing room was always intended to contain the finest of Lord Scarsdale's Old Masters. Many of these were acquired in Italy by the art dealer William Kent (no relation of the architect) – including the Lodovico Carracci above the chimneypiece, the large Benedetto Luti biblical scenes at either end of the room, and the Bernardo Strozzi overdoors on the south wall. However, there are also two contributions from the Low Countries, both of outstanding quality: Cuyp's *Landscape in the Rhine Valley* and its pendant, *Mountain Scene with the Story of St Peter and Cornelius*, by Joos de Momper and Frans Francken the younger, flanking the fireplace.

While the drawing room was deliberately feminine in character with its pink and blue ceiling and blue damask walls, the library beyond was intended to be more sombre and masculine. In the drawing room, the order was

Corinthian; here it is the bolder Doric. As with many of the other rooms, there are Adam drawings for all four walls, and the so-called 'Mosaic Ceiling' – based on the kind of antique mosaic pavements which Adam had seen both in Rome and in Ravenna. The bookcases, again part of Adam's design, still contain the 1st Lord Scarsdale's leather-bound books, demonstrating his interest in all the arts and sciences – but particularly in architecture. It is easy to imagine him sitting at the huge double-sided desk in the centre to study Adam's *Ruins of Spalatro*, or drawing up a leather-covered reading chair with a copy of Virgil or Ovid to catch the last of the light on a summer's evening.

On the other side of the saloon, at the south-west corner of the main block lie the three rooms known collectively as the state apartment – dressing room, bedchamber and wardrobe – used on occasion to lodge the most distinguished guests, but otherwise part of the usual circuit of show rooms. Just as Rebecca's *grisailles* in the saloon linked the Curzons with the Plantagenet kings, so the family portraits grouped here, going back to the seventeenth century, were intended to link them with the Stuarts. Nathaniel Hone's double portrait of the Scarsdales – an interesting precursor of Gainsborough's *Morning Walk* – occupies pride of place over the dressing-room chimneypiece, and it may be that the view of the little parish church from the bedchamber windows was a conscious reminder of the similar pantheon of family tombs that it contains. Dynastic dreams may also have been encouraged by the punning motto above the

Nathaniel Curzon 1st Lord Scarsdale, and his wife Lady Caroline Colyear, painted by Nathaniel Hone in 1761, the year when Curzon was raised to the peerage.

Robert Adam's Fishing Room on the Upper Lake, built in 1770–72, is flanked by a pair of boathouses. The window allowed ladies to cast for trout without having to expose themselves to the sun.

old sundial in the east gable of the church, which reads: 'Wee shall' leaving the spectator to add 'soon die all'.

The palm tree motif which runs through the furniture in these rooms may derive from an earlier set of chairs here, probably made by the London cabinet-maker William Bradshaw in the 1740s, and among the few pieces retained from the old house at Kedleston. However, the vast palm branch mirror on the west wall of the dressing room, placed on the long axial view through from the saloon, also performs an architectural function, extending the apparent length of the enfilade – cut off when Adam's southern pavilions were finally abandoned. The state bed in the room beyond is even wilder, with its scaly treetrunk posts (carved out of cedar) each with gilded roots. Palm branches were always a symbol of fame in classical mythology, and ostrich plumes (like those on the canopy) were an attribute of temporal power, so their combination here can be seen as a nice compliment to the favoured occupant of the main guest room.

If Lord Scarsdale was thoroughly up-to-date in his taste for Neo-Classicism, his Toryism may have led him to be old-fashioned in other respects. Kedleston not only has one of the greatest Baroque beds in England, it also has one of the last formal 'buffets' of plate in the dining room, once again recalling seventeenth-century practice. The idea for a niche or alcove to display it seems to have originated with 'Athenian' Stuart, who designed a magnificent ormolu perfume burner, and a plate warmer in the shape of a large Greek vase, both still in the room. However, the final arrangement was entirely due to Adam, and the three curved tables to fit the apse are among his earliest designs for furniture in the Neo-Classical style, dating from 1762.

The room itself, described by Horace Walpole six years later as 'the Great Parlour in the best taste of all', is one of the architect's greatest triumphs. The elaborate ceiling inset with roundels by Zucchi, Hamilton and Morland, the marble chimneypiece by Spang, with caryatid figures of Ceres and Bacchus, and William Collins's roundels of *Harvest* and *Vintage* over the doors on the west wall, were all carefully chosen for their suitable symbolism – as were the pictures. Adam once again set them all into the walls in uniform plaster frames, both adding to the decorative

unity of the room and ensuring that their arrangement should never be altered. At the upper level, still lifes of fruit and dead game by Snyders, Fyt and others represent the pleasures of the table, while below them landscapes reflect the Arcadian views of the park seen through the windows – scenes of horticulture, hunting and fishing, whence these pleasures come.

Beyond the dining room the curving west corridor led to the kitchen pavilion, which also contained the still room, scullery, laundry and other domestic offices. Although used by servants bringing food, it was also one of the rooms generally seen by visitors, including the Duchess of Northumberland, who in 1766 found it 'hung with prints & 3 models of ships in Glass Cases'. Two of these survive and have recently been replaced here, reminders of Lord Scarsdale's passion for naval affairs – extending to mock battles on the lake, with frigates manned by gamekeepers and farm-hands. Nor was a tour of Kedleston complete without a view of the kitchen itself, from the gallery at the southern end. '48 ft. by 24 ft. and very lofty', as noted by Sir Christopher Sykes in 1794, it must be one of the most perfectly proportioned rooms of its type in any English country house. Even the elaborate spit mechanism over the hearth was embellished with chaste Neo-Classical urns.

Although the interiors of Kedleston rank among the finest of all Robert Adam's achievements, the landscape setting of the house is unique in being formed largely to his designs at the same time. The wholesale removal of the old village to the edge of the park, and the diversion of the public turnpike way to the north, the building of the new North Lodge, the bridge and fishing pavilions, were all achieved by 1775, together with the three lakes replacing Bridgeman's formal canals and ponds. Again, rivalry with Chatsworth was paramount: the bridge was re-designed with three arches instead of one (and a cascade below it) to outdo James Paine's Chatsworth bridge, built in 1762; Adam's design for a 'prospect tower' was clearly a Neo-Classical version of the Cavendishes' Elizabethan hunting tower; and the sash-bars of the windows on the north front were gilded, just as Talman had done for the 1st Duke of Devonshire.

In the end, the Curzon family estates were never a match for the vast territorial possessions of the Devonshires – particularly after the gambling debts run up by the 2nd Lord Scarsdale, and the intestacy of the 3rd. But that, and the conservatism of its later owners, accounted for the miraculous survival of Kedleston in the nineteenth century, when so many other great houses were altered or remodelled beyond recognition. The twentieth century has brought its own problems of restoration and upkeep, but now that the house is safe in the hands of the National Trust (with the present Lord and Lady Scarsdale still occupying the family pavilion, and maintaining the long association of the Curzons with Kedleston) it looks set to survive for future generations. AMICIS ET SIBI ('For his friends and himself'), the 1st Lord Scarsdale's inscription carved high on the south front, remains a fitting testimony to one of the greatest of Georgian connoisseurs, and to the value of his life's work.

Castle Coole

C O U N T Y   F E R M A N A G H

WHEN WE THINK OF IRISH HOUSES, it is usually their eccentricity that first comes to mind: whether the immensely extended *palazzo* façade of Castletown, or the turrets, pinnacles and pepperpots of Tullynally; whether the Neo-Norman of Gosford, the Neo-Tudor of Crom, or the Neo-Greek of Ballyfin. As in American colonial houses, style here is often skin-deep. At Castle Ward in County Down for instance, the house is Gothic on one side and Classical on the other, apparently the result of a matrimonial disagreement that was to end in separation. Elsewhere, as at Florence Court in County Fermanagh, the exuberant plasterwork decoration based on Palladio and Serlio suggests a copybook architect with a touch of genius: bold, naive and charming in its rusticity.

In this company, and in the wild and lonely beauty of the Fermanagh landscape, Castle Coole is of a very different order. Nothing could be less provincial, or more assured, than this balanced masterpiece of late eighteenth-century architecture: a culmination of the Palladian traditions, yet strictly Neo-Classical in its chaste ornament and its noble austerity. Nor is it simply the design that seems so effortlessly 'right'. The quality of the craftsmanship is breathtaking, from the masonry of the walls, with scarcely a hairline of mortar showing between the great ashlar blocks, to the carving of the massive Ionic capitals of the portico, from the exquisitely modelled plasterwork ceilings and friezes, to the huge mahogany double doors, and even their chased brass escutcheons and key plates. '*Un palais superbe*', as a French visitor described it in 1797, even if he felt obliged to add, '*il faut laisser les Temples aux Dieux*'.

So perfect is Castle Coole that its building history seems scarcely credible. Begun by one architect, it was completed to quite different designs by another – who never visited the site, and who never saw the house that most people regard as his masterpiece. Moreover the estimates were exceeded to such an extent that it remained virtually an empty shell for a generation. The sumptuous furnishing then undertaken, close in style to the Prince Regent's

Carlton House in London, may strike a very different note from the classical austerity of the earlier period. But it was also responsible for humanizing Castle Coole, and turning a temple for the gods into a palace fit for princes.

Such distinctions would have seemed strange to the hard-boiled soldiers and planters who first established themselves here in the early seventeenth century. As its name suggests, Castle Coole was originally a fortified house, built near the shores of Lough Coole and only a short distance from the nearby town of Enniskillen, a vital strategic centre between Upper and Lower Lough Erne. This castle, built about 1613, was burnt in the rebellion of 1641, and again during the Williamite wars of 1689, and was finally replaced in 1709 by a symmetrical double-pile house (like a smaller and less sophisticated version of Belton), designed by an architect named John Curle. By this time the estate belonged to James Corry, son of a Scottish immigrant who had made a fortune as a merchant in Belfast, and had bought Coole in 1656. However, the male line of the Corry family died out in 1741, when the spoils were divided among James's four grand-daughters, Martha, Sarah, Mary and Elizabeth – whose somewhat forbidding portraits still gaze down from the walls of the dining room. The future of Castle Coole might have been very different if these sisters had all produced heirs, but in the event only Sarah, who was married to Galbraith Lowry of County Tyrone, managed to produce a son – and it was he who was to inherit all his mother's and aunts' estates, greatly augmented by those of their husbands, in 1779.

Armar Lowry Corry (called after one of these beneficent uncles, Colonel Margetson Armar) had married a daughter of the 1st Earl of Carrick, but her early death in 1776 left him one of the most eligible widowers in Ireland. So it was no surprise to contemporaries that in 1780 he should land a spectacular catch in the shape of Lady Harriet Hobart, one of the daughters of the then Lord Lieutenant of Ireland, the Earl of Buckinghamshire: 'a young lady possessed of youth,

Armar Lowry Corry, 1st Earl of Belmore. It is possible that he conceived Castle Coole as a monument to the new Irish nationalism.

beauty, elegance of manners, and a fortune of £30,000', as *Walker's Hibernian Magazine* succinctly put it, adding the 'pleasing reflection that a native of this country has been destined to enjoy such supreme felicity'. As well as her dowry, Lady Harriet brought her husband a title (that of Baron Belmore) acquired through the Earl's influence in the following year, and still greater expectations in the future as one of her father's co-heirs. Sadly, material gains were not to be matched by spiritual ones, for the eighteen-year-old bride soon grew tired of her forty-year-old husband, and a divorce was eventually obtained by Act of Parliament in 1793 – at a critical time in the building of the house.

Lord Belmore's advance in the peerage – to a viscountcy in 1789 and an earldom in 1797 – was probably due to his rent-roll of £12,000 a year (among the two dozen largest in the country) and his control of five seats in the Irish House of Commons. Despite the large compensation offered to landowners for the loss of these seats, the 1st Earl and his son were to remain convinced supporters of Grattan and opponents of the Act of Union, and Castle Coole may well have been conceived in the optimism of the 1790s as a monument to a new Irish

nationalism, consciously rivalling the earlier seats of the English Whigs.

When the Belmores decided to rebuild the modest Queen Anne house down by the Lough, it is also easy to see why they chose a new site with wider and more picturesque views on the ridge to the south. The very choice of their new title (derived from a mountain seen in the distance beyond Enniskillen) shows a fashionable awareness of Romantic scenery, and in the early 1780s they employed a landscape gardener called King – who had earlier worked for the Bishop of Derry at Downhill, and Lord Enniskillen at nearby Florence Court – to sweep away the formal gardens and avenues round the old house, and to re-plant in the more naturalistic manner of Capability Brown. From the start, the new house was conceived in terms of the landscape, and, like the classical buildings in many of Claude's pictures, its straight lines and perfect all-round symmetry were in intentional contrast to the rounded shapes of hills and woods, the uneven shores of the lake, and the mountain peaks beyond. The works of man and nature, the one improving the other, appealed to a generation brought up on Rousseau's theories of individual liberty, while the idea of houses based on the temples of antiquity, each within its sacred grove, came naturally to those who saw the origin of such theories in ancient Greece and Rome.

Work on preparing the site began as early as 1788, though the earliest known designs, by the Dublin architect Richard Johnston, are dated October 1789. The older brother of the more famous Francis Johnston, Richard was a safe choice of architect for an Irish landowner at the time, with buildings like the Rotunda Assembly Rooms (1784) and Daly's Club House (1789) to his credit. Like his Castle Coole designs, these buildings owed much to Sir William Chambers and to James Gandon, applying French-inspired Neo-Classical ornament to what were essentially Palladian structures. Indeed the end pavilions that Johnston proposed for Castle Coole would have been miniature versions of Chambers' most celebrated Irish work, the Casino at Marino, near Dublin.

Just as Lord Scarsdale changed horses at the last moment, however, commissioning Robert Adam to complete the house which Brettingham and Paine had begun, so Lord Belmore went to Adam's chief rival, James Wyatt, for an entirely new set of designs in May 1790 when the building of Johnston's basement was already far advanced. A comparison between the two architects' drawings shows this basement virtually unchanged. But Wyatt's revised façades and upper-floor plans represent an altogether higher level of artistic achievement – all the more amazing given the limitations of his predecessor's plan. As C. R. Cockerell later put it, 'Wyatt liked to meet with those difficulties and accidents from which agreeable circumstances of effect might be derived.' Here at Castle Coole, where the relationship with his patron was too distant to be soured by his usual unpunctuality and lack of business acumen, he rose to the challenge in a remarkable way, producing not just a solution to a problem but a work of genius in its own right.

As a young man, James Wyatt had become famous almost overnight as the architect of the Pantheon in Oxford Street, a 'winter Ranelagh' built in 1770, almost immediately after his return from six years' study in Italy. The diarist, Farington, records a later conversation in which Wyatt told George III that 'there had been no regular architecture since Sir William Chambers – that when he came from Italy he found public taste corrupted by the Adams and he was obliged to comply with it'. There may be some truth in this, for his later buildings, like the mausoleums at Cobham in Kent and Brocklesby in Lincolnshire, and houses like Castle Coole and Dodington in Gloucestershire, show a development of Chambers' style in a bolder, more masculine, direction – looking forward to the Greek Revival, as well as backwards to Palladian practice. Wyatt's ability to work in almost any style, and his particular interest in the Gothic, also gave his architecture an abstract quality, suppressing purely ornamental detail and concentrating on the effect of larger masses.

At Castle Coole, his revision of Johnston's design does just this, pruning and tightening up the elements of the façades until there is not a single superfluous line. Thus, the string course below the first-floor windows is continued as the entablature of the colonnades and pavilions, tying the whole composition together; the windows are simply voids in the walls without any surrounds; while, instead of Johnston's urns, festoons and pilasters, attention is concentrated on fewer, more telling,

projections and recessions. The giant Ionic columns of the portico on the south and the bay window on the north gain impact from being set close against the sheer unrelieved face of the main block, and there is a satisfying contrast too between its contained mass and the lines of fluted Doric columns marching off on each side and carried through into the end pavilions, like little temples in their own right. As Edward McParland has written, 'form contrasts with form; light and shade are exploited to heighten the contrast; and all is worked out with the precision of impeccable stonework'.

In many ways, the 'Attic Simplicity' of the overall effect is misleading, for there are many more references to Palladio here than to the incipient Greek Revival. The idea of the straight colonnades and pavilions is itself Palladian, recalling those which Davis Ducart added to Florence Court (for Lord Belmore's brother-in-law) in the 1770s; and the same can be said of the Venetian windows on the north side of the end pavilions. The baseless Doric columns come from Palladio's engravings of the order (copied from the theatre of Marcellus and other Roman monuments) rather than the heavier and squatter versions found on Greek temples. A strict Revivalist might also find the Ionic capitals of the giant columns distinctly impure, with big curly volutes projecting out on the diagonal in an old-fashioned, almost Baroque, manner.

On the other hand, there are aspects of Castle Coole which are unmistakably Neo-Classical: to begin with, the way it sits directly on the ground. Unlike Kedleston,

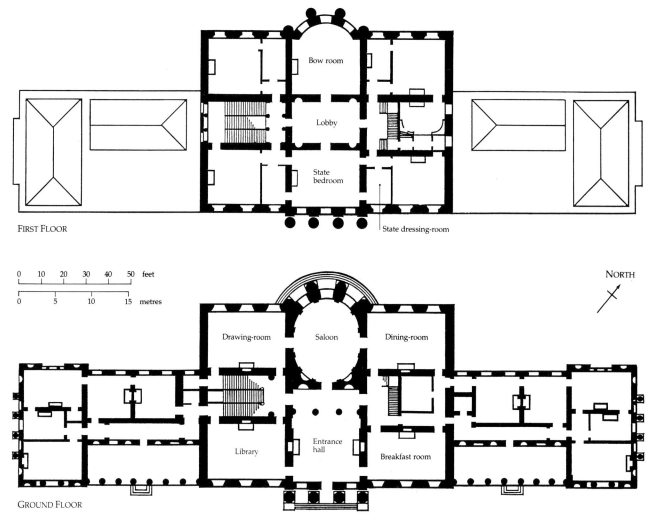

FIRST FLOOR

GROUND FLOOR

NORTH

Johnston's design for the north front, 1789. The urns, carved festoons and moulded window surrounds were removed in Wyatt's design.

James Wyatt's more severe design. There are fewer façade projections, and the pilasters on the bow are replaced by giant columns.

where the state rooms occupy a *piano nobile* set above the 'rustic' and approached by great flights of steps, here the servants' quarters in the basement are completely sunk below ground level, and approached by a huge tunnel on the east – also used to bring stone into the foundations during construction. This abandonment of the 'rustic', pioneered by Chambers at Duddingstone, near Edinburgh, was once again a response to Picturesque values. The fact that you could step from any of the main rooms straight into the landscape increased that sense of 'communion with nature' so strongly urged by Repton and his contemporaries, while the concealment of the servants and their means of access meant that all four sides of the house could enjoy the same advantages. Just as the rooms flowed out into the garden, so the garden flowed back, with the increasing popularity of vases and pots of flowers, plant stands and *jardinières*, as well as schemes of floral decoration. It is interesting to find that on Wyatt's ground plan of Castle Coole, the deep *loggie* behind the colonnades on the south are labelled 'Green houses', and it is possible that tall windows like those in the end pavilions could have been inserted between the columns in the winter months, turning them into sunny conservatories where orange trees and other tender exotics could be kept. In this respect, too, Wyatt was anticipating a Regency fashion.

In the eighteenth century Irish houses tended to have more servants than their English counterparts, but fewer who were educated or presentable. So the idea of a basement under the whole house, lit through gratings in the surrounding paving, continued well into the nineteenth century, when in England these pits or dry moats had been generally abandoned in favour of better-appointed servants' wings, usually tacked on to one corner of a house asymmetrically, and concealed by dense shrubberies – as for instance at Wyatt's Dodington, built in 1797. Improvements in the household bell system lay behind this development (enabling servants to be summoned from much further away) and almost entirely

dispensed with the need for servants' rooms anywhere on the principal floors, a characteristic of Castle Coole.

Although the foundation stone of the house was only laid on 17 June 1790 – a month after Wyatt's earliest plans – this may well have been the first Portland stone block of the main elevation, laid above a basement that was largely complete. Instead of finding a contractor to carry out the work at a fixed price, Lord Belmore took the rather unusual step of building with direct labour, hiring the individual craftsmen, and obviously keeping a very close watch on progress. His own perfectionism may well account for the high standards achieved, but in the absence of Wyatt, who came to Ireland only once, in 1785, he also had an outstanding executant architect or clerk of the works in Alexander Stewart – later to act in a similar capacity for Soane at Baronscourt and Dance at Mount Stewart. Unfortunately these high standards also had a high cost. The original estimate was £30,000, but by June 1795 the Earl had already spent £54,000, with several expensive items like Richard Westmacott's marble chimneypieces still to come. The work also took double the expected time.

One of the major factors here was his superbly impractical decision to clad the house entirely in the finest Portland stone, using the local quartz from the deer park only for the basement and interior walls. The initial cost of procuring, quarrying and sawing the stone at Portland was £12,000 but then the brig *Martha* had to be chartered to bring it all the way from Dorset to a specially constructed quay at Ballyshannon, in Donegal Bay. Thence it was dragged by teams of oxen ten miles overland to Lough Erne, transported by barges or lighters from there to Enniskillen, and finally by more oxen up the steeply sloping park to the site of the new house.

Another of Lord Belmore's extravagances was his choice of leading London craftsmen like the plasterer Joseph Rose and the scagliola worker Domenico Bartoli, both previously employed at Kedleston and in many other Adam and Wyatt houses. In one letter of May 1793 Rose

Castle Coole

1 Hall
2 Library
3 Staircase
4 Drawing-room
5 Saloon
6 Lobby
7 Lord and Lady Belmore's apartments
To nurseries, with kitchen under

NORTH

110

The north front, strictly Neo-Classical in its simple ornament and noble austerity.

writes to Lord Belmore, 'I have (at last) sent you 4 more plasterers (very good men I believe) but I have been obliged to give them more wages otherways they would not have left England. . . . Mr. Wyatt has also sent the drawings [presumably ceiling designs] by them. They have been made these twelve months. My men are rather afraid of being pressed [i.e. press-ganged] – why they should I cannot tell as none of them are sailors. If anything of the kind should happen I hope Yr Lordship will stand their friend.' These were not the only problems, for only a month later Rose reported 'some difficulty in getting the orniment men to come because I understand that there are letters come to London from the last men I sent saying that it is an unhealthy place, that most of them are ill and that there is not lodging for them but in damp rooms'. Rose himself visited the house on two occasions (once in 1794), but savings were also made by having the more complicated elements, like the frieze and the Corinthian capitals of the pilasters in the saloon, made in London under his supervision, and shipped over via Liverpool and Dublin.

If Lord Belmore was not prepared to skimp in the decoration of the state rooms, the same applied to the servants' quarters in the basement below, unseen by the vast majority of his guests, but just as impressive for their sheer size and for the quality of their plasterwork and woodwork. Following Johnston's lead, Wyatt provided a kitchen and scullery in the east pavilion, but sank them lower than the rest of the basement so as to provide the necessary height, while still leaving room for the nurseries above. Lit by three huge sash windows, as tall as the pavilion windows on the south front, the kitchen is surprisingly light – despite the fact that it looks into a covered area at the entrance to the tunnel, with daylight filtered down through cast-iron gratings. The massive stone vaulted ceilings here and throughout the basement were intended as a fire precaution, as well as a means of insulating the noise and hurly-burly of this subterranean kingdom from the civilized calm of the state rooms above.

Throughout the nineteenth century servants could only approach the house from the huge stable and estate yards concealed below the brow of the hill to the south-east, up the long barrel-vaulted tunnel, 14 feet wide and 12 feet high, with store rooms for peat and firewood off it: a scene

Part of the tunnel leading from the stables to the kitchen, the only means of approach to the house for servants and tradesmen.

reminiscent of Piranesi's *Carceri* engravings, with ropes and chains suspended from the ceiling, and shafts of light piercing the gloom from an occasional oculus. Skirting the kitchen, they would then enter the basement by a wide, stone-paved lobby under the east colonnade, with the larder, pantry and cooks' rooms leading off it, together with water closets and a plunge bath – modern conveniences shared by few other Irish houses at this date. In the main block, the servants' hall and steward's room (where the lower and upper servants respectively met for meals) lay below the dining and breakfast rooms, while the menservants' barrack room lay below the drawing room and the butler's rooms below the library. The beer and wine cellars occupied the central space below the hall and saloon, since the portico on one side and bow window on the other made them difficult to light. Finally, the housekeeper, lady's maids and valets had rooms below Lord and Lady Belmore's own apartments in the west wing.

On the ground floor of the main block Wyatt kept Johnston's layout virtually unchanged, though amalgamating the 'Breakfast Parlour' and Lord Belmore's 'Audience Room' (for interviewing tenants) in the south-west corner, so as to give all four corner rooms identical dimensions. Following Palladian precedent, these are based on a six-foot module – 36 by 24 feet, and 18 feet high – the so-called 'harmonic proportions' that theorists equated with the regular intervals of musical chords. The dining room and breakfast room conveniently adjoined the back staircase, used by servants bringing food up from the kitchen in the east wing, while the drawing room and library flanked the main staircase, next to the family's private apartments in the west wing.

Separating these two pairs of rooms were the hall and saloon, forming an old-fashioned 'state centre' on the central axis, distinguished on the exterior by the portico and bow. In earlier Palladian houses like Holkham, Nostell and Kedleston, however, these rooms were double-height, and there was a state bedchamber and dressing room on the *piano nobile* forming part of the circuit of the main rooms. By contrast, Wyatt's principal bedchamber at Castle Coole is also part of the 'state centre', immediately above the hall, and the highly architectural treatment of the staircase and first-floor lobby provides a grand processional route leading up to it: a series of spaces flowing into each other, and giving a sense of mounting excitement to the ascent. Originally hall, staircase and lobby seem all to have been stone colour, but about 1811 the 2nd Earl repainted them in a warmer terracotta, according well with Bartoli's scagliola columns in the hall, which imitate porphyry.

Wyatt's drawings for the hall, dated 1791, show the room very much as executed though with fluted rather than plain Doric pillars (perhaps intended to echo the colonnades outside) and with a tall niche, possibly for a stove, in place of one of the two fireplaces. The rich Doric entablature over the columns is carried as a frieze all round the room, and repeated in the doorcases and in Westmacott's white statuary chimney surrounds. Plaster, carved wood and marble thus contribute to the

Cross-section through the centre of the house, looking north-east.

1 Hall	**5** State bedroom
2 Saloon	**6 and 7** Great bedrooms
3 Lobby	**8** Wine cellar
4 Bow (or Work) room	**9** Beer cellar

feeling of decorative unity, restrained but elegant, as Wyatt's interiors so often are. The architect also designed the four tripod candlestands which were made by the carvers at the house in 1797–8, and (probably) the six mahogany armchairs bearing the Belmore crest, thought to have been made soon afterwards by the London cabinet-maker William Kidd.

The screen of columns in the hall, emphasizing the main cross-axis of the house and pointing the way to the main staircase, also acts as a fitting ante-room to the oval saloon straight ahead. Here, Wyatt's drawings show a far richer decorative treatment, with marbled walls, Corinthian pilasters (which Bartoli executed in mottled grey and white scagliola) and painted pier tables between them. The ceiling was to be the most elaborate in the house, costing £119 according to Joseph Rose's estimate of 1793. The drawing closest to its present appearance is in Rose's own hand, and he may also have added the delicate plasterwork in the heads of the two niches containing Wyatt's cast-iron stoves.

While it is true that the 1st Earl never properly completed the furnishing of Castle Coole, the emptiness of the saloon reflected its function as a ballroom used almost exclusively for parties. On such occasions the great curved double doors could be flung open, allowing the guests to pass from the buffet in the dining room to the card tables in the drawing room on one long enfilade, to the accompaniment of waltzes and polkas from the musicians stationed in the bow window.

Within twenty years, however, a taste for heavier and more magnificent decoration had been introduced by the Prince Regent at Carlton House, and in particular a fashion for chairs, couches and tables placed in the middle of rooms, where previously they had been set rigidly round the walls. Apparently unconcerned by the large debts which his father had left in 1802, the new Lord Belmore approached the upholsterers John and Nathaniel Preston of Henry Street, Dublin, in 1807, and over the next eighteen years was to spend the then massive sum of £26,367 with the firm, clothing Wyatt's chaste Neo-Classical interiors in the most sumptuous and colourful Regency garb.

The saloon, one of the last rooms to be tackled, was also the most extravagantly treated, taking a number of years to complete. The four 'Grecian style' sofa tables and couches were sent from Dublin in 1815, but the large circular centre table made to match only arrived in 1821, and its 'rosewood top with finely executed Bhul border' took two more years. The most expensive items were the four mirrors costing £880 and the four candlestands at £944, but the sophistication and the immensely high prices of these pieces compared to those supplied in the previous decade suggest that Preston may have been importing furniture from London makers like Marsh and Tatham, or Morel and Hughes.

An undated note from Preston, written in London, contains various references to goods shipped via Liverpool and to customs duties on calico bought in

England, while a postscript to the accounts of 1816–25 talks of 'the heavy expense incurred in sending several articles to London to be regilt, in consequence of great damage sustained'. A John Preston, upholsterer and auctioneer, is recorded as living at 349 Rotherhithe Street between 1804 and 1825, and he may therefore have had premises in both London and Dublin.

If he relied on others for carcass pieces, Preston's detailed bills for upholstery suggest that this remained his own province. The '3 French Window Curtains' in the saloon were of immense elaboration, made of 'Rich Striped Crimson Watered Satin' and with drapery (or pelmets) of crimson silk velvet, trimmed with gold lace, fringe and tassels. Their effect must have been to impart a feeling of warmth as well as luxury to Wyatt's perfectly proportioned but somewhat frigid interior. There was naturally a much greater sense of formality here than in the other main rooms, for the one invariable ceremony that had survived from the Baroque period was the gathering of family and guests in full evening dress in the drawing room, and their procession, two by two, through the saloon to the dining room. In an earlier period, the oval shape of the saloon would have been ideally suited to the circle of chairs usually arranged in the centre for 'conversations', when visitors called, or guests were being entertained. By the end of the eighteenth century this rigid etiquette had been abandoned, and the 2nd Earl's couches and sofa tables round the walls would have encouraged the company to split into smaller, more intimate groups. Halfway between the male territory of the dining room and the female territory of the drawing room, this was, after all, a place where the sexes could meet on equal terms.

Wyatt's dining room still has an austere and masculine character, little altered since the house was first built, and a perfect example of the restrained taste of the 1790s. There were originally no curtains here, for at this date it was still feared that textiles might harbour the smell of food. Nor were there any pictures, either at this time or later in the nineteenth century. Instead, the subtle rhythm of the wall panels and the exquisite detail of the plasterwork ceiling, cornice, doorcases and window frames were to speak for themselves. The wreath motif, seen in large scale on the ceiling, is repeated in the oak and ivy garlands of the frieze, above the doors, on the dado rail and on Westmacott's marble chimneypiece, giving a decorative unity to the room, and perhaps also recalling the wreath of the Lowry crest. Little bowls or *tazze* also incorporated in the frieze and ceiling are the only discreet references to the room's use, together with Bacchus's garlanded *thyrsus* or staff on the jambs of the chimneypiece.

Wyatt almost certainly designed the sideboard, its flanking urns on pedestals and its sarcophagus wine-cooler, and these were all made by the carvers at the house in 1797, after their work on the joinery had been completed. As at Kedleston, where the house carvers also produced pieces to Adam's design, the sideboard would have been set with the finest pieces of family plate, like an altar at the far end of the main enfilade: a touch of

A corner of the hall. Wyatt's screen of scagliola colums support a rich Doric entablature which is carried as a frieze all round the room.

ostentation particularly telling in these chaste surroundings.

The drawing room, on the other side of the saloon, took up more of the upholsterer's time, as one might expect. In his *Cabinet Dictionary* of 1803, Thomas Sheraton argued that 'the Drawing Room is to concentrate the elegance of the whole house, and is the highest display of richness of furniture. It being appropriated to the formal visits of the highest in rank, nothing of a scientific nature should be introduced to take up the attention of any individual from the general conversation that takes place on such occasions. Hence the walls should be free of pictures, the tables not lined with books, nor the angles of the room filled with globes; as the design of such meetings are not that each visitant should turn to his favourite study, but to contribute his part towards the amusement of the whole company.' Wyatt's designs, made in 1792, suggest a pink and blue ceiling, light blue walls and elaborate swagged curtains within the arched window reveals. But the room was probably unfurnished at the time of the 1st Earl's death in 1802, and it was only in 1815–18 that Preston decorated and furnished it in the most elaborate Regency taste.

The walls were lined with blue paper, without pictures (following Sheraton's advice); the frieze was picked out in a stronger blue with silver-gilt mouldings; and a huge, continuous set of curtains made of 'Rich Striped Salmon-Color Watered Satin' was hung over the three windows. The same material was used to cover quantities of new seat furniture, including '2 Very Superb Grecian Couches' (costing £490), thirteen gilt armchairs and twelve single chairs. Such a crowded arrangement, familiar from the contemporary drawings of rooms furnished by Gillows of Lancaster, had much to do with changes of fashion in costume. Wide paniers and hoops had now been abandoned for the slimmer and high-waisted 'Grecian' gowns, while men's coats and trousers also tended to be closer cut and better adapted for sitting in deep sprung chairs, or lounging on sofas.

The uneven number of armchairs here supports the tradition that Lord Belmore acquired one on his visit to Paris in 1802–3, during the Peace of Amiens, and had the others made by Preston to match. Like his contemporaries, William Beckford and the Prince Regent, the 2nd Earl may indeed have been one of the pioneers of the 'Louis Revival', for French influence can clearly be seen in the Neo-Rococo scrolls of the couches, and the 'Boulle' borders to the tables – not to mention the copy of a medal cabinet designed by Oppenordt for Versailles, which could be the 'rich French Cabinet' listed here in 1816. With mass-manufactured furniture becoming more readily available, French pieces which defied cheap imitation had a natural appeal for the upper classes, particularly in the wake of the sales following the French Revolution.

By contrast with the grand reception rooms on the north, the library and breakfast room on the south (flanking the hall) were noticeably less formal and more comfortable. The pictures, books and globes forbidden by Sheraton in the drawing room came into their own in the cluttered arrangement of the library. Like Sir Richard Colt Hoare's at Stourhead, this was no mere retreat for the scholar, enjoined to silent study, but an everyday living room equipped in 1816 with a 'large Harpsichord' and 'large Tea Table', besides two sofas and sofa tables, eight armchairs, six side chairs, four carpet-covered hassocks and no fewer than six firescreens.

Wyatt's drawings for the room show landscapes alternating with oval portraits above the bookcases, which were somewhat altered in execution by the joiners. They also show a far more conventional chimney surround than the great swags of marble drapery which Westmacott finally supplied – perhaps intended to echo the original curtains on the opposite side of the room. The walls were again pale green in the 1790s, but altered to grey about 1811, to go with Preston's new curtains and chair covers – made of chocolate-coloured calico with a yellow scroll pattern.

His bills describe the two sofas as 'large Egyptian couches', and this is particularly appropriate since the 2nd Earl took his family on an extended tour of the Mediterranean, Egypt and the Near East in 1818–21, bringing back a notable collection of sculpture (now in the British Museum) on his yacht, the *Osprey*. Books on Egyptology, testifying to his serious interest in archaeology, still fill many of the shelves; and there is also a two-volume account of the tour published in 1822, under the title *Travels along the Mediterranean*, by the family's physician, Dr Robert Richardson.

The breakfast room on the other side of the hall had a still more exotic chinoiserie theme after Preston had finished with it. The curtains, with another vast continuous drapery over the three windows, were made of chintz, with vivid red and green figures on a mustard-yellow ground, reminiscent of the materials used in the Prince Regent's Brighton Pavilion. The French ebonized pier tables were married (somewhat curiously) to a pair of pagoda-topped breakfast cabinets, hung with bells, and these later contained the 2nd Earl's 'large Collection of Early Egyptian Curios, Idols, Beasts, Beetles &c.'. The seat furniture, including a 'Grecian Couch', was also ebonized and chintz-covered, while the walls were painted blue and hung with '21 Large Paintings of Various Views'. From the inventory descriptions there can be little doubt that the room was used as a morning sitting room, though it also contained two oval tables at which breakfast and other informal meals could be taken. At another Irish house, Carton in County Kildare, the Duchess of Leinster had recorded not long before that 'we breakfast between ten and eleven, though it is called half past nine. We have an immense table – chocolate – honey – hot bread – cold bread – brown bread – white bread – green bread – and all

Wyatt's design for one wall of the library, where all the elements contribute to its symmetry.

The state bed supplied by John Preston in 1820, probably in anticipation of a visit by George IV.

coloured breads and cakes. After breakfast . . . the chaplain reads a few short prayers, and then we go as we like.'

The essence of house-party life by this date was the freedom of guests to follow their particular pursuits – reading, writing or embroidery, cards, billiards, or outdoor sports – meeting up again only at about six-thirty or seven for the formal assembly in the drawing room before dinner. The ground floor of Castle Coole clearly demonstrates this division, with its informal, daytime rooms facing south-east to catch the morning sunlight, and its grander evening quarters looking north-west to the sunset, with the greylag geese returning to the still waters of the lake. On the upper floor this situation is reversed, for the windows of the state bedroom are set between the Ionic capitals of the south portico, while the Bow Room, intended as an informal sitting room for the afternoon and evening, lies above the saloon, with the best views in the house.

Wyatt's staircase, very much in keeping with the austere architecture of the hall, is of the so-called 'imperial' type – rising in one central flight, and then dividing into

two, cantilevered out from the side walls. However, his ceiling design was revised by Joseph Rose to make allowance for an extra screen of Doric columns on the top landing, supporting a landing in the attic above. It is not clear how these columns were first treated, but about 1821, when the walls were painted the same terracotta colour as the hall, they were coated in yellow scagliola (to look like Siena marble) by craftsmen sent over from the Coade manufactory in Lambeth. Apart from this touch of opulence the decoration is kept purposely low-key, for Wyatt's *coup de théâtre* is still to come: the wide lobby at the head of the stairs rising through the attic storey and with pairs of marbled Doric columns marching all round at gallery level.

A number of earlier Irish houses have top-lit bedroom lobbies in the centre of the first floor, so the idea may initially have come from Lord Belmore. On the other hand, nothing like it appears in Richard Johnston's plans, and Wyatt's aim may have been to divert attention from the generally rather low ceiling heights at this level. Masterly in its handling of light and shade, with vistas through to further skylights on the east and west, it has all the nobility of a great temple atrium, recalling the superimposed columns inside the Parthenon or the Temple of Poseidon at Paestum. Even the stoves set in niches round the walls are in the form of sacrificial altars, carefully designed by the architect to enhance the feeling of classical solemnity.

At the end of this long processional route, the state bedchamber would be an anti-climax were it not for Preston's magnificent bed-hangings and window curtains. The finest draperies in the house, and also the most expensive, these miraculously survived until the 1960s when the original 'Rich fire-coloured Mantua' was replaced by a matching silk taffeta – re-using the old braids and fringes. The crimson flock wallpaper, another remarkable survival, was made in 1812 by the Dublin paper-stainers J. & P. Boyland, according to a stamp on the back. But otherwise the entire contents of the room, and its adjoining dressing room, were sent by Preston in one large consignment in 1821. The 'French Canopy Bedstead' in the dressing room, and the equally typical French Empire commodes in the bedchamber, appear in the bills, and prove that he was importing Parisian as well as English furniture.

The date also supports the tradition that the two rooms were prepared for a possible visit by George IV, for the King came to Ireland that year and stayed at Slane Castle in County Meath, Wyatt's other major Irish house. However, he was so captivated by its *châtelaine*, Lady Conyngham (who happened to be his current mistress), that he strayed no farther north. One can well imagine Lord Belmore's disappointment. Like Lord Burghley and Sir Christopher Hatton way back in the reign of Queen Elizabeth, he had exceeded his purse in the hopes of entertaining his sovereign. Already £70,000 in debt by 1812, he may well have undertaken his Mediterranean expedition on the *Osprey* for reasons of economy, and in 1828 he was forced to sell his London house for £30,000 and accept the governorship of Jamaica – which he held for four years.

Re-crossing the lobby to the Bow Room is to go back in time from the last of Preston's work at Castle Coole to the first. In the bills and in the 1816 inventory this is called the 'Work Room' and indeed the wide bay window facing north-west must have been ideal for needleworkers. The comparatively low ceiling meant that it would also be warmed more easily than the high ground-floor rooms, and it must regularly have been used as an informal family drawing room in the winter. As in the Breakfast Room, the decoration had a chinoiserie theme, though using more delicate patterns on a smaller scale.

The grey and white wallpaper featuring miniature pagodas amid flowering trees and shrubs was hung in the summer of 1807, having been supplied by a paper-stainer named Robert Dyas who had premises a few doors away from the Prestons in Dublin. Sections of it survived intact behind the pier glasses (put up three years later), and it has thus proved possible to copy it accurately, together with its green, pink and black border – originally flock. The 'French Window Curtains', made of 'Chinese Chintz' with 'rich Silk Cotton Parisian fringe', were also hung in

1807 from '3 sanguined Spear Shafts rosewood'. Miraculously these too had survived, though in tatters, and the material – an English glazed cotton, printed in four colours on a white ground – has again been copied.

The Bow Room still contains most of the furniture listed in 1816, including twelve satinwood chairs with lion's paw feet, recognizable in a Preston bill of 1809, the pier tables with gilt lion supports of 1811, the two sofas upholstered to match the curtains, and the bamboo settee. There was also a large amount of china, appropriate to the decoration of the room and useful for taking tea; matting as well as rugs on the floor (the latter perhaps produced by the needleworkers); more hassocks covered in Brussels carpet; and '30 Glaizd and framd Prints' on the walls.

The five other main bedrooms on this floor were decorated in the same light colours, with satinwood and painted furniture, printed cottons, chintzes and muslins. Rather surprisingly the bedrooms in the attic above, reached from the back stair beyond the lobby, were also intended for guests and not for servants. Writing in 1797, long before the 2nd Earl's campaign of redecoration and refurnishing, de la Tocnaye found that, in this respect, 'comfort has been almost entirely sacrificed to beauty . . . rooms intended for visitors are like cellars, although at the top of the building. Light comes to them only through little windows eight feet below the level of the ceiling, and against these windows there is a stone balustrade, so that they may not be perceived in the design from the outside.' In the late nineteenth century they were occupied by the three bachelor sons and eight spinster daughters of the 4th Earl of Belmore: an Anglo-Irish household straight from the pages of Somerville and Ross.

Anna Walker, wife of a colonel posted in Enniskillen in 1805, also found the attic rooms 'very bad', though admiring the house as 'one of the most Beautiful and Correct Grecian Buildings I ever saw'. Better than any novel, however, her diary entry for 11 July, describing one of the 2nd Earl's house parties, brings back the flavour of life at Castle Coole in the second decade of its existence – filling its silent rooms for a moment with the laughter and gossip of another age. 'Lord and Lady Belmore', she writes, 'improve excessively on Acquaintance, are extremely good humoured, and are good enough to express great Regret at our leaving Enniskillen. We Worked in the Evening very Sociably [presumably in the Bow Room], & staid very late. . . . No-one dined with them but ourselves, excepting the Party staying in the house, which consisted of Mr and Mrs Brooks of Colebrook – good humoured pleasant people – Mr Brooke of the 18th Dragoons – their sister Miss Brook, a very fine girl of 16, Lady Kilkenny, a very pleasant Woman, Tho' rather Masculine in appearance. Poor Thing, her Situation is a Melancholy one, Lord Kilkenny having lost his Reason very soon after they were married, and is now confined. Major Waters of the 3rd Dragoons made up the Party. The latter is on a visit to Castle Coole previous to his Marriage with Miss Corry, a very charming Little Girl, Natural Daughter of the Late Lord Belmore. We stayed Supper & took leave of their charming family with great Regret.'

Ickworth

S U F F O L K

AFTER THE UNEXPECTED ENGLISHNESS of Castle Coole, set in the wild Fermanagh landscape, there is an Irishness about Ickworth that is equally surprising among the hedgerows and cornfields of domestic Suffolk. Nor does the paradox end there. Castle Coole was designed by an English architect who never saw it; Ickworth was built under the supervision of an Irish architect for a patron who never saw it. The one is noble, restrained, austere; the other eccentric, extravagant, impractical. They might seem at opposite ends of the spectrum of late eighteenth-century taste. Yet their builders had much in common – both were typical products of the Enlightenment, both steeped in the traditions of Classicism, both strong supporters of Irish nationalism at a time (perhaps the only time) when the problems of that country were truly capable of resolution.

The differences between these two great buildings are best explained in terms of intention, illustrated by one of the great texts of the Enlightenment, Edmund Burke's *Enquiry into the Origins . . . of the Sublime and Beautiful*. For Burke, the attributes of the Sublime were obscurity (even 'delightful Horror'), power, vastness and infinity. At the same time he maintained that the Sublime depended for its effect on surprise, while Beauty also acted instantaneously, relaxing the nerves and fibres, and thus inducing a kind of sensual languor.

Surprise and 'delightful Horror' are the last things on your mind arriving at the little village of Horringer, near Bury St Edmunds. With its lime-washed cottages, thatched roofs and weather-boarded barns it gives no hint of what is to come. It is only after passing the neat lodge gates on the village green, as you drive through typical East Anglian parkland dotted with grazing cattle, that the great dome with its balustraded platform suddenly comes into view above the trees.

Your initial feeling is one of disbelief, as if this huge bulk had newly arrived from another planet, having floated down to rest among the ancient oaks and ilexes. The road skirts the thick belt of surrounding woodland, and only as

you approach it at close quarters are you aware of the curving wings and pavilions forming great arcs on either side, tying the rotunda to the ground. The effect is crushing and invigorating. No wonder that science fiction comes to mind, for after the idealized 'Beauty' of Castle Coole, here we are, face to face with the 'Sublime'.

Begun only five years after Castle Coole, Ickworth transports us from the sylvan landscapes of Claude to the mountains and precipices of Salvator Rosa; from Gainsborough's Suffolk portraits (so easily imagined on our drive through the park) to the dramatic intensity of De Loutherbourg and the megalomania of John Martin. It is a change of mood that Burke anticipated. According to him, 'a *Rotund* form, in presenting no checks to the eye, simulates Infinity'. Whether in a building or in a plantation of trees (Capability Brown's 'clumps' for instance), it had a noble effect. 'Nothing', he wrote, 'is so prejudicial to the grandeur of a building than to abound in angles.' But more than that, Ickworth represents a move from Classical balance towards Romantic asymmetry, from the pure reason of the Encyclopaedists to the untrammelled emotions of the French Revolution.

In the past it has been the fashion to dismiss Ickworth as an overgrown folly, and its creator, Frederick Hervey, 4th Earl of Bristol and Bishop of Derry, as a frivolous and irresponsible eccentric. However, both verdicts are wide of the mark. No other English building of the period comes so near to the colossal geometry of Boullée and Ledoux, and no other individual of the time was so willing to abandon traditional social conventions in favour of a rationally enlightened individualism. It is high time that both were treated seriously, and to do so we have to go back to the Earl-Bishop's antecedents.

The Herveys acquired Ickworth by marriage as early as 1467, and soon became pre-eminent in local politics. From 1628, when Sir William Hervey was elected Member of Parliament for Bury St Edmunds, every direct male descendant of his, down to the 4th Marquess in 1906, sat either for the borough or for West Suffolk. The only

A distant view of the Rotunda from the park. Begun in 1795, it reflects the Earl-Bishop's passion for circular and oval buildings.

exception was the Earl-Bishop, whose cloth debarred him from a role he would doubtless have enjoyed. This parliamentary interest encouraged the family to keep a large town house in Bury as well as the fifteenth- or early sixteenth-century manor which stood near Ickworth church, but which was demolished about 1710. Its then owner, John Hervey, created Baron Hervey in 1703 and Earl of Bristol in 1714, owed his peerage to his support of the Protestant succession, and in particular to his patroness, the Duchess of Marlborough. He had also married two considerable heiresses, and retired early from public life to spend his days at 'sweet Ickworth', commissioning first Talman and then Vanbrugh to draw up grandiose plans for a new house.

Why these plans were never achieved remains something of a mystery. The reason may lie partly in the 1st Earl's parsimony and partly in the extravagance of his numerous and mostly unsatisfactory sons, in particular Carr, Lord Hervey, his eldest son by his first marriage, who died in 1723, and Thomas and William, younger sons of his second marriage. The last two, although dissolute to a degree, were nevertheless befriended by Dr Johnson, who went so far as to claim: 'If you will call a dog Hervey, I shall love him.'

The architect Sir Thomas Robinson visited Ickworth in 1731 and found the Herveys living in the lodge, 'a tenant's old house in the park, so very bad a habitation, that I am astonished how so large a family have so long made a shift in it'. Robinson also records that 'the old mansion house was pulled down about twenty years ago, and those materials and others sufficient to build a new house were led to another situation, and the new one determined to be built; but an ill run at play (as fame reports) stopped the design, and most of the wood, brick and stone have since been used in tenants' houses.'

The 1st Earl's eldest son by his second marriage was perhaps the most brilliant member of an exceptionally gifted family. John, Lord Hervey, despite his early death at the age of forty-seven (eight years before his father),

was one of the best-known figures of his time – a politician and pamphleteer of the Walpole faction who became Vice-Chamberlain of the Royal Household and Lord Privy Seal. A close personal friend of Queen Caroline, Lord Hervey is best remembered today for his vivid, outspoken memoirs of the court of George II. His mercurial temperament and ambivalent nature forced Lady Mary Wortley Montagu to conclude that there were three human species – 'men, women and Herveys' – but he nevertheless made a love match with the beautiful and, by all accounts, delightful Molly Lepel, one of the Queen's maids of honour.

Lord Buckinghamshire later wrote that 'no one contributed more to the cheerful elegance of her age than Molly Lepel, Lady Hervey . . . with nothing natural about her she pleas'd like a french flower garden, where art appears in every fancy'd Border. In her youth she affected

Frederick Augustus Hervey, 4th Earl of Bristol and Bishop of Derry (1730–1803). Painted in Naples, about 1792, the Earl Bishop is holding an elevation of his Irish house, Ballyscullion.

the manners of that country, and in her age acquired them.' She bore Lord Hervey eight children, of whom the three eldest sons – destined, conventionally enough, for politics, the Navy and the Church – were to succeed as 2nd, 3rd and 4th Earls of Bristol after their grand-father's death in 1751.

The 2nd Earl followed in his father's footsteps, becoming Lord Privy Seal in 1768 after serving as ambassador in Turin and Madrid and as Lord Lieutenant of Ireland. His inordinate pride, said to be the reason why he never attained higher office, might have encouraged him to build the long-awaited new house at Ickworth – but for the fact that he remained unmarried. He did, however, employ Capability Brown to carry out work on the park and garden, in preparation for what was to come.

On his death in 1775 the 2nd Earl was succeeded for a brief period by his next brother Augustus, Vice-Admiral of the Blue, whose great portrait by Gainsborough still hangs in the drawing room at Ickworth. The Admiral's memoirs of his life as a naval captain, recalling warlike adventures afloat and amorous adventures ashore, are almost as entertaining as his father's, but his chief claim to fame was as husband of the notorious Elizabeth Chudleigh, who afterwards contracted a bigamous alliance with the Duke of Kingston – involving him in one of the most famous scandals of the eighteenth century.

In 1779 Lord Hervey's third and most remarkable son, Frederick Augustus, Bishop of Derry, finally succeeded as 4th Earl of Bristol. The inheritor of his father's intelligence and wit, and his mother's cosmopolitan charm, the Earl-Bishop (as he was soon known) was already a rich man. Thanks to his eldest brother's influence as Lord Lieutenant of Ireland, he had obtained first the Bishopric of Cloyne and subsequently (in 1768, when he was only thirty-eight) that of Derry. By clever management he increased the income from this see to £20,000 a year, leasing Church lands to his own trustees, and pocketing the fines payable by tenants on the renewal of sub-leases. These procedures were considered neither unusual nor dishonest at the time, and indeed the Bishop's notable enthusiasm for diocesan reforms and Irish nationalism – and his assistance of Roman Catholics and Presbyterians alike – earned him enormous popularity in the early years of Grattan's campaign for an independent Irish parliament.

The high point of this acclaim was reached in 1783 when he arrived in Dublin for the Convention at the head of the Volunteer Corps, whose cannon were said to be engraved, 'O Lord open thou our lips and our mouth shall show forth thy praise'. However, the Earl-Bishop's mercurial temperament did not in the end fit him to play a serious political role in Ireland, as the more statesmanlike Lord Charlemont had foreseen. Indeed, even his ecclesiastical duties seemed to many to be undertaken in an incurably frivolous manner: on one famous occasion he organized a curates' race along the sands at Downhill, the winners to be rewarded with benefices then vacant in his diocese. His passion for travelling and collecting works of art also led to more and more prolonged absences from Ireland, and he soon became a well-known figure bowling

along the roads of Germany and Italy in his great coach, causing Hotels Bristol to be called after him in towns all over the Continent.

Two of the Bishop's consuming interests, geology and architecture, were combined at Downhill, the vast mansion which he began about 1775 on the wild north coast of County Londonderry, only a short distance from that most famous of natural phenomena, the Giant's Causeway. A Cork architect, Michael Shanahan, was responsible for carrying out the building, possibly to initial designs by James Wyatt or Charles Cameron, later to become famous in the service of Catherine the Great. As usual with his houses, the Bishop's practice of taking up and dropping architects with equal rapidity makes it difficult to disentangle the origins of their design. But it must have been his own predilection for 'sublime' scenery that led to the choice of this exposed cliff-side site, and to the way that the house (now reduced to a shell) hugs the contours of the hill, with great semicircular bastions, castellated to resemble an ancient castle, projecting at the back towards the ocean.

Even more important for the future was the Mussenden Temple (called after his *chère cousine*, Frideswide Bruce, married to Daniel Mussenden), which Shanahan built in 1783–5 on the model of the circular Temple of Vesta at Tivoli. Perched spectacularly on the very edge of the cliffs, with the roar of the Atlantic rollers breaking on the rocks below, this was equipped as a library, and the inscription from Lucretius carved round the frieze reads '*Suave, mari magno turbantibus . . .*', 'Sweet it is, when on the high seas the winds are lashing the waters, to gaze from the land on another's struggles'. The trouble was that 'on occasions', as an early visitor recorded, 'the wind on the plateau was so strong that servants could get back to the house only on their hands and knees'.

From an early date the Bishop seems to have developed a passion for circular and oval buildings, perhaps encouraged by Burke's *dicta* on the subject, and he was soon in a position to indulge this curious taste to the full, for his brother's death in 1779 doubled his income to about £40,000 a year. At this time he had just met the young John Soane in Rome, and on their trip to Naples in 1779 Soane is recorded as designing for the Earl-Bishop both a 'doghouse' in the form of a rotunda with curving wings, and an oval dining room for Downhill. These unusual ideas may perhaps have stemmed from their mutual admiration for Piranesi, known to have been experimenting with similar ideas, and to have been particularly inspired by the oval form of the Colosseum. Soane returned to Ireland with his patron in 1780, but in the following year (when the Bishop contributed 50 guineas to the building of the oval First Presbyterian church in Belfast, designed by Roger Mulholland) they quarrelled, and any thought there may have been of building a new house to Soane's designs was forgotten.

In the winter of 1781–2 the Earl-Bishop stayed at Ickworth for the first time since inheriting his ancestral estates. He evidently considered his grandfather's long-delayed schemes for rebuilding quite seriously, despite what he considered the unsuitability of the flat

A lithograph of Ballyscullion, the Earl-Bishop's Irish house, which was the prototype of Ickworth, although on a much smaller scale.

Suffolk landscape for 'sublime' architecture. 'A thousand thanks to you, my dear friend, for your recollection of me', he was to write to the agriculturalist, Arthur Young, 'but no thanks at all to you for wishing me back to the foggy, ferney atmosphere of Ickworth, in preference to the exhilarating and invigorating air, or rather ether, of the Downhill.' Nevertheless he received two visits from Capability Brown at this time, on the second of which Brown brought 'Plans and Elevations for an Intire New House'. The reason that nothing immediately came of these plans may have been the Bishop's final separation from his long-suffering wife, said to have taken place after a bitter exchange in their coach while driving through Ickworth park. The Countess thereafter lived a retired and melancholy existence at Ickworth Lodge, while her husband returned with renewed zest to his European travels and to building operations in Ireland.

The next house to be built there was Ballyscullion,

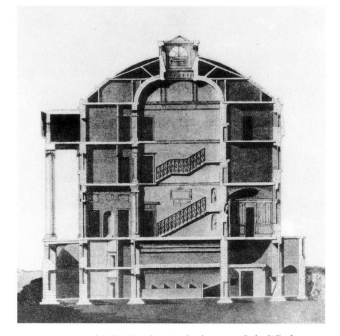

A cross section of Belle Isle, the circular house on Lake Windermere, which was the inspiration for Ballyscullion, in Ireland.

begun in 1787 on the shores of Lough Beg, and of interest as being the prototype of Ickworth. The design, probably again by Shanahan, although this time carried out by a pair of brothers called Francis and Joseph Sandys, was inspired by a circular house that the Bishop had seen on an island in Lake Windermere – John Plaw's Belle Isle, built in 1775. Like Belle Isle, Ballyscullion had a domed rotunda with a pedimented portico projecting from it on the entrance side: the significant differences were the oval shape of the rotunda and its continuous giant order round the outside (based on the Colosseum), the high pitch of the dome, terminating in a circular balustrade rather than a lantern (like the Pantheon), and the long curving corridors, never actually executed, but intended to lead to galleries for German and Italian pictures respectively. All of these features were to recur later at Ickworth, though on a far larger scale: a façade of 600 feet as against 350 feet at Ballyscullion. The rotunda at Ballyscullion was roofed and furnished, but the Bishop lost interest in it and the house was never completed; it was dismantled in 1813 and only the portico now survives, removed to the façade of a church in Belfast.

In 1792, after an absence of ten years, the Bishop visited Ickworth again, and it was during this stay (in fact to prove his last) that he determined to embark on the grandiose building scheme which was begun three years later in 1795 and was ended abruptly by his death in Italy in 1803. The site chosen may well have been that suggested by Capability Brown ten years earlier – on a slight rise in the park, halfway between Ickworth Lodge and the church, and with wide views to the south. As his executant architect the Bishop employed Francis Sandys, who had already worked for him at Ballyscullion and whose brother, the Rev. Joseph Sandys, acted as a kind of clerk of the works both there and at Ickworth. Francis Sandys was almost certainly the 'young student of Ireland' present at a dinner party in Rome in November 1794, at which the Bishop met C. H. Tatham, protégé of Henry Holland, then studying in Rome. 'To my great surprise', wrote Tatham, 'he commissioned me to make him a

Ickworth

1 Hall
2 Dining-room
3 Library
4 Drawing-room
5 Pompeian room

NORTH

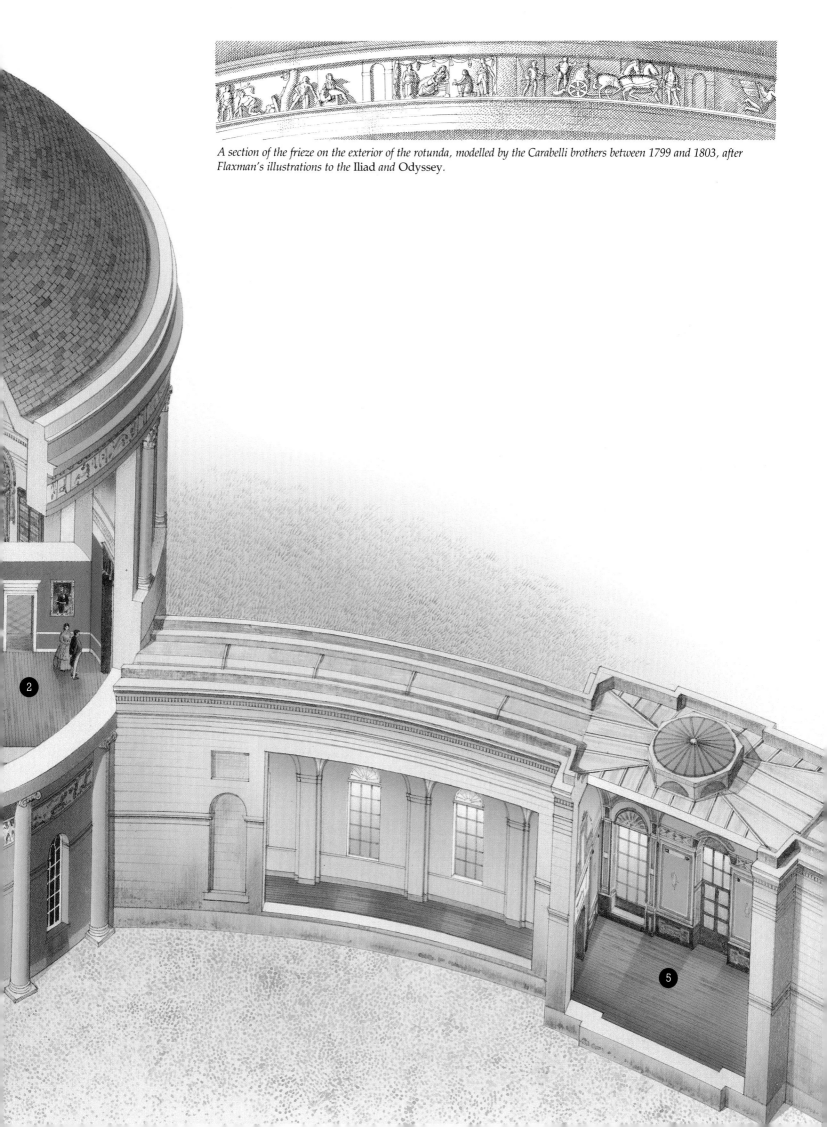

A section of the frieze on the exterior of the rotunda, modelled by the Carabelli brothers between 1799 and 1803, after Flaxman's illustrations to the Iliad *and* Odyssey.

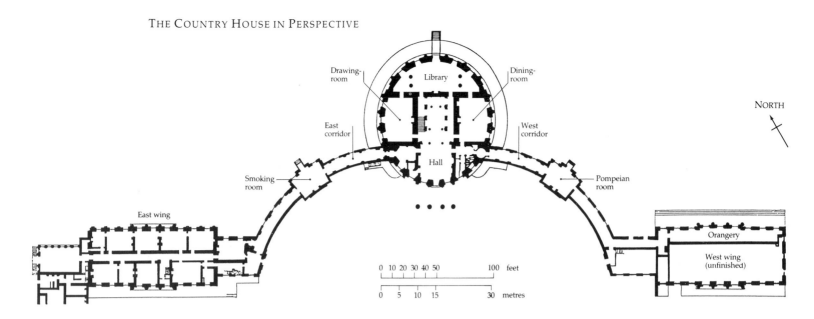

NORTH

Drawing-room

Library

Dining-room

East corridor

West corridor

Hall

Smoking room

Pompeian room

East wing

Orangery

West wing (unfinished)

0 10 20 30 40 50   100 feet

0   5   10   15   30 metres

design for a villa to be built in Suffolk, extending nearly 500 feet including offices . . . the house being oval, according to his desire.' Poor Tatham's period of favour was, however, to be as brief and as unproductive as Soane's had been. From the existence of two drawings of elevations close to the final model of the house, and from the evidence of several contemporary accounts, the Bishop's final choice of architect now seems certain to have been an Italian, Mario Asprucci the younger, with whom Tatham was then studying.

Asprucci, the son of the curator of the Borghese collections, was also the architect of numerous buildings in the grounds of the Villa Borghese and an influential figure among the Neo-Classical artists and designers then gathered in Rome. Of his two surviving designs related to Ickworth, that in the Cooper-Hewitt Museum in New York appears to be a preliminary scheme, made in 1794 or early in 1795, with a two-storey portico and a shallower dome to the rotunda than was finally adopted, but with east and west wings significantly identical to those shown in Francis Sandys' engraving of the house, made in September 1795. In the other drawing, now at Chatsworth (perhaps given by the Bishop to his daughter Elizabeth, who later became Duchess of Devonshire), the dome, rotunda, portico (not yet pedimented) and curving corridors are exactly paralleled in Sandys' engraving.

If Mario Asprucci can now be confidently accepted as the originator of the design of Ickworth, the contributions of the Sandys brothers and of the Earl-Bishop himself must not be under-rated. Asprucci certainly never came to England, and in execution his designs were modified in several important respects: the lavish sculptural embellishment he suggested was confined to the rotunda and not continued round the curving corridors and wings, the portico was reduced in size and given a pediment as at Ballyscullion, and, most important of all, the curving corridors were made to join the rotunda farther north, rather than in the centre – a concession to the English climate, which at the same time somewhat reduced the impact of the whole composition. All these changes can be seen in the model, now in the Pompeian Room at Ickworth, which the Sandys brothers constructed in 1796, presumably to send to the Bishop in Italy for his approval.

The Earl-Bishop's own interest in the architectural details of his new house can be judged by his voluminous

correspondence on the subject. In September 1795, for instance, he writes about the two great friezes on the rotunda: 'My only difficulty now is how to get the basso-rilievos executed. The upper ones must certainly be painted as Dear Canova suggested, being beyond the reach of the eye's accuracy, but the lower ones must be bold and I suppose in gesso. . . . As the extent of our basso-rilievos is immense we must blend Oeconomy with our Magnificence or we shall wreck the Vessel.' In the event, the lower and most of the upper reliefs were carried out in terracotta between 1799 and 1803 by two brothers, Casimiro and Donato Carabelli, recorded earlier as making statues for the west front of Milan Cathedral. They were modelled on Flaxman's famous illustrations to the *Iliad* and *Odyssey*, apart from the panels within the portico itself which are said to have been designed by the Bishop's eldest grand-daughter, Caroline, Lady Wharncliffe. The small section of the upper frieze not finished by the Carabellis at the time of the Bishop's death in 1803 was completed later by the Coade manufactory.

In March 1796, the Earl-Bishop expressed himself even more vehemently on the subject of materials for the building of the house, writing to his daughter, Lady Elizabeth Foster, 'You beg me on your knees that Ickworth may be built of white stone bricks – What! Child, build my house of a *brick* that looks like a sick, pale, jaundiced red brick, that would be red brick if it could, and to which I am certain our posterity would give a little rouge as essential to its health. . . . I shall follow dear impeccable old Palladio's rule, and as nothing ought to be without a covering in our raw damp climate, I shall cover the house, pillars and pilasters, with Palladio's *stucco* which has now lasted 270 years. It has succeeded perfectly well with me at Downhill on that temple of the winds. . . . It has resisted the frosts and rains of Vicenza – *c'est tout dire* – and deceives the most acute eye till within a foot.' Unfortunately this sanguine view of the durability of stucco in England was unjustified, and the exterior of Ickworth has given trouble ever since it was built. The family wing was re-faced in stone by Reginald Blomfield in 1909, but the rotunda and corridors are still of stucco, in constant need of renewal.

What were the Earl-Bishop's motives in building a palace on so large a scale? The ever-increasing size of his income must have been a major inducement; besides the

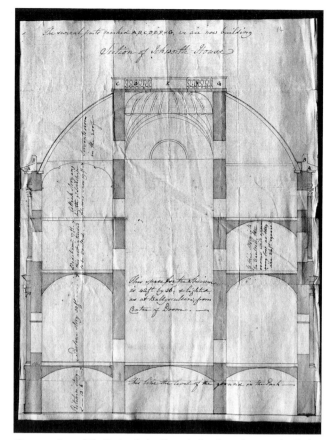

Cross-section of the Rotunda by Francis Sandys who was the Earl-Bishop's executant architect at Ickworth.

revenues from the bishopric of Derry, he enjoyed the rents of some 30,000 acres in England which, from the outbreak of war with France in 1793, yielded steadily rising profits. Dynastic ambition may also have played a part. In 1796, just as the foundations of Ickworth were being dug, he was in the middle of negotiations to marry his eldest surviving son to an illegitimate daughter of the King of Prussia who would, he claimed, 'bring into our family £5,000 a year, *besides* a principality in Germany, an English Dukedom for Frederick or me . . . a perpetual relationship with both the Princess of Wales and her children . . . the Embassy to Berlin, with such an influence and preponderance in favour of dear England as no other could withstand.' It may well have been with a view to entertaining royal relations that he conceived such a gigantic house; if so, he was (not for the first time) being over-optimistic: in 1798 Frederick married Elizabeth Upton, the Irish girl with whom he had for a long time been in love.

A far more compelling reason both for the size of the house and for its curious plan, however, was the Earl-Bishop's mania for collecting. His vision of a house, which has been aptly described as 'combining the uses of the National Gallery with those of the British Museum', is an early and fascinating example of the spirit which, in the Neo-Classical period, began to see the value of museums as educational institutions. This attitude is already clear in the Bishop's letter about Ickworth written in July 1796 to John Symonds, a Cambridge professor who lived at Bury and whom on other occasions he asked to settle a dispute between 'my young Hounds' – the Sandys brothers. 'I wish to unite magnificence with convenience and

simplicity with dignity – no redundancy – no superfluity – not one unnecessary room, but the necessary ones to be noble and convenient, to have few pictures but choice ones, and my galleries to exhibit an historical progress of the art of Painting both in Germany and Italy, and that divided into its characteristical schools – Venice, Bologna, Florence, etc.'

In another letter to Symonds, a few months later, he took this idea even further, writing: 'Galleries in general are both confused and uninstructive. Mine, by classing the authors under the different schools, will show the characteristick Excellence of each, instruct the young mind and edify the old.

Venice – Coloring, Titian
Bologna – Composition, Guido
Roman – Sentiment, Rafael
Florence – Drawings, M. Angelo
Naples – Extravagance, Salvator Rosa, Polimea . . .

I have been if possible more fortunate as well as more copious in the German than even the Italian School, having by means of the King of Prussia acquired masterpieces of Wohlgemuth, instructor of the Divine Homerican Albert Durer.'

In the next two years the Bishop feverishly collected works of art for Ickworth. His chief admiration was for the painters of the later Renaissance; but he must have been almost unique, in his period, in not neglecting the Primitives, of whom, even if he did not like them, he at least saw the historical interest – 'Cimabue, Giotto, Guido da Siena and all the old pedantry of painting that seemed to show the progress of art at its resurrection'. Among his other acquisitions he mentions 'large Mosaick pavements, sumptuous chimneypieces for my new house, and pictures, statues, busts, and marbles without end, first-rate Titians and Raphaels, dear Guidos and three old Carraccis – *gran Dio che tesoro*'.

Sadly, though, Ickworth was never to become the treasure house he had intended, for in 1798 the French invaded Italy and occupied Rome; the Bishop's collections (worth by his own account £20,000) were confiscated and he himself imprisoned in Milan for nine months. A petition asking for the restitution of all his goods, signed by 323 artists living in Rome, appears to have had no effect; no list seems ever to have been made of them, and their fate is unknown. The Bishop did not return to England after his release, to see the progress of his new house. Instead, he leased a house in Florence and continued to travel about Italy. It was on one of these journeys, on the road to Albano, that he died, in 1803, in the outhouse of a peasant who could not admit a heretic prelate into his cottage. By a final stroke of irony that would probably have delighted him, when his coffin was shipped back to the family vault at Ickworth it had to be disguised as the packing case for an antique statue, for the superstitious sailors refused to have a corpse on board.

It is possible that some of the sculptures and chimney-pieces now at Ickworth may have been bought by the Bishop in the last four years of his life, reaching England after his death. A large bill for storing 'certain chimney pieces, marbles etc. late belonging to the late Frederick,

The Earl-Bishop, with the Bay of Naples and the smoking cone of Vesuvius in the background, painted by Madame Vigée le Brun in 1790. The Earl-Bishop climbed the volcano every day during his visit.

Earl of Bristol' was paid by his son in 1812, when the items (unfortunately not specified) were brought to Suffolk. However, these must have included the chimney surrounds in the dining room, drawing room and library – all described as Italian when they were finally installed by the mason John Field in 1829. The most elaborate, in the library, has pairs of lovers framed in Doric 'tabernacles' either side of the fireplace: both are versions of famous Canova groups, respectively his Capitoline Eros and Psyche, and his Bacchus and Ariadne from Marbury Hall in Cheshire. But despite Canova's friendship with the Earl-Bishop, these are probably replicas by another Roman sculptor of the day, possibly a member of the Cardelli family. Other pieces of sculpture, acquired earlier on, include a bust of the Earl-Bishop carved by the Irish sculptor Christopher Hewetson in Rome about 1770, and the dead child reclining on a dolphin, now in the West Corridor. This was bought, again in Rome, about 1765, and highly prized by him as a work of Raphael – though it is almost certainly by Nollekens, after an original by the sculptor and 'antique restorer' Cavaceppi.

The most important single work of art at Ickworth

commissioned by the Earl-Bishop is undoubtedly Flaxman's colossal marble group entitled *The Fury of Athamas*, which stands in the very centre of the rotunda at the bottom of the main staircase. However, this was among the many items confiscated by Napoleon, and was only re-acquired by the 1st Marquess in Paris in the early 1820s – as an act of filial piety. The sculpture, carved in Rome in 1790 at a cost of £600, represents the scene from Ovid's *Metamorphoses* when Athamas, driven made by the gods, snatches his infant son Learchus from the arms of his mortal mother Ino and dashes out his brains upon a rock. There could hardly be a subject which better illustrates Burke's theory of the 'Sublime', with its heightened emotions, yet frozen Neo-Classical grace, and it seems perfectly at home here at the heart of the Earl-Bishop's own 'sublime' work of architecture, already decorated with friezes after Flaxman on the exterior.

At the time of the commission, the sculptor wrote to Sir William Hamilton that 'I shall be detained here three years longer by the noble patronage of Lord Bristol, who . . . has reanimated the fainting body of Art in Rome.' In fact the work took much longer, and caused Flaxman so much trouble that, after its completion, he complained of being seriously out of pocket. Lord Bristol was, however, delighted with the result, considering that 'it exceeded the Laocoön in expression' and was 'the finest work ever done in sculpture'.

Other mementoes of the Earl-Bishop's time in Italy include three portraits now hung in the drawing room: his own by Madame Vigée le Brun, painted at Naples in 1790; and those of his daughter, Lady Elizabeth Foster, and his daughter-in-law, Elizabeth Drummond, Lady Hervey, both painted by Angelica Kauffmann – the first in Naples in 1785, and the second in Florence three years later. More than any other likeness, the Vigée le Brun captures the Earl's affable and convivial character. Seated on a balcony overlooking the Bay of Naples, and with the smoking cone of Vesuvius in the background, he seems to be enjoying a joke with the spectator, while his rubicund complexion may be due to his daily exercise in climbing the volcano. As Sir Brinsley Ford has observed, its appearance here is particularly appropriate, for in addition to his interest in the 'Sublime' and the geological aspects of volcanoes, this energetic cleric 'caused eruptions wherever he went'.

The only other memorial to him at Ickworth, representing a more serious side to his character, is the great obelisk in the park, just visible from the south side of the house and rising above the trees of Lownde Wood. It was erected in 1817 by the People of Derry, and it is a testimony to Lord Bristol's immense popularity within his diocese that the subscribers included both the Roman Catholic bishop and the Nonconformist moderator. 'His great patronage', runs the inscription, 'was uniformly administered upon the purest, and most disinterested principles . . . and hostile sects which had long entertained feelings of deep animosity towards each other, were gradually softened and reconciled by his influence and example.' Would that such lessons could still be learned.

At the time of the Bishop's death, the rotunda at Ickworth had attained a considerable height (though it had only a temporary roof), but the walls of the wings, which were to have contained picture and sculpture galleries, were only a few feet above ground. Work was brought to an immediate halt by the 5th Earl while he disentangled his father's affairs, and it was almost twenty years before he felt able to resume. Francis Sandys had meanwhile developed an independent practice as an architect in Bury, designing the Assembly Rooms (now the Athenaeum) there in 1804, and Finborough Hall and Worlingham Hall, also in Suffolk. He moved to London in 1808 and was still exhibiting at the Royal Academy in the following year, although after that nothing is known of him. Since work on the completion of Ickworth did not gather momentum until at least 1824, it is unlikely that Sandys played any part in it. There are no payments to any other architect in the account books of the 5th Earl (who was created 1st Marquess of Bristol in 1826), but the most probable explanation is that he relied on local Bury craftsmen to make the necessary adjustments to Asprucci's and Sandys' original designs. The mason family of De Carle (who had built the obelisk)

were responsible for most of the stone and stucco-work, while William Hall, John Field and the carpenter John Trevethan were the other main contractors. Some idea of the scale of the operations is given by the fact that nine hundred thousand bricks were paid for in 1827. Two years later, in August 1829, the family at last moved into their 'magnificent new mansion at Ickworth'.

The 1st Marquess's most important decision had been to abandon his father's idea of picture and sculpture galleries in the wings, to adapt the east wing instead as the usual family residence (which it has remained ever since), and to furnish and decorate the great rooms in the rotunda principally for entertaining. The west wing and corridor were for the time being left unfinished. Despite these modifications, the cost was prodigious, and the Marquess was enabled to undertake it only by the increasing revenues from his large estates in the years before the repeal of the Corn Laws.

In 1803, when work on the house stopped, the hall was no more than an empty shell, while a temporary wooden spiral staircase behind it gave access to the first floor and roof. The Bishop's intentions for the staircase are not entirely clear, although the Sandys brothers' model shows an arrangement similar to that at Ballyscullion: two quite separate spiral flights concealed from each other (one for family and guests, the other for servants), but lit by the

One of a pair of eighteenth-century Portugese 'trumos' or combined pier-tables and glasses in the Drawing Room.

Painted decoration in the Pompeian Room, based on Roman wall-paintings discovered in 1777 at the Villa Negroni on the Esquiline.

F.C. Penrose's theatrical design for a new staircase in the centre of the Rotunda, which was never executed.

same skylight in the middle of the dome. Ten years before, in 1788, the Bishop had ordered drawings to be made of the staircase at Chambord, and this seems to have been the inspiration for the scheme.

The 1st Marquess completed the hall in 1827, installing a screen of Ionic scagliola columns imitating porphyry at the southern end, not unlike Wyatt's screen in the hall at Castle Coole. Beyond this lay a separate walled-off staircase only completed in 1832 and evidently very simple, with flights climbing round the four walls and enlivened by an elaborate cast-iron balustrade. A highly theatrical Neo-Baroque design for a new staircase made by the architect F. C. Penrose in 1888 came to nothing, but in 1909 a complete remodelling of the space was carried out for the 4th Marquess of Bristol by Reginald Blomfield, who replaced the dividing wall by a second pair of giant scagliola columns and pilasters – opening up a vista from the hall to Flaxman's *Fury of Athamas* in the staircase well – and built the present oak stairs, concealed by screens on each side. Though more 'Wrenaissance' than Neo-Classical in style, with its *oeils-de-boeuf* lighting the mezzanine landings, it was an ingenious solution to the problem of providing a grand staircase in such a high, but dark and confined, space.

The dining and drawing rooms on either side of the staircase were described in 1821 as being 'the only

apartments bounded by an interior wall'. Their decoration and furnishing were carried out by the 1st Marquess later in the same decade, but his father can take credit for their somewhat eccentric shape and their height – over 30 feet. The Earl-Bishop always claimed that his 'lungs played more freely' and his 'spirits spontaneously rose much higher, in lofty rooms than in low ones where the atmosphere is too much tainted with . . . our own bodies'.

The estimate for the dining room drawn up by the builder W. B. Hall in 1824 included the 'Cornice of the Ionic order from Minerva [i.e. the Temple of Minerva at Athens] with its proper enrichments', and the solid mahogany doors and window jambs. Here and in the drawing room, much of the equally solid rosewood and mahogany furniture was made by the firm of Banting, France & Co. of Pall Mall, who in the same decade supplied furniture for George IV at Windsor Castle. There are also more exotic Portuguese and Turinese pieces acquired by diplomats in the family including the 1st Marquess's son, Lord William Hervey, and French pieces probably bought through the dealer Baldock, whose acquisitions for Lord Hertford began to make 'Louis' furniture fashionable in the same period.

At a time when libraries had become the usual living rooms for large country houses, it is appropriate that the one at Ickworth should be the largest interior in the rotunda, with a central door leading out to the garden terrace on the south – in the best Reptonian fashion. The curve of the wall is more obvious here than in the other main rooms, since it is on the main axis of the oval. But the Marquess made a virtue of this by introducing screens of yellow scagliola columns at each end and by putting in a deep coved ceiling which somewhat reduced its enormous height.

As we have seen, Lord Bristol's main concern was to make the half-finished house at Ickworth habitable, and to this end the east wing was made into comfortable, self-contained living quarters for the family, which are still occupied by his descendants. The linking corridor between this wing and the rotunda widened out at its centre to form a smoking room, where male members of the family and guests would be permitted to indulge a habit still considered unsuitable for ladies to witness. The corresponding west wing was never finished, apart from a narrow conservatory along its southern façade, and still remains an empty shell. The corridor leading to it was also left incomplete until 1879, when the 3rd Marquess of Bristol employed the architect F. C. Penrose and the fashionable decorator John Diblee Crace to create a Pompeian Room at its centre, balancing the smoking room on the other side. The elaborate painted decoration here was conceived as a tribute to the Earl-Bishop by his great-grandson, for it was based on an antique source: the Roman wall paintings discovered in 1777 at the Villa Negroni on the Esquiline. Not only was the Bishop to acquire fragments of these frescoes, but the engravings of the complete series, carried out by Mengs and other leading artists of the day, were dedicated to him. For an Englishman who had 'reanimated the fainting body of Art in Rome', there could be no more fitting memorial.

Cragside

NORTHUMBERLAND

Imagine a great hill covered from bottom to crest with huge grey boulder stones, and half way up, cut out of a steppe on the hill side, the site and placing of a building of the most picturesque kind imaginable. Then having chosen the site and placed the house, call forth your gardeners by the hundreds, and bid them make amongst and around those crags and boulders cunningly-winding walks, every one formed of steps of the natural grey stone. . . . Form two artificial lakes in the valley near the house, so that you can defy suspicion of the manufacture. Make a carriage approach from opposite ends of the valley, so easy and pleasant that it might have been transplanted from Hyde Park; and, beside these, let there be rolling along the hill, at the heights above, carriage drives that for views and healthful breezes shall be immaculate. Along the valley let there be a brooklet teeming with fish, and covered and bordered with trees and rocks forming a veritable glen: span the stream by rustic and iron bridges, which form the centres of a score of perfect pictures.

LINES LIKE THESE could have been written by a late eighteenth-century disciple of the Picturesque, by Richard Payne Knight, or by Humphry Repton in one of his famous 'Red Books', proposing a new seat for an old landed family. So it is a surprise to find that they actually come from an article in *The British Architect* written by Raffles Davison as late as 1881, and that they describe Cragside, a house built not by a duke but by an industrialist – not on the proceeds of broad acres, but on those of engineering and the manufacture of armaments.

Influenced by Ruskin, we tend to think of the Industrial Revolution as a break with the past, the dawn of a prosaic age replacing the poetry of an idyllic, agrarian society. Yet to most of his contemporaries it conjured up a very different picture. There was a feeling of romance, even of magic, in the belching factory chimneys, the clanking wheels of machinery, the ships and trains that were helping to bring prosperity to the masses, while the lot of the peasantry grew worse in the years of agricultural depression and famine. Thus in the hall at Wallington, only a few miles away from Cragside, the painter William

Bell Scott's scenes from Northumbrian history end with a celebration of *Iron and Coal*, showing the young heir, Charles Trevelyan, wielding a hammer in a smoky Tyneside colliery – seen in the same romanticized light as *The Building of the Roman Wall*; *Bede's Death at Jarrow*; and *Grace Darling Rescuing the Men of the 'Forfarshire'*.

Cragside itself was built on the profits of Lord Armstrong's Elswick works, the biggest on the Tyne. To one contemporary the house represented 'the romance of science, of hard struggle with nature, of power and determination overcoming seemingly insuperable difficulties', while to another it was simply 'the palace of a modern magician'. The earliest house in the world to be lit by electricity derived from water power, it was full of other inventions that were to revolutionize domestic life in the next half-century. Yet, as we have seen, Cragside looked backwards to eighteenth-century ideas of the Picturesque as well as forward to twentieth-century ideas of the house as a 'machine for living'. Nor did it escape the high aestheticism of its own time. The mock-medieval inglenook in the dining room, the *japonaiserie* of the library, the grand French Renaissance of the drawing room, represent that nineteenth-century search for the best of the past still found in the 'period rooms' of our older museums. A synthesis of old and new, English and Continental, Oriental and Occidental, it exudes the self-confidence and optimism of Imperial expansion, and the character of the man who, more than almost any of his contemporaries, made that expansion possible.

William George Armstrong was born in Newcastle-upon-Tyne in 1810, the son of a corn-merchant who was also a distinguished mathematician and later alderman and mayor of the city. Although trained as a solicitor, the young Armstrong showed an increasing interest in mechanics, particularly after 1835 when, during a fishing expedition on the Craven, he observed the inefficiency of an overshot water wheel and began to turn his mind to the study of hydraulics. From then on, his family found that 'William had water on the brain'. Working in collaboration

The west front of Cragside, 'cut out of a steppe on the hill side, the site and placing of a building of the most picturesque kind imaginable.'

with Henry Watson, contractor for the new High Level Bridge in Newcastle, he soon evolved a hydro-electric machine which generated electricity from effluent steam, and which earned him his fellowship of the Royal Society while he was still a solicitor. In 1845 he had his first practical success when he master-minded a new water company to supply the city – a foretaste of the dams, reservoirs and pumps he was later to create at Cragside – and, with the resulting pressure, invented the world's first efficient hydraulic crane for the Newcastle Docks, 'making a column of water lift a hundred tons'.

In 1847, having for fifteen years 'swung like an erratic pendulum between the Law office and the Lathe', Armstrong decided to turn manufacturer: he set up the Elswick works initially to produce hydraulic machinery, though later it branched out to build bridges and even locomotives. However, it was the Crimean War which transformed the company into a vast industrial concern. As an early biographer put it, 'difficulty was experienced at the battle of Inkerman in bringing up heavy artillery . . . within a month Armstrong had solved the problem, convincing the War Secretary, and commenced making a light gun . . . its success was conclusive and a fortune was at his feet. He gave the fruit of his genius to his country without fee or consideration, and was knighted in return'. Armstrong's new guns were not simply lighter than their predecessors: they were breech- rather than muzzle-loaded, fired shells rather than balls, and had rifled instead of smooth barrels. They were also constructed of

coiled and welded steel rather than cast iron.

From 1859 onwards the firm dealt primarily with armaments, as its successor, Vickers Armstrong, continues to do today. It also combined with the shipbuilders, Charles Mitchell, to develop naval artillery and to make some of the world's first ironclad warships. By 1887, when its founder was raised to the peerage, Armstrong's was one of the two biggest manufacturers of arms in the world, with only Krupp's of Germany as a rival. A succession of presidents, prime ministers and crowned heads thus descended, first on Jesmond Dene, the Armstrongs' Newcastle house, and then (after that house was given to the city in 1884) on Cragside, to pay their compliments to the man who remained chief partner until his death in 1900 – and to present their orders.

Many Victorian industrialists, having made their pile in Birmingham, Manchester or Leeds, were anxious to forget their origins and to set up as country gentlemen, acquiring an estate and building a seat in a suitably 'antique' style, where their descendants could live free from the stigma of trade. But Lord Armstrong was motivated by no such thoughts in building Cragside. Straightforward and unpretentious as always, he initially intended it simply to be a small lodge for fishing and shooting holidays. Only later did its enlargement and improvement become a consuming hobby, and even then its character was to remain that of a large villa surrounded by pleasure grounds, rather than a proper country house at the centre of a landed estate.

The site itself, acquired in 1863, could hardly have been less promising: a bleak stretch of moorland strewn with boulders, looking from early photographs almost like a lunar landscape, on the upper part of the Debdon Burn (a tributary of the Coquet), above the dour little market town of Rothbury. But there were childhood memories which gave it a particular attraction. 'I believe I first came to Rothbury as a baby in arms', Armstrong later recalled, 'and my earliest recollections consist of paddling in the Coquet, gathering pebbles from its gravel beds, and climbing amongst the rocks on the Crag. For many years I annually visited Rothbury with my parents, and under well-known local celebrities I learned to fish. The Coquet then became to me a river of pleasure. As I grew up I extended my explorations of it from its mouth to its source, and acquired an admiration for its scenery which has been a source of enjoyment to me through all my life . . . moreover, as a boy, my health was very delicate, and more than once an apparently incurable cough was quickly removed by coming to Rothbury, and had it not been for its curative effect there would have been no Cragside nor any Lord Armstrong. My annual visits were continued with rare exceptions up to the time of my abandoning the profession of the law and commencing my present business, the exigencies of which for the first fifteen years prevented my taking any holiday whatever. After that interval [in 1863] I again visited my haunts and decided to build for myself a small house in the neighbourhood for occasional visits in the summer time. I well knew the site upon which Cragside now stands, and by good fortune I was able to purchase it, together with a few acres of adjoining land'.

The first Cragside was a modest two-storey lodge in rock-faced stone, which still exists almost buried by later extensions and alterations at the centre of the present house. Its designer is not known, and in any case it had few architectural pretensions. As a contemporary writer put it, 'there is little to be said of the original building erected at Cragside. In fact, both whilst it was building, and afterwards, when its owners had entered upon its occupation, more attention was devoted to covering the bare hill sides with foliage than to building anything great

The original lodge built by Sir William Armstrong in 1864–66.

in the shape of the house.' Between this date and his death in 1900, Armstrong's original 20 acres grew by systematic purchases to over 1700 of pleasure ground and a further 76 of water – while in the same period he made 31 miles of carriage drives and walks and planted in the region of seven million trees, giving employment to a large proportion of the male population of Rothbury. On the higher slopes the planting consisted mainly of conifers, but lower down shrubs predominated, with 'the finest and rarest of Alpine plants, saxifrages, and stonecrops, heather, heath and ferns'.

Besides this intensive landscaping work, Armstrong began from the start to introduce the latest in hydraulic technology. After the water shortage which occurred when the Debdon Burn dried up in 1865, he dammed the stream to form Tumbleton Lake; below it he installed a ram which pumped water up to the house, supplied the gardens and even rotated the pots in his extensive glasshouses at Knocklaw. A few years later Debdon Lake was created higher up the stream, with a turbine running a sawmill and providing electricity to the house, and later still an aqueduct was constructed from the Black Burn high above and to the east of the house so as to form the two Nelly's Moss Lakes, connected to a new power house at Burnfoot.

In 1869 it was announced that the Northumberland Central Railway was to be extended to Rothbury, and this was probably the decisive factor in persuading Armstrong to enlarge the house. Less and less concerned with the day-to-day management of the business in Newcastle, he could afford to spend more time on his scientific experiments – so often to be combined with his domestic comforts. But in order to entertain friends and clients he obviously needed far more bedroom accommodation and far larger reception rooms than the little lodge with its steep gables, fretted bargeboards and pantiled roofs could offer. Richard Norman Shaw (1831–1912), the architect he chose for this task, could hardly have been better equipped to read his mind and to produce a building that matched his aspirations. Born in Edinburgh, and first apprenticed to William Burn – purveyor of 'Tudorbethan' and 'Scottish Baronial' piles to the Tory aristocracy – Shaw had later worked in the offices of Anthony Salvin and G. E. Street before setting up in partnership with Salvin's nephew, William Eden Nesfield. The two young architects had learned much of their craft through sketching tours all over Britain and the Continent, developing an interest in the painterly qualities of architecture more than the rulebook Gothic Revival.

Armstrong probably came to know Shaw through the painter J. C. Horsley, a brother-in-law of Isambard Kingdom Brunel, and nicknamed 'Clothes Horsley' for his vociferous disapproval of naked figures. Following Brunel's death in 1859, Armstrong had helped support the great engineer's son, Henry. At the same time he was becoming interested in contemporary English painters, hanging their work in the Banqueting Hall at Jesmond, designed for him by the Newcastle architect John Dobson.

Norman Shaw was first commissioned to enlarge this room so as to house a huge new picture by Horsley,

One of the perspective drawings for raising the central tower, which Shaw exhibited at the Royal Academy in 1872.

having already worked for the artist and for the marine painter E. W. Cooke, another of Armstrong's friends. Both of their houses, Willesley in Kent (of 1864–5) and Glen Andred in Sussex (of 1868–9), had been designed in the 'Old English' style, which Shaw and Nesfield had virtually invented. A reaction against the hard 'Modern Gothic' then favoured by most country-house architects, hardly distinguishable from the town halls and railway stations of the time, 'Old English' represented a return to the Picturesque tradition, taking its key from vernacular rather than high-style buildings of the past, and preferring eclecticism to scholarship. Leys Wood in Kent, which Shaw also designed in 1868 for J. W. Temple, a partner in his brother's Shaw Savill shipping line, repeated the pattern on a much larger scale and still more clearly anticipated the new Cragside.

Instead of the standard formula of a high main block joined to a lower servants' wing, and with formal gardens and terraces round it, both houses followed the contours of their rocky sites and were conceived as a cluster of different elements and roofs of different heights around a courtyard. In Mark Girouard's words, 'leaded lights and plate glass, large windows and small ones under the eaves, high rooms and low rooms, were skilfully mixed up together . . . with Gothic arches, Tudor windows, seventeenth-century chimneystacks, half-timbering and tile-hanging artistically sprinkled with panels of sunflowers and other aesthetic trimmings'. The result was not the imitation of a particular style, but the creation of an atmosphere – which contemporaries were quick to characterize as 'quaint': so successful was this idiom that its effects are still with us in the half-timbered gables of semi-detached houses and the inglenooks of pretentious pubs all over England. The very word 'quaint' has become debased, and it is hard for us to grasp the real charm it once represented, and to understand what a breath of fresh air Shaw and Nesfield (and their contemporary George Devey) blew through the pompous portals of mid-Victorian architecture.

There were, of course, particular reasons why Shaw's

brand of 'Old English' was so well adapted to Cragside. To begin with, the crazy site of the house, burrowing into the hillside on the east (with the aid of explosives) and projecting out above the ravine on the west (with the aid of massive piles), necessitated constant changes of level and a veritable warren of passages, corridors and staircases within. Then there was Lord Armstrong's restless addition of one wing after another, from 1870 right up to the 1890s. Built with little in the way of an overall plan, these contribute to the rambling nature of the building and help to suggest the organic development of earlier houses, added to by several different generations. Yet at the same time it is a measure of Shaw's genius that, despite a few compositional weaknesses (especially on the north), the building reads as coherently as it does.

To some extent this is due to his masterly sense of balance and picturesque grouping: on the south side for instance, the long drawn-out horizontal of the picture gallery range is matched by the soaring verticals of the chimneys and the two flanking towers; while the large expanse of blank stone wall is relieved by the fussy half-timbering of gables and 'hutches' above, originally left silvery-grey rather than being stained black. The fact that half-timbering is virtually unknown in Northumberland shows that Shaw never worried unduly about the authenticity of his vernacular details: as Mark Girouard has put it, he simply 'reached out for it like an artist reaching out for a tube of colour'.

To see exactly how the paintbrush was applied, and to follow the way the final composition gradually emerged, it is worth starting in the small, low-ceilinged rooms of the original lodge and then exploring Shaw's additional wings in turn. The least changed of the early interiors are the Japanese Room, originally Sir William Armstrong's 'Business Room', the Study, which was his wife's sitting-room, and the Boudoir immediately above, which served as a first-floor drawing room. All three enjoyed spectacular views south-west over the Debdon Burn towards Rothbury, now largely obscured by the growth of the huge conifers in the glen below. The Study and Boudoir both had projecting bay windows, moulded plasterwork ceilings (the latter coved and compartmented in a vaguely Italianate fashion), and heavy mid-Victorian chimneypieces: the one in an unusual combination of scagliola on slate, and the other of red Italian marble. The only evidence of the Armstrongs' artistic sensibilities at this date were the flock wallpapers supplied by the London firm of Cowtan and Sons (the successors of J. G. Crace) in 1866. These were overpainted in white in the early twentieth century, but fragments with the original colours were found behind radiators during the National Trust's restoration of the house in the 1970s, and it was then possible to reprint them using the firm's contemporary wood-blocks. At the same time partly used rolls of William Morris papers, one dated 1864, were found in the attics, and copies of these were made (again from original blocks) for the Yellow and White Bedrooms adjoining the Boudoir.

On his first visit to Cragside in October 1869, Norman Shaw is said to have stayed behind while the rest of the

Cragside

1 Staircase (and entrance hall below)
2 Gallery
3 Watercolour gallery
4 Tower room (Gilnockie tower above)
5 Drawing-room
6 Billiard room
7 Gun room

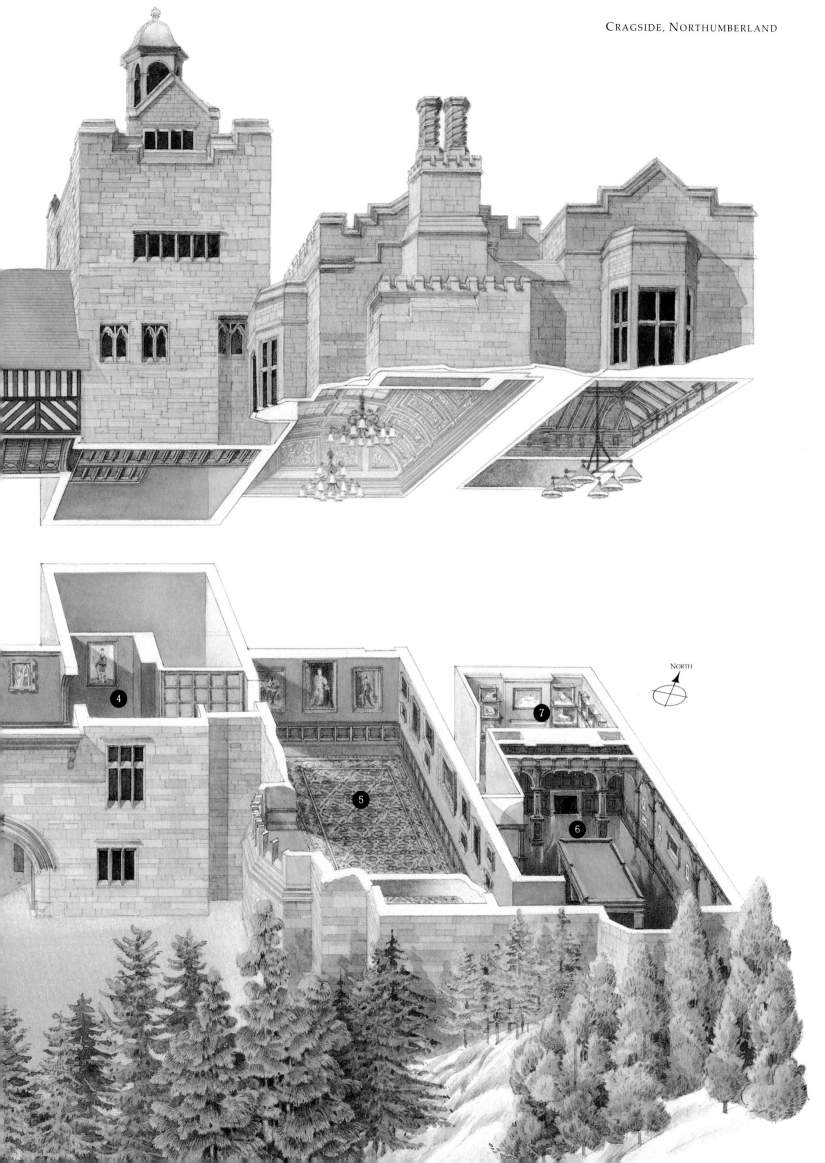

NORTH

4

5

6

7

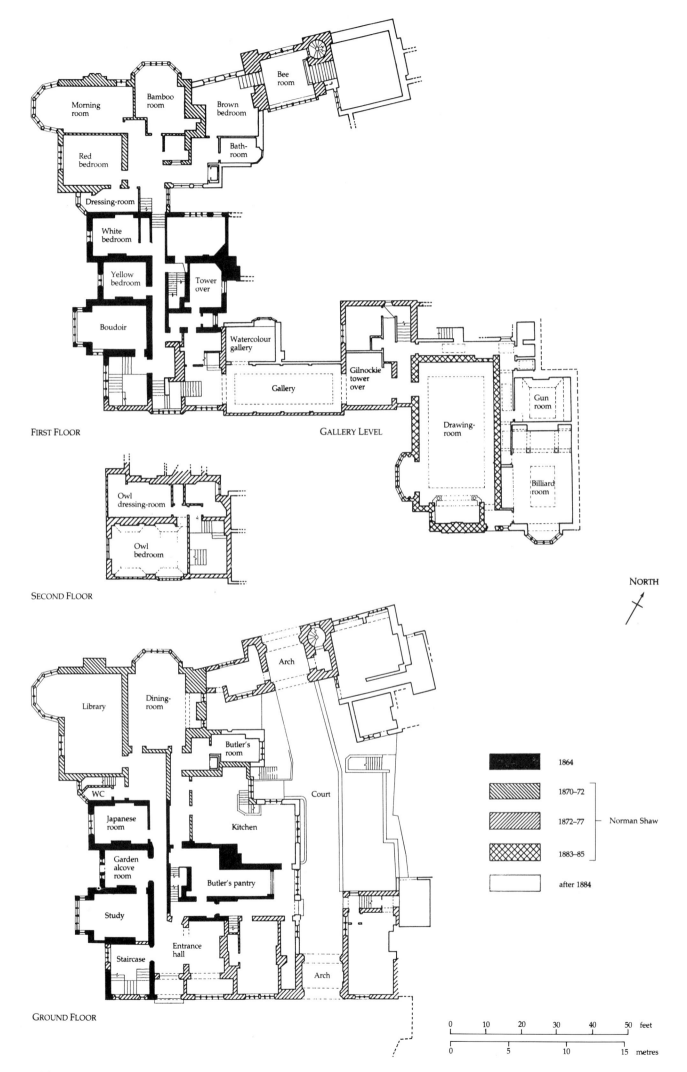

FIRST FLOOR

GALLERY LEVEL

Morning room

Bamboo room

Brown bedroom

Bee room

Red bedroom

Bath-room

Dressing-room

White bedroom

Yellow bedroom

Tower over

Boudoir

Watercolour gallery

Gilnockie tower over

Gallery

Gun room

Drawing-room

Billiard room

SECOND FLOOR

Owl dressing-room

Owl bedroom

NORTH

GROUND FLOOR

Library

Dining-room

Arch

Butler's room

WC

Court

Japanese room

Kitchen

Garden alcove room

Butler's pantry

Study

Entrance hall

Staircase

Arch

	1864
	1870–72
	1872–77	Norman Shaw
	1883–85
	after 1884

0   10   20   30   40   50 feet

0   5   10   15 metres

weekend guests went out shooting, and to have drawn up a complete scheme for the enlargement of the house by the time they returned. No such drawing survives, but it is certainly possible that he visualized extensions to the north and east of the original lodge at this early date – already having the broad outlines of the finished building in his mind's eye. On the other hand, Armstrong's immediate concern was simply to provide a more substantial dining room and library on the north, with extra bedrooms above, and it was this addition which occupied the builders for the first two years.

On the outside, this new wing was to be on an altogether bigger scale than the old lodge, with smooth ashlar facing instead of the latter's self-conscious rock-faced blocks, and large mullion-and-transom windows, culminating in a huge five-sided bay window at the north-west corner. Due to the steep descent of the cliff face, the building had to be supported by an extra basement storey at this corner; Shaw made a virtue of this by providing hot-air, plunge and shower baths, together with a cooling and dressing room, below the library. At ground-floor level the gloomy, unlit passage forming the central spine of the old lodge was improved by opening up a large arch through to the central vestibule, now known as the Garden Alcove Room, and Shaw also added a colourful dado of majolica tiles here and in the corridor, with wallpaper above. At its northern end the passage broadens out into an inner hall, with the new dining room straight ahead and the library to the left, a processional route that was to be almost doubled by the 1880s.

The dining room is a wonderfully untouched example of Shaw's 'Old English' manner, using Gothic, Renaissance and Pre-Raphaelite details yet achieving a unity and a rugged character that is wholly of its own time. Lit by a broad bay window on the north, and with tawny oak panelling and ceiling beams, it is dominated by the huge stone inglenook fireplace on the east. A picturesque feature of yeoman homesteads in the sixteenth century and earlier, the inglenook had originally been designed to trap heat in at least a corner of an inefficiently insulated room at the expense of the rest – and it had disappeared when better-fitting joinery and windows helped to warm the whole room. By the time Shaw and Nesfield revived the form at Willesley, Glen Andred and Farnham Park, their clients could afford to keep the heat of a fire in the inglenook and warm the rest by central heating. The inglenook was thus employed purely for its associations: it spelt the hospitality and good cheer of the 'olden tyme', when mead was quaffed, yarns were spun, and pages and damosels trysted.

The idea of the broad Gothic arch with its heavy stone apron beneath comes from the medieval kitchen at Fountains Abbey, which Shaw had sketched in 1861, but the decorative elements, including the pierced frieze carved with dogs hunting among the foliage, are entirely his own invention. The massive stone lintel over the fireplace itself is inscribed with the suitably homespun North Country proverb 'East or West Hame's Best'; the corbels that support it are appropriately carved with cocks on one side and wolves on the other. The andirons

Sir William Armstrong, painted by H.H. Emmerson, sitting in the huge stone inglenook that dominates the dining room.

with their embossed brass discs are again symbolic rather than practical, for instead of supporting huge logs they stand in front of a grate always intended to burn coal. Dated 1872, they were probably designed by Shaw himself, together with the two oak settles within the alcove, decorated with circular 'pies', as he and Nesfield christened them – a favourite form of the Aesthetic Movement, based on the sun-and-petal ornaments found in Oriental porcelain and prints. H. H. Emmerson's charming portrait of Lord Armstrong shows him sitting in the inglenook, reading the newspaper and with his two dogs at his feet. Blue and white pots are arranged on the mantelpiece and on the shelf behind him, the firelight picks out the polychrome tiles within the hearth, and stained-glass figures from William Morris's studio cast a rich glow in the background. Sentimental but down-to-earth, high-minded but plain-speaking, the great inventor seems at one with his surroundings – as if his material gains (he is no doubt engrossed in the stock-market reports) have earned him a spiritual reward.

Emmerson's other pictures in the room, including portraits of a sheepdog named 'Silky' (otherwise entitled *Waiting for Orders*), and two short-horn calves, add to the sober, masculine character of the room. A large sideboard is built into the panelling at the southern end of the room, conveniently placed between the doors to the kitchen passage and the inner hall, and there are shelves above it to display more porcelain, or (on special occasions) an old-fashioned buffet display of gold and silver plate. Round the rest of the room the panelling is only chest-height, with intricate reliefs of flora and fauna carved by James Forsyth, one of Shaw's favourite craftsmen, in the top panels, and a Cowtan wallpaper in two shades of green hung on the walls above. The furniture includes an

The library, designed by Norman Shaw, was the first room in the world to be lit by electricity produced from water-power.

expanding 'Capstan' dining table, whose ingenuity must have appealed to Armstrong the engineer. This too may have been made by Forsyth, though it is similar to an earlier patented design by Robert Jupe.

In many of Norman Shaw's later houses, built from scratch, he revived the idea of the great hall as the main living room, placed at the centre of a hub of staircases, galleries, corridors and vestibules, with as many entrances and exits as the set for a West End farce. But at Cragside, where he had to incorporate the old lodge at the centre of the house, the library was always intended to be the everyday living room – as it might have been way back in the Regency period. Generally more delicate and 'aesthetic' in treatment than the neighbouring dining

room, its dominant feature (the answer to the latter's inglenook) is nevertheless a huge five-sided bay window built out over the rock face above the Debdon Burn, and reminiscent of the great oriel lighting the dais end of a fifteenth- or sixteenth-century hall or great chamber. The resemblance is made more striking by the stained glass in the upper lights, showing episodes in the life of St George, made by Morris and Co. after some earlier designs by Rossetti.

Otherwise the room is an extraordinary mixture of different elements. The panelled oak ceiling is in a vaguely Italian Renaissance style, though with elaborate Gothic bosses carved by Forsyth. On the other hand, the compartments of the frieze are painted with delicate

without being prosaic, opulent without being vulgar, crammed with furniture and works of art without ever seeming incoherent. Perhaps the only visible sign of tycoonery is the magnificent glass and ormolu cigar casket on the table in the bay window, shaped like a giant corded bale of tobacco and supported by bronze figures representing Havana, Maryland, Virginia and Brazil.

The bookcases here were deliberately kept low so that some of Sir William's finest pictures, including Albert Moore's *Follow My Leader*, could be hung above the high dado. Raphael Sorbi's *A Girl with Doves*, dated 1866 and hanging between the windows, is one of the few survivors, but the majority – among them Millais's *Jephtha* and *Chill October*, a Turner seascape, O'Neil's *Death of Rafaelle* and Bonheur's *Forest of Fontainebleau* – were sold in 1910 following some unwise speculations by his great-nephew and heir. Their places have been taken by some notable Pre-Raphaelite pictures lent by the William de Morgan Foundation, including many by de Morgan's wife Evelyn and her uncle, John Roddam Spencer-Stanhope. More 'aesthetic' and highly charged than their predecessors – recalling the 'greenery yallery, Grosvenor Gallery' school satirized in Gilbert and Sullivan's *Patience* – they nevertheless seem at home in Shaw's 'Old English' interiors.

It would be easy to leave the library without noticing the most remarkable objects in it: four large *cloisonné* enamel vases placed on the bookcases. These first functioned as oil lamps, but in 1880 were connected to Armstrong's electric generator in the grounds and supplied with the incandescent light bulbs newly invented by his friend Joseph Swan of Newcastle. These bulbs were concealed by globes of clouded glass, and each vase had a bowl of mercury at its base; the current then passed up a wire in the centre and back through the copper sides of the vase itself. 'Thus', as Sir William wrote to the editor of *The Engineer*, 'the lamp may be extinguished and relighted at pleasure merely by removing the vase from its seat or setting it down again.' With four more bulbs hanging in one large globe in the bay window (replaced by a more ornate electrolier in the 1890s), the library at Cragside was the first room in the world with a permanent system of electric lighting powered by water: a development almost as momentous as the hydraulic cranes, the five-pounder guns and the ironclads produced at the Elswick works.

Above the library and dining room, Shaw's northern extension also contained two floors of bedrooms, off large landings corresponding with the Inner Hall below – and equipped with electric 'dressing gongs', operated from the butler's pantry, to warn guests of approaching mealtimes. But these rooms were still not enough for the numbers the Armstrongs needed to entertain and in 1872 Shaw went on to add an extra storey to the old lodge, enlarging and heightening the tower behind. A second, rather lower, tower was added soon afterwards to the north of the dining room, above the archway to the courtyard, and this too helped swell the number of guests' and servants' rooms. By 1873 work had also started on a long new south wing, to the east of the entrance, containing Armstrong's 'museum' (the present picture gallery) at first-floor level,

sprays of leaves and flowers on a gold ground, recalling the new taste for *japonaiserie*, championed by Whistler. The Oriental pots and plates arranged on the low bookcases continue this theme. But the large set of ebonized chairs supplied by Gillow's (to Shaw's design) are based on Goanese seventeenth-century prototypes; the fireplace has a bold and simple surround of Egyptian onyx (probably procured during the Armstrongs' visit to Egypt in 1872); and the bright blue majolica tiles flanking the hearth, after a design by Alfred Stevens, go back to the *cinquecento* and bring the wheel full circle. It says much for the sure taste of architect and patron that the room has a feeling of such unity and such individuality. Never descending to the level of pastiche, it is comfortable and ending in a third large tower. Called the Gilnockie Tower, this was supposedly based on an early sixteenth-century keep built by John Armstrong of Gilnockie, 'that mosstrooper so famous in Border song', whom Sir William claimed as an ancestor. Initially crowned by the dome of the latter's observatory, it was only in about 1887 that the gable and cupola were finally built to Shaw's design.

Together, the museum and observatory originally formed a private wing away from the rest of the house for Armstrong's studies. But by 1879 the museum had been cleared of its scientific, geological and natural history specimens and had become a picture gallery, lit by an electric arc-light that prefigured the use of Swan's bulbs in the library. The staircase at the south-west corner of the house had already been reconstructed by Shaw in about 1876, as a worthier approach to his new guest quarters above the old lodge, known as the Owl Rooms. Again the approach is witty and romantic, combining bulbous 'Queen Anne' balusters with castellated Gothic newel posts, crowned by heraldic lions. The latter

originally carried pierced brass banners, but in 1880 these were replaced by stubby poles looped over to hold large electric light bulbs – still a source of wonder, so not yet covered by shades. As one contemporary put it, 'the lamps . . . present a very beautiful and star-like appearance, not so bright as to pain the eye in passing, and very efficient in lighting the way'.

From first-floor level the flights meander off in different directions, with bronzes, majolica tiles and stained glass adding to the picturesque effect. The Owl Rooms on the second floor take their name from the furniture designed by Shaw and decorated with figures of owls: like the lions on the staircase, these pieces were probably carved by W. H. Lascelles, another of the architect's favourite craftsmen. Despite the fact that they are attics, with panelled ceilings reflecting the shape of the pitched roofs above, the Owl Rooms were given to the Prince and Princess of Wales on their visit to Cragside in 1884: a sign of the 'homely' qualities then more appreciated than the icy splendour of a state apartment.

The oak staircase was designed by Shaw in about 1876. Electric lighting was introduced here in 1880; the present shades date from about 1894.

Shaw's French Renaissance style is apparent everywhere in the drawing room, right down to the lockplate on the door.

The last and grandest of Norman Shaw's additions to Cragside was the drawing-room wing built in 1883–4, partly in anticipation of this royal visit, partly because the Armstrongs had now decided to give Jesmond Dene to the city of Newcastle and to make this their permanent home. Originally consisting of one gigantic room at first-floor level, this wing adjoins the east side of the Gilnockie Tower and stretches southwards, helping to enclose the entrance courtyard. Inside, the oriel window is like a separate room, approached through a massive arch of streaky sandstone quarried within the Cragside grounds. But the room is flooded with light from a series of huge curved skylights incorporated in the barrel-vaulted ceiling. Here the 'Old English' style has at last been abandoned, and the room is in a freely interpreted French Renaissance style, reaching a climax in the vast inglenook at the far end, said by one contemporary to weigh 10 tons. Designed by W. R. Lethaby, Shaw's brilliant chief assistant at this period, it is made of Italian marbles, exquisitely carved by the firm of Farmer and Brindley, with a riot of nymphs and cupids, garlands and strapwork inspired by the famous gallery of François I at Fontainebleau. As with the dining room, there are seats and even little windows within (this time concealed in the side walls), but the difference in mood could hardly be more apparent: festive grandeur has replaced homely cheer, and high art has finally vanquished the sturdy vernacular.

The Armstrongs' art collection had of course been growing in the fifteen years since Norman Shaw's first visit to Cragside, and the drawing room was also intended to house many of the best pictures brought from Jesmond Dene: hence its skylights, and hence the dark red damask on the walls supplied by J. Aldam Heaton, Shaw's favourite decorator of the 1880s. Heaton also designed much of the furniture for the room, happily blending Arts and Crafts and Neo-Georgian motifs, and even persuaded Armstrong to buy a life-size marble *Undine* (by Alexander Munro) from his widowed sister, placing it in the oriel window on a revolving pedestal. The drawing room was thus a worthy extension of the old picture gallery, which now became a passage leading to it – its iron stanchions boxed in with woodwork and decorated with stencil patterns so as to make it seem less functional.

One particularly happy result of the drawing-room addition was the long processional route of almost a hundred yards between it and the dining room. With its changes of axis and level, this was guaranteed to impress visitors at a time when ladies were still formally 'handed in' to dinner by their gentleman partners, two by two. From this time onwards there were regular state visits to Cragside by potential purchasers of arms from the Tyneside works: among them the King of Siam, the Shah of Persia (1889) and the Crown Prince of Afghanistan (1895). Of course there were also large weekend parties, for servants' wages were still low and the nationwide railway network encouraged frequent travel. So if Shaw's loose planning, with wings spread out like a series of limbs, seems absurdly wasteful of space by twentieth-century standards, it made a great deal of sense in its own day. Different suites of rooms in towers, up staircases or along corridors could be filled up for house parties and then forgotten about in the intervals, without the house seeming empty. As Mark Girouard has written, too, 'inglenooks, bay windows, galleries and changes in level provided a series of different focuses, of recesses for different groups to retire to, giving scope for a complex and sophisticated social life'. A great admirer of Dickens, Shaw must have known, and delighted in, the description of Mr Wickstead's drawing room in *David Copperfield*: 'it seemed to be all old nooks and corners; and in every nook and corner there was some queer little table, or cupboard, or bookcase, or seat, or something or other, that made me think there was not such another good corner in the room; until I looked at the next one, and found it equal to it, if not better'.

Although Norman Shaw's association with Cragside came to an end after 1884, Lord Armstrong continued to make additions – notably a new billiard room and 'Electrical Room' (used for his late experiments on high-tension current), behind Shaw's drawing room; a small watercolour room off the picture gallery, looking into the inner courtyard; and large extensions to the kitchen and other domestic offices in the courtyard itself. The powers of the 'modern magician' were shown again here, in the hydraulic spit above the main range in the kitchen, powered by gravity feed from the water of Nelly's Moss Lakes high above the house, in a service lift connecting with the basement, and in a passenger lift introduced some time before 1880, also worked by a hydraulic ram. The central-heating system was another triumph, with the boilers buried under the hillside to the east where a great chimney still rises inexplicably from the rocks: a surreal sight for walkers who chance upon it.

Another spectacular achievement was the steel footbridge, 150 feet in length, that spanned the burn below the house and is thought to have been made at the Elswick works between 1870 and 1875. Suspended, apparently weightless, over the gorge, and with the gables, towers and chimneystacks of the house looming above, there could be no more powerful symbol of Victorian England: confident in the march of science, yet sentimental, romantic, dreaming still of a golden age.

Castle Drogo

D E V O N

'CONSULT THE GENIUS of the place in all', Pope's famous advice to landscape gardeners, is a principle that English country house builders and their architects have always taken to heart. The way in which the perfect symmetry of Bodiam is doubled in the reflection of its still moat may be fortuitous, but there is nothing accidental in the way the towers of Hardwick crown their high ridge, or the curving wings of Kedleston reach out like arms to embrace the amphitheatre of woods and lakes spread out below. There is the same dramatic sense of 'place' in the great dome of Ickworth, seeming to reflect the huge arc of the East Anglian sky, and in the jagged outlines of Cragside with gables, towers, chimneys and weathervanes looming eerily above the dark firs of its Northumbrian hillside.

Castle Drogo represents, in this context as in so many others, a culmination of a long tradition. Its architecture is fused both with the natural beauty and the historical associations of its site; romantic and backward-looking, but also unmistakably of the twentieth century, and with a promise for the future that is only now (sixty years after its completion) becoming evident.

Like Cragside, Drogo was built on the proceeds of a trading fortune, gained in the heady days of Imperial expansion, not exactly by a *nouveau riche*, but by a member of a respectable middle-class family who had the sense to employ one of the best and most original architects of his day. Julius Drew was born in 1856, the sixth child of an Evangelical clergyman, the Rev. George Smith Drew, who eventually became a don at Cambridge. George Drew's father had been a tea-broker in Marylebone, and this would explain his own marriage to Mary Peek, from a well-established family of tea importers then living at Loddiswell in South Devon.

Having left school at seventeen, Julius was given a job as buyer for his uncle's firm of Francis Peek and Winch in the Far East, returning to England shortly after his twenty-first birthday when he joined its staff in Liverpool. This was a time when multiple stores were being started, by Thomas Lipton and George Sainsbury among others. With his experience in China and in India Drew saw that, if he joined their ranks and was able to buy his goods direct from the country of origin rather than through middlemen, success was assured.

By 1878 he had opened his first shop in Liverpool, the Willow Pattern Tea Store. In 1883, in partnership with John Musker, an experienced retailer, he moved to London and set up a shop in the Edgware Road. The business developed so rapidly under the name of the Home and Colonial Stores that by 1890 there were 106 branches all over the country, undercutting competitors particularly with their own brands of Indian tea (now preferred to China tea for the first time in England), butter, and later margarine. In 1889 both partners decided they could afford to retire, retaining the majority of the shares but leaving the running of the new limited company in the capable hands of Drew's brother-in-law, William Capel Slaughter.

Still only thirty-three, Julius Drew was now able to set up as a country gentleman, and in 1890 – a few months before his marriage to Frances Richardson, daughter of a Derbyshire cotton manufacturer – he bought an early nineteenth-century castellated mansion near Tunbridge Wells called Culverden Castle, a house that may well have influenced his later architectural tastes. By 1899, however, Frances had already borne her husband three sons, and in that year he acquired Wadhurst Hall, a far larger Victorian house just over the border in Sussex, which had been the home of Adrian de Murietta, a banker of Spanish origins and a friend of the Prince of Wales (later Edward VII). Murietta's bankruptcy had forced him to sell the place lock, stock and barrel, and the Drews thus acquired many of the pieces of Spanish furniture, the French and Flemish tapestries, and other eclectic works of art which they were later to move to Castle Drogo.

It was Julius's elder brother William, a barrister of the Inner Temple, who first consulted a professional genealogist to establish the family's ancestry, and who

*Edwin Lutyens (centre), Julius Drewe (left) and John Walker, the
Clerk of Works (right), inspecting progress on the site, around 1912.*

thus inadvertently paved the way for what was to come.
The family tradition was that their great-grandfather
Thomas, a surveyor, had come to London from Devon,
and the genealogist convinced them that they were indeed
descended from the Drewes of Broadhembury near
Honiton, some of whose original estate then happened to
be on the market. In 1901 Julius bought part of this
property and enlarged a farm to make Broadhembury
House, in which he installed his brother William.

More than this, however, the pedigree produced for the
family showed its descent from Drogo, or Dru, a Norman
baron who accompanied William the Conqueror to
England, and whose descendant, Drogo de Teigne, living
in the reign of Henry II, gave his name to the parish of
Drewsteignton (Dru's-town-on-the-Teign). By happy
coincidence, Julius's first cousin, Richard Peek, was rector
of Drewsteignton, and Julius had stayed with him on
several occasions. It must have been on one of these visits
that he conceived the idea of building a castle here, on the
home ground of his remote ancestor. The opportunity
finally arose in 1910, when he was able to buy the greater
part of the glebe lands of the parish, about 450 acres to the
south and west of the village – at the same time changing
his name by deed poll to Drewe. He added to this
purchase in subsequent years, and by the time of his
death in 1931 had built up an estate of 1500 acres.

From the outset, Julius Drewe decided that his castle
should not be a theatrical pastiche like Culverden,
but a solid fortification built in a defensible position.
The obvious place was not difficult to find: a granite

outcrop, formerly part of the rector's Twenty Acre Fir
Plantation, that formed a narrow ridge commanding the
Chagford Vale to the north, and the gorge of the River
Teign to the south, with magnificent views westward to
Dartmoor. With a site to hand, Drewe next sought an
architect. Exactly why he chose Edwin Lutyens is
uncertain, but it was probably on the advice of
Edward Hudson, the proprietor of *Country Life*, for whom
Lutyens had built Deanery Garden in Surrey and,
more significantly, remodelled Lindisfarne Castle in
Northumberland in 1903. Hudson was fond of
introducing Lutyens as 'the only possible architect',
and Lindisfarne would have appealed to Drewe for its
craggy qualities – as would Lambay, another small house
incorporating sixteenth-century castle ruins, created for
the Baring family in 1908 on an island off the Irish coast.

At a family picnic in the summer of 1910, Lutyens and
the Drewes pegged out the site for the house and for a
drive following the only possible route along the ridge to
the east. By early August the architect could report to his
wife: 'Mr. Drew writes a nice and exciting letter. I go on
with drawings not more than £50,000 and £10,000 for the
garden. I suppose £60,000 sounds a lot to you but I don't
know what it means. If I look at Westminster Abbey it is
an absurd – a trivial amount. If I look at a dear little old
world two roomed cottage it merely looks a vast and
unmanageable amount. Only I do wish he didn't want a
castle – but just a delicious loveable house with plenty of
good large rooms in it.' Though this was the biggest single
commission he ever received for a private house, one can
well sympathize with Lutyens's initial misgivings,
not only on account of the vast scale of the original project
– three times the size of the present building – but
because he had progressed from the early vernacular
mode of his Surrey houses to become increasingly
interested in what he called the 'high game' of classicism.
To respond to the drama of the site, and to the emotional
commitment of Drewe's vision, he needed to recapture
the passion that always lay beneath his formidable
intellect, the romantic nature beneath his humanism.

In another of his letters written to Lady Emily in August
1910, he summed up his view of the great country house
in a way which goes far to explain the genesis of Drogo:
'I feel so for Mrs. B. [i.e. Mrs. Baring, of Lambay], through
you, for her antipathy to the big house and all it means
from one point of view. I look at the big house from the
other, and best, point of view:– a centre for all the charity
that should begin at home and cover henwise with wings
of love all those near about her that are dependent and
weaker and smaller. A house with the soul of a Wilton
gives me a choke of veneration, at its unending
possibilities of giving and receiving love. Neither the
loveliness nor the love of such can be bought, not by all
the millions in the world.'

The first plans for the castle to be worked out in detail
were made during Lutyens's voyage to South Africa in
November, when he and his assistant, Hall, had a deck
cabin fitted up as a drawing office. Adopting the heroic
scale of the Johannesburg buildings he was to plan with
Herbert Baker, or his recently rejected scheme for County

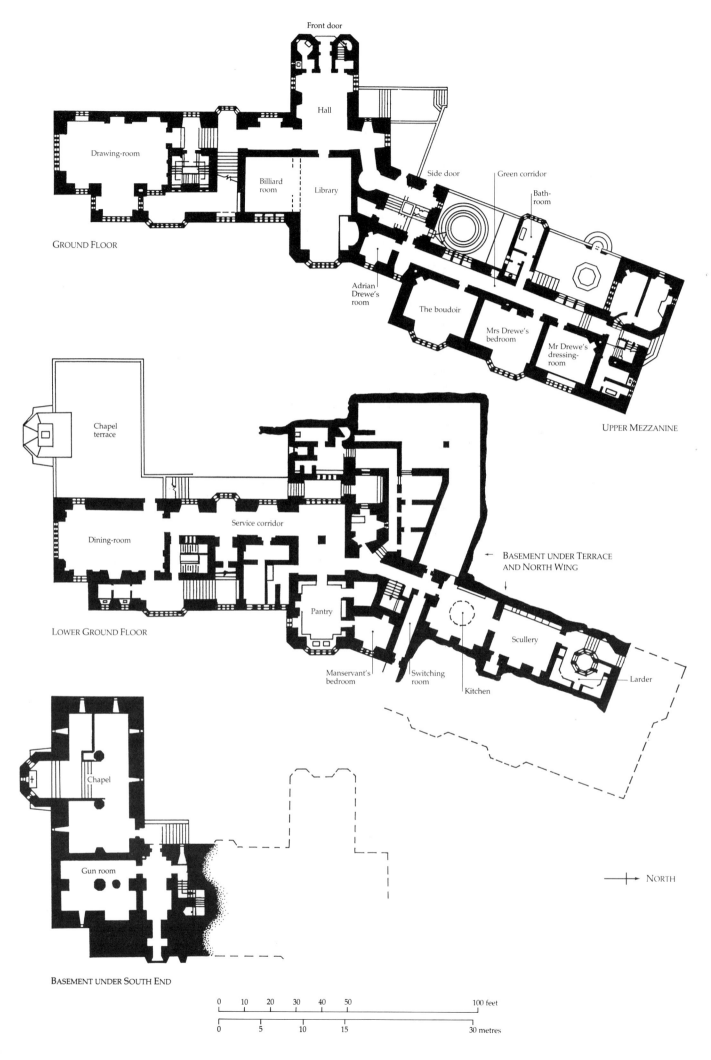

Front door

Hall

Drawing-room

Billiard
room

Library

GROUND FLOOR

Side door

Green corridor

Bath-
room

Adrian
Drewe's
room

The boudoir

Mrs Drewe's
bedroom

Mr Drewe's
dressing-
room

UPPER MEZZANINE

Chapel
terrace

Service corridor

Dining-room

BASEMENT UNDER TERRACE
AND NORTH WING

LOWER GROUND FLOOR

Pantry

Scullery

Manservant's
bedroom

Switching
room

Kitchen

Larder

Chapel

Gun room

NORTH

BASEMENT UNDER SOUTH END

0   10   20   30   40   50   100 feet

0   5   10   15   30 metres

The original proposal, in a rare watercolour by Lutyens himself, had batteries and a great hall looking south.

Hall in London, they proposed a colossal courtyard house occupying the whole neck of the cliff-top promontory. The slight broadening of the ridge behind also allowed for great splayed wings, like open arms welcoming the visitor to the forecourt: that on the east containing servants' quarters and that on the west a billiard room, cloisters and chapel. The three principal rooms – a great hall with an open timbered roof, flanked by a barrel-vaulted drawing room and hammer-beamed dining room, both lit by bay windows – were to occupy the south range, jutting out over the cliff-face and built over large vaulted crypts. Seen from the valley, the build-up of projecting bays and buttresses, of parapets and towers at different levels, may have been inspired by his tour of 1911, when he helped design the British Pavilions at the Rome and Turin exhibitions. 'The great buildings on the hilltops I see excite me fearfully,' he wrote, 'high, high up against the sky, and how the devil do they get to them, still more *at* them to build them?'

Early sketches of Drogo were made in a Tudor vernacular style, incorporating a gabled roof and tall chimneystacks. But this was soon abandoned, perhaps at the client's instigation, in favour of a massive simplicity, more like a real castle. No guttering, downpipes, window-sills or string courses were to disfigure the smooth planes of the granite walls, while the straight lines of the parapets, only occasionally varied by an irregular castellation, gave a feeling of power and solidity without simply aping medieval fortifications.

Just as Lord Armstrong had built a tower at Cragside in honour of his ancestor Johnnie Armstrong of Gilnockie, so one of Lutyens's letters to his wife reveals that Julius Drewe 'wants to build a large keep or commemorative

tower to commemorate the first Drogo and this will be over and beyond the £60,000 castle'. Lutyens complied with this request by designing a great curtain wall and barbican at the entrance to the courtyard, and this idea was only rejected after a full-scale mock-up had been made out of timber and tarpaulin in the summer of 1913, to show how it would look.

The foundation stone of the castle was laid on 4 April 1911, Julius Drewe's fifty-fifth birthday, under what is now the north-east corner of the house. But the plans went on being developed by architect and client, reaching their climax in by November, when more detailed drawings show the vast scale of the hall, with two chimneypieces, each 12 feet wide, a gallery 160 feet long, and a chapel rising from a lower level through three storeys. Lutyens's enthusiasm had over-reached itself, and although the idea of economy had not entered Drewe's head at this stage, he and his wife were already worried about occupying such huge spaces in reasonable comfort. There was also another reason for reconsideration. To achieve the massive effect which Lutyens wanted, his earlier drawings show 2-foot-thick granite walls either side of a 2-foot cavity in many parts of the house. But Drewe was still obsessed by authenticity: this was not the way castles were wont to be built, and he decided to have solid stone walls 6 feet thick in the south range, and not much less elsewhere. Bricks, even though intended to be hidden, were entirely banned. The extra cost involved meant that some reduction was now inevitable, and by October 1912 it was decided to abandon the whole west range, resulting for the first time in an asymmetrical composition.

The south wing with the great hall remained on the

Castle Drogo

1 Hall
2 Library
3 Billiard room
4 Drawing-room (with dining-room below)
5 Chapel
6 The boudoir
7 Mrs Drewe's bedroom
8 Mr Drewe's dressing-room
9 Kitchen
10 Scullery
11 Larder

NORTH

agenda until the First World War, but then, with two-thirds of the workforce away on active service, and with the death of Julius's eldest son, Adrian Drewe, in the trenches in 1917, it too disappeared. The massive undercroft already built in preparation for it was converted into a chapel, and in 1919 Lutyens made final revisions to the plan, providing bedrooms for the family in the north-east wing (previously intended as servants' quarters), and a dining room and drawing room one above the other at the southern end of the house. A greatly reduced band of craftsmen worked slowly away in the succeeding years, and the building was finally completed in 1930, only a year before Drewe's own death.

With a lesser architect, and a less complex original scheme, these constant abbreviations might have been disastrous, but Lutyens had a knack of turning such setbacks to advantage. As his biographer, Christopher Hussey, put it, Drogo is 'even more of a castle, even more dramatic for being an unresolved fragment', and in its present state it shares that 'sublime irrationality produced in medieval castles by forgotten military needs, catastrophic truncation, and the domestic accretions of centuries'. In many ways the culmination of the Picturesque country house, it is also, paradoxically, the building that architects of the Modern Movement admire most in Lutyens's *oeuvre*. The geometry of its

gridiron windows set against advancing and receding planes of uninterrupted granite can be compared with the abstraction of a Mondrian painting; the feel for the colour and texture of stone, inside and out, recalling the strength of primitive art, has much in common with the sculpture of Henry Moore; and the working out of spatial problems, levels and axes, so as to produce a constant feeling of excitement and revelation, looks forward to the public buildings of Stirling and Foster.

The approach to the building, and its surroundings, contribute to its spell. The narrow, twisting, high-banked Devon lanes gradually ascend from the valley to reach a *rond point* within clipped beech hedges at the start of the drive. But apart from the formal circles of ilex here, and halfway to the castle where the road curves to the west, the effect is of wild open moorland, with the blue flank of Dartmoor in the distance. Credit for this must go to Julius Drewe, who in 1915 wrote to Lutyens, 'so far as the Drive is concerned . . . what I want is heather, bracken, broom, holly, brambles, foxgloves, etc.'. Lutyens agreed, but suggested that Drewe should consult his long-time friend, Gertrude Jekyll, 'who is a great designer and Artist, old and experienced in the way of plants and a lover of the wilderness and of moorland'. Though now in her seventies and almost blind, she not only produced a planting scheme, but also advised on the design of the yew 'bastions' flanking the entrance to the forecourt, substitutes for the curtain wall and barbican Lutyens had intended.

Originally, there were to have been elaborate gardens cut into the hillside immediately below the east front of the castle. But by 1920 these plans had been discarded, and a new layout by George Dillistone of Tunbridge Wells (probably drawn up with advice from both Lutyens and Jekyll) was adopted for the hillside to the north of the drive: three formally planted terraces like separate 'rooms', leading up to an immense circular croquet lawn, surrounded by high walls of clipped yew. This change preserved the rough landscape of heather and Scots pines from which the walls of the castle rise sheer, gaining immeasurably in drama and in contrast.

From the east, indeed, the building looks its most impressive. The walls are a full storey higher than on the forecourt side, where the ground level is raised; and the way in which the two wings are joined at an angle of 160 degrees, following the natural bend of the hilltop, increases its apparent length. There is also a subtle counterpoint in the rhythm of the windows: smaller in the right-hand wing containing the private family rooms and servants' quarters; far larger in the left-hand block containing the main reception rooms – and culminating in the cathedral-sized bay lighting the great staircase. Moreover, the number of surfaces at different angles to each other, some in full light, some in half light, some in shadow, as the morning sun moves across the valley, gives a feeling of endless variety and movement.

From virtually any viewpoint Castle Drogo tends to look bigger than it actually is, and this too is part of Lutyens's artistry. Like the outline of his famous Cenotaph in Whitehall, starting vertical but then tapering towards the

The site for Drogo was chosen on a picnic in 1910. Lutyens and Drewe shared a vision of a fortress overlooking the Teign gorge.

The mock-up for the barbican and curtain walls made of timber and tarpaulin in 1913. This part of Lutyens's scheme was later abandoned.

top, many of the key angle-walls at Castle Drogo are subtly 'battered' so as to exaggerate their height – particularly when seen in conjunction with the vertical mullion windows which they adjoin. One of the oldest architectural tricks in the world (even found in the slight curvature of the walls of the Parthenon), it can seldom have been used to greater effect. In the south front, for instance, one massive projecting bay, the wall surface cut back at each storey, leaves the corners to stand proud like great angled fins. These corners are battered both at ground-floor and at second-floor level, so that the vertical bay which they frame seems to jut out from the hillside like a great ship's prow. The walls themselves seem to grow out of huge boulders, which give every impression of being a natural feature. In fact, the rocks were specially moved here in 1912 with the aid of a notoriously unstable sheerlegs crane that caused a number of accidents.

The quality of the stonework, seen in the razor-sharp edges of the corner walls here, is one of the great features of Castle Drogo. Astonishingly it is the work of only two men, the Devon masons Cleeve and Dewdney who, after the first year's work, mainly concerned with foundations, laid every single stone. Naturally, they had a large team of labourers who hewed and dressed the granite blocks, some quarried locally in Whiddon Park just across the valley, and brought up to the site by traction engine or steam lorry, and some (of finer quality) from the Dartmoor quarries of Merivale, Blackinstone and Pew Tor, near Tavistock. They were supervised by a remarkable man, the Clerk of Works, John Walker, who had himself trained as a stonemason, working for the Duke of Portland at Welbeck before moving to Devon. Walker's eye for detail ensured the highest standards of craftsmanship inside and out, and his presence enabled Drewe to work economically with direct labour, instead of by contract.

An exchange of letters between architect and client in the autumn of 1912 shows the thought that went into the character of the masonry, and the differences that still existed between them: Lutyens anxious not to produce a mere pastiche; Drewe was still determined to have a castle in the most literal sense. 'May I ask *why* you have altered your opinion as to preparation of the granite facing?' Drewe writes, continuing: 'From the commencement you

expressed your firm decision that only rough granite should be used. You told Jenkins that no tool marks were to be visible on any piece. He went on with what you told him to do and would have gone on doing so had you been detained at Delhi [where work had just begun on Lutyens's Viceroy's House]. To my mind . . . the building should be continued to your pre-Delhian instructions. What might have happened to us if you had also seen the Pyramids as well makes us quake to think about.' To this Lutyens replied firmly, 'the big lumpy blocks are right for the lower courses but quite impossible to carry them up . . . it will mean a barbaric building worthy of a small municipal corporation. When a barbarian built a fortress he heaped up rocks and hid his women behind them. If those hard, wide stones are what you think I meant I am the Barbarian! I am very keen about your castle and must 'fight' you when I KNOW I am right.'

The texture of the granite, cut with such precision, is best appreciated on the west front when the evening sun falls on the entrance tower, catching the silvery quartz within the blocks but leaving the angled north-east wing to the left still plunged in shadow. The tower itself, marching out into the forecourt, is the most overtly Romantic feature of the whole castle, recalling the keep or barbican which Julius Drewe originally wanted 'to commemorate the first Drogo'. The low walls each side give the impression of a moat behind them, but actually conceal the skylights of the kitchen and scullery on the left, and a secret garden leading from the servants' quarters to the chapel on the right.

The octagonal turrets flanking the doorcase have a marked 'batter', rather like the entasis of two giant classical columns, contrasting with the straight lines of the flattened oriel between. Lutyens also took great trouble with the design of the heraldic Drewe lion carved in a bas-relief panel over the door by Herbert Palliser, a Yorkshireman teaching at the Royal College of Art. Not unlike the lion which he later designed as a symbol for the British Empire Exhibition at Wembley, it also has the family motto *Drogo Nomen et Virtus Arma Dedit* ('Drewe is the name and valour gave it arms') carved below, linking the oriel with the turrets in a playfully 'unstructural' way. Still more playful is the working portcullis guarding the front door, and wound up by a special winch: the only conscious anachronism in the house, and quite possibly an idea of the client's rather than the architect's.

Inside the castle, the hall and corridors, and many of the main rooms, again have bare granite walls and unpainted woodwork, continuing the solid strength of the exterior. In these surroundings, the furniture brought from Wadhurst by the Drewes – largely Spanish and French pieces acquired by Adrian de Murietta – can seem rather out of character. On the other hand the joinery, most of it by the Crediton firm of Dart and Francis, is as accomplished as the masonry, and shows the same attention to detail. The most exciting spaces are inevitably the corridors and staircases, offering constant surprises in the form of long vistas, changes of axis and level, and contrasts of light and shade. The intricacy of the plan is also deliberately counterbalanced by the massive simplicity of the execution.

In many ways, the key to this plan is the private staircase at the point where the two wings meet – although the actual internal 'hinge' is the little circular lobby adjoining, where the whole axis of the house changes, catching you almost unawares. With its entrances and exits at every half-landing, the staircase ingeniously resolves the difference in floor levels: the southern block (with the main reception rooms) consisting of three storeys, and the north-eastern block (with the family's and servants' rooms) consisting of four. In addition the great open arches give a Piranesian sense of grandeur and mystery to the ascent.

The main corridor, passing through the far end of the hall, 'arched, vaulted and recessed in a series of perfect cubic spaces', owes more to Lutyens's favourite architect, Wren. But if the crypt and side aisles of St Paul's come to mind, the force of Lutyens's genius is a guarantee against any sense of incongruity. Like his contemporary, church architect Ninian Comper, he could mix castle and cathedral, Romanesque and Classical, to achieve a wholly individual 'unity by inclusion'. At the point where the corridor begins to ascend to the drawing room, another great flight of steps plunges down to the left, leading to the dining room. Here there is also a *coup de théâtre* in the way the ceiling remains at the same level: first as a coffered granite vault, then as a saucer dome over the landing (easing the change of direction), and finally as an oak-beamed structure above the lower flight. By this time the distance to the floor is 27 feet, allowing an east bay window of gigantic size, made up of no fewer than forty-eight lights with transoms subtly graded to create different proportions in each of its six stages. So vast is the space that two other large internal windows look into it from the drawing room above, borrowing light from the bay.

This great processional route from hall to drawing room to dining room made sense at a time when servants were still plentiful, and when the Drewes could expect to entertain house parties as well as neighbours on a lavish scale. From a social history point of view, remarkably little has changed since Norman Shaw's Cragside, and indeed Shaw was a formative influence on the young Lutyens, both in his 'modified Tudor' idiom and in the axial but asymmetrical plans of houses like Flete, one of Castle

Drogo's near-neighbours. The way in which the servants' movements were hidden from view seems to go back even further, to the late eighteenth century. Thus, both the staircases at Drogo appear to have solid cores, but, as the Earl-Bishop intended at Ickworth, there is a complete secondary flight for servants concealed within the main stair (lit by windows through the core walls), while a lift rises unseen through the centre of the private stair.

In some ways, the two main reception rooms are disappointing after the spatial excitement of the approach. The drawing room, panelled in a loosely seventeenth-century style, painted a conventional 'Georgian green', and furnished with flowery chintz-covered chairs and sofas, is most memorable for its great mullion windows on three sides, giving panoramic views over the Teign Valley and Dartmoor. The dining room below was originally intended to rise through two storeys, but was finally reduced to a long, low room panelled in dark cigar-box mahogany, rather like a City board room. The heavy plasterwork ceiling, with its great wreaths of fruit and flowers in Lutyens's favourite 'Wrenaissance' manner, seems to emphasize the lack of height. By contrast, the giant pilasters round the room are carved with strapwork decoration in a more literal Jacobean vein (recalling those in the Cartoon Gallery at Knole), and may have been one of Julius Drewe's purchases which he instructed the architect to incorporate. The only sign of Lutyens's usual individuality and playfulness is the broad band of granite emerging behind their Corinthian capitals, immediately below the cornice – as if, even here, the solid stone walls of the castle have pushed their way through, to reassert the building's rugged grandeur.

Much more successful is the combined library and billiard room, entered from the hall. Here, the walls are again unadorned granite, only partly covered with bookcases and with tapestries brought from Wadhurst. The room is L-shaped, with an immense granite arch between the two arms. This was built with the aid of a crane in January 1915, and John Walker reported its completion to Drewe with some relief: 'with an arch of this size one is always anxious that the key is in. There are 49 stones in it, the weight being over thirty tons.' The oak-beamed ceilings were finally put in place five years later, by Dart and Francis, and soon afterwards Burroughs and Watts supplied the massive billiard table in the shorter arm, made specially to Lutyens's design. Lutyens was always more concerned with aesthetic than practical considerations, and the gigantic fireplace in the longer library section has always smoked unless the door to the hall is kept open. But far more serious problems than this emerged during the course of the building work. Rainwater penetration of many of the granite blocks on the exterior was first noticed in 1913 (and is still being tackled today), while faults found in the asphalt used for waterproofing meant that all this work had to be done again by Italian specialists the following year.

These difficulties, and the shortage of labour during and after the First World War, caused long delays. But it says much for Julius Drewe's determination that he persevered despite these blows, and despite a threefold rise in

Part of the great staircase. Below the window, which helps to light the drawing room, is a portrait of Mrs Drewe by C.M. Hardie.

building costs. On 22 December 1925 Lutyens's faithful office manager, Albert Thomas, wrote to Walker noting that 'the Last Stone of the Castle proper will be fixed today and the crane taken down; I should say this is "some" termination to the Year. Congratulations!' Two years later the family were finally able to move in to the north-east wing, occupying the rooms off the long, tapestry-hung Green Corridor – with the nurseries on the floor above, staff quarters on the floor below, and kitchen, scullery and larder on the floor below that.

There are unmistakeable Lutyens touches in this family wing, like the deep granite window embrasures in the Green Corridor itself, with sills at different levels for the display of ceramics, and the arrangement of stepped ledges in the bay window of the bathroom overlooking the forecourt, probably intended for the same purpose. Another bathroom in the guest quarters – which the architect may jokingly have intended for his own use – has a gigantic Doric column in the centre, placed in such a way that it has to be contemplated from the bath.

On the other hand, Mrs Drewe's bedroom and boudoir, and Julius Drewe's own dressing room, oak-panelled and modest in size, are more interesting for the personal tastes they display than for their architecture: the pedimented

cigar cabinet, the morocco-bound albums recording 'Motor Trips', the faded family photographs. There is a particular poignancy also in the small room arranged by Mrs Drewe to commemorate her son Adrian, killed in Flanders in 1917. Back in 1910, as a boy of nineteen, he had helped Lutyens peg out the drive and plot the site of the castle that he was never to inherit. School and college mementoes line the walls, witnesses to a life tragically cut short.

True to Lutyens's vision of the country house preserving some of the best aspects of feudalism – covering 'henwise with wings of love all those near about her that are dependent and weaker and smaller' – the rooms 'below stairs' were designed with just as much attention to detail and just as much grandeur of scale as the rest. The kitchen is reached by way of a broad service corridor from the dining room, alternately arched and vaulted like the main corridor above, and with granite ribs just as immaculately finished. Passing the pantry (under the library), with oak cupboards, table and teak sinks all made to Lutyens's designs, the passage then changes course on axis with the wing and from comparative darkness enters the domed kitchen, flooded with light from its circular lantern. Despite the width of this skylight,

The dining room was intended to be very grand, rising through two storeys, but was reduced to a long low room panelled in mahogany. Family portraits line the walls, including that of Julius Drewe by George Harcourt at the far end.

One of the great cast-iron ranges in the Lutyens's kitchen.

Mrs Drewe complained that it never received 'a glint of sun', due to the massive ranges towering above it on the south and west. But Lutyens could argue that this did not apply to the servants' hall or to their living quarters, and that the heat from the great ranges and ovens would be quite enough to warm this cavernous space.

The circular table in the centre was specially designed to reflect the lantern above, and drawings for the dressers – and even the pastryboards – were sent down from his London office in Queen Anne's Gate. Like his Arts and Crafts predecessors, Lutyens loved the idea of domestic order, writing to the thoroughly undomesticated Lady Emily during their engagement in praise of simple oak tables, linen presses, brass candlesticks, and 'the kitchen, where the pots and range glisten in the light, where the cheery cook turns mountains into molehills and frugal fare into a feast. The breadpan with his father oven open and shut in busy intercourse, the larder restocked from Smithfield Mart, and the wood washed bins are filled with clean fresh vegetables from Covent Garden.' At Drogo, the markets were not necessary for the supply of food, but his beautiful vegetable racks wait by the larder door for the produce brought daily from the kitchen garden.

The scullery is placed below the tower which projects from the north-east wing towards the forecourt, with two bathrooms above it. Again the treatment is monumental, with the centre section rising through two storeys, this time forming a square lantern with a vaulted ceiling, lit by two large therm windows: a Neo-Classical touch that again brings Piranesi to mind. On the other hand, the lantern is supported by rock-solid granite columns, with 'primitive' capitals looking back to Byzantine and even earlier models. A plate rack big enough to take several services at once runs above the three large sinks, with their gleaming brass taps and teak draining boards. The room was used for preparing food as well as washing dishes, however, and this explains the enormous pestle and mortar which Lutyens also provided, the matching hexagonal chopping block, and the lift which transported food to the servants' hall on the floor above and to the nurseries two floors above that.

The third and last of these great subterranean chambers is the larder, which was ingeniously built round an open octagonal well that allowed fresh air to enter, but only a shady, subdued light. Granite walls and traditional slate shelves add to the coolness, and there are steps up to the back door where gardeners and tradesmen would call.

One last port of call remains: the chapel, formed within the undercroft of the south range when the great hall was finally abandoned, but not consecrated until September 1931, only two months before Julius Drewe's death. The effect of its 6-foot walls, its tiny splayed windows and massive groin vaults is appropriately crushing and tomb-like, almost as if it was cut out of the solid rock. Above the apse, Lutyens's bell tower, growing out of the steeply sloping roof, looks like a miniature version of his great war memorial arch at Thiepval in Flanders. Rooted in his sculptural understanding of his materials, it is abstract, but at the same time deeply moving: its bell tolling not just for Adrian Drewe, lost in the trenches, but for the passing of a whole way of life, a chapter of British history that had already closed.

Glossary

Angel tester   canopy over a bed unsupported by posts at the foot; otherwise known as a flying tester

Armatures   wooden or metal brackets used to support decoration, usually of plasterwork

Ashlar   masonry of large stone blocks cut with even faces and square edges

Barbican   outwork defending the entrance to a castle

Bas-relief   carving in relief, usually in wood or stone

Battering   inward inclination of a wall

Bolection moulding   convex moulding covering the joint between two planes and overlapping both, especially on panelling and fireplace surrounds of the late seventeenth and early eighteenth centuries

Boulle   marquetry using inlaid metals, usually brass and pewter, on a wooden or tortoiseshell veneered ground, called after the French *ébéniste*, André Charles Boulle (1642–1732)

Buttery   room adjoining the great hall of a medieval house or castle, used for the dispensing of wine, beer and other beverages under the supervision of the butterer, or butler

Caffoy   a rare form of cut wool velvet, described in various eighteenth-century inventories

Close stool   chair or armchair used as a privy, with a removable pan of porcelain, pottery, silver or pewter below the seat; sometimes called a commode

Coving   concave soffit like a hollow moulding, but on a larger scale, usually employed to act as a junction between walls and ceiling

Cruck   piece of naturally curved or crooked timber combining the structural roles of an upright post and a sloping rafter e.g. in the building of a cottage where each pair of crucks is joined at the ridge

Dado   lower part of a wall or its decorative treatment

Dumb-bell   mechanism similar to a church-bell, with weights in place of the bell, used as a form of exercise

Enfilade   alignment of doors on one axis, to give a vista through several rooms

Entablature   collective name for the three horizontal members above a column in classical architecture (i.e. the architrave, frieze and cornice)

Garderobe   medieval privy or lavatory, sometimes also called the wardrobe

Grisaille   Form of painted decoration in black and white or shades of grey

Gun loop   opening for a cannon or firearm

Ha Ha   concealed ditch with retaining wall also acting as a fence to keep out livestock

Jettying   form of building with upper storeys projecting out beyond lower ones

Lime cement   mortar made out of slaked lime mixed with sand, gypsum and other materials

Machicolations   in fortified medieval buildings, a series of openings between the projecting brackets of a parapet (usually in a gatehouse), through which missiles or boiling liquids could be dropped on the heads of attackers

Mansard roof   form of double hipped roof, built at a steep angle in the lower stage (often pierced by dormer windows), and at a much shallower angle in the upper stage; called after the French architect, François Mansart (1598–1666)

Meurtrières/ **murder holes**   holes cut through the vaulted roofs of passages, usually in the gatehouses of medieval castles, enabling missiles and liquids to be dropped on the heads of attackers

Mullion   vertical member between the lights in a window opening

Newel   central post in a spiral staircase; likewise the principal post when a flight of stairs meets a landing

Oeil de boeuf   small circular or oval window, also known as a bullseye or (in the seventeenth century) as a lucerne

Oriel   bay-window on an upper floor, built out on corbels or brackets

Pediment   formalized gable derived from that of a temple in classical architecture, also used over doors, windows etc.

Piano nobile   principal floor, usually with a ground floor or basement underneath

Pilaster   flattened version of the classical column, applied to a wall

Postern   gateway at the back of a building

Purlin   roof timber, laid horizontally to support rafters, and held in places by braces, queenposts, or other struts

Rustic   name sometimes given to the ground floor or basement of a classical house containing servants' quarters or less important family rooms, called after the rusticated stonework of its exterior face (see below)

Rustication   treatment of masonry or timber to resemble blocks with recessed bands between, so as to give an effect of strength

Scagliola   decorative surface treatment applied to columns, table tops, etc., achieved by mixing marble dust and colour pigments with a bonding agent, and subsequent polishing

Screens passage   screened-off entrance passage at one end of the great hall of a medieval house

String course   intermediate stone course or moulding projecting from the surface of a wall

Stucco   smooth external rendering of a wall; sometimes also used (particularly in the eighteenth century) to describe internal decorative plasterwork

Tester   canopy, usually over a four-post bedstead

Transom   horizontal member between the lights of a window

Trompe l'oeil   form of illusionistic painted decoration, intended to deceive the eye

Venetian window   tripartite window with arched central section flanked by smaller rectangular openings, often framed by columns; the form was made popular by the Venetian architect Andrea Palladio (1508–80)

Select Bibliography

The primary source of information on each of the twelve houses featured here is the current National Trust guidebook, available at the property, from the regional offices or from the Trust's headquarters at 36 Queen Anne's Gate, London, SW1H 9AS.

For English country houses generally, the following are indispensable:

John Cornforth and John Fowler, *English Decoration in the Eighteenth Century*, 1974
John Cornforth and Oliver Hill, *English Country Houses: Caroline*, 1966
Mark Girouard, *Life in the English Country House*, 1978
Mark Girouard, *The Victorian Country House*, 1971
Christopher Hussey, *English Country Houses: Early, Mid and Late Georgian*, 1955–59
James Lees-Milne, *English Country Houses: Baroque 1685–1715*, 1970

BODIAM

H.M. Colvin, (ed.) *The History of the King's Works*, vols. I-III, 1963–70
Marquis Curzon of Kedleston, *Bodiam Castle*, 1926
Paul Johnson, *The National Trust Book of British Castles*, 1978
Sydney Toy, *The Castles of Great Britain*, 1954

KNOLE

V. Sackville-West, *Knole and the Sackvilles*, 1922
C.J. Phillips, *History of the Sackville Family*, 2 vols., 1929

LITTLE MORETON HALL

C.F. Stell, 'Little Moreton Hall' *Report of the Summer Meeting of the Royal Archaeological Institute at Keele*, 1963
H. Avray Tipping, 'Little Moreton Hall, Cheshire' *Country Life*, 1929

HARDWICK

Lindsay Boynton and Peter Thornton, 'The Hardwick Hall Inventories of 1601', *Journal of the Furniture History Society*, vol. VII, 1971
David N. Durant, *Bess of Hardwick*, 1977
Mark Girouard, *Robert Smythson and the Elizabethan Country House*, 1983
Mark Girouard, *Hardwick Hall*, The National Trust, 1989

BELTON HOUSE

Geoffrey Beard, 'Edward Goudge, "The Beste Master in England"', *National Trust Studies*, 1979
John Cornforth, 'Belton House, Lincolnshire, I, II & III', *Country Life*, 3, 10 & 17 September, 1964
Lady Elizabeth Cust, (compiled by), *Records of the Cust Family, Series II: The Brownlows of Belton*, 1909
Lionel Cust, (compiled by), *Records of the Cust Family, Series III: John Cust, Third Baronet*, 1927
David Green, *Grinling Gibbons*, 1964

PETWORTH HOUSE

Rev. James Dallaway, *The Parochial Topography of the Western division of the County of Sussex*, vol. II, part 1, 1832
Gervase Jackson-Stops, 'The Building of Petworth' *Apollo*, May 1977
Gervase Jackson-Stops, 'The Furniture at Petworth' *Apollo*, May 1977
Gervase Jackson-Stops, 'Petworth and the Proud Duke', *Country Life*, June 28, 1973
James Lees-Milne, *English Country Houses: Baroque 1685–1715*, 1970
Hugh Wyndham, *A Family History – The Wyndhams of Somerset, Sussex and Wiltshire 1688–1837*, 1950

STOURHEAD

Sir Richard Colt Hoare, *A Description of the House and Gardens at Stourhead*, 1818
Sir Richard Colt Hoare, *The History of Modern Wiltshire, The Hundred of Mere*, 1822
Christopher Hussey, 'Stourhead, Wiltshire', *Country Life*, 11 and 18 June, 1938 and 5 January, 1951
Christopher Hussey, *The Picturesque: Studies in a Point of View*, 1927 (reprinted 1967)
Howard Stutchbury, *The Architecture of Colen Campbell*, 1967
Kenneth Woodbridge, *Landscape and Antiquity: Aspects of English Culture at Stourhead 1718 to 1838*, 1970

KEDLESTON HALL

Arthur T. Bolton, *The Architecture of Robert and James Adam*, 1922
John Fleming, *Robert Adam and His Circle*, 1962
Leslie Harris, *Robert Adam and Kedleston: The Making of a Neo-Classical Masterpiece*, 1987

CASTLE COOLE

The Earl of Belmore, *The History of Two Ulster Manors*, 1881, revised 1903
Christopher Hussey, 'Castle Coole I & II, County Fermanagh', *Country Life*, 19 and 26 December, 1936
Gervase Jackson-Stops, 'A Temple Made Tasteful', *Country Life*, 10 April, 1986

ICKWORTH

W.S. Childe-Pemberton, *The Earl Bishop*, 1924
Brian Fothergill, *The Mitred Earl – An Eighteenth-Century Eccentric*, 1974
Christopher Hussey, 'Ickworth, Suffolk', *Country Life*, 10 March, 1955
Peter Rankin, *Irish Building Ventures of the Earl Bishop of Derry*, Ulster Architectural Heritage Society, 1972
Pamela Tudor-Craig, 'The Evolution of Ickworth', *Country Life*, 17 May, 1973

CRAGSIDE

Mark Girouard, 'Cragside, I & II', *Country Life*, 18 and 25 December, 1969
Mark Girouard, *The Victorian Country House*, 1971
Andrew Saint, *Richard Norman Shaw*, 1976

CASTLE DROGO

Christopher Hussey, *The Life of Sir Edwin Lutyens*, 1950
Peter Matthias, *Retailing Revolution*, London 1967

Index

NOTE: References in **bold type** denote illustrations; there may also be text references on these pages

Picture Credits

The illustrations on the following
pages are reproduced by kind
permission of: British Architectural
Library/RIBA 57; Country Life 22, 28
(top), 104, 125; Courtauld Institute of
Art 76, 85; The National Library of
Ireland 111 (bottom); The National
Portrait Gallery, London 96; The
National Trust Photographic Library 9
(Unichrome), 14, 18 (Tim Stephens),
25, 28, 29 (John Bethell), 30, 33
(Vernon D. Shaw), 40, 43, 45 (John
Bethell), 49 (Angelo Hornak), 53 and
58 (Graham Challifour), 60, 64, 65, 69
(A.C. Cooper), 70, 74, 81 (Charlie
Waite), 83, 88, 93 and 97 (Andrew
Haslam), 100, 101, 102, 103, 107, 109
(A & C Photography), 115, 116 (Chris
Hill), 119, 121, 126 (Angelo Hornak),
128 (Mark Fiennes), 129, 132, 133, 137,
140 (Charlie Waite), 143, 145, 149, 152;
Woodmansterne 41 (bottom), 43; Mel
Wright 112.